M000168384

Beginning Git and GitHub

A Comprehensive Guide to Version Control, Project Management, and Teamwork for the New Developer

Mariot Tsitoara

Beginning Git and GitHub

Mariot Tsitoara
Antananarivo, Madagascar

ISBN-13 (pbk): 978-1-4842-5312-0   ISBN-13 (electronic): 978-1-4842-5313-7
https://doi.org/10.1007/978-1-4842-5313-7

Copyright © 2020 by Mariot Tsitoara

This work is subject to copyright. All rights are reserved by the Publisher, whether the whole or part of the material is concerned, specifically the rights of translation, reprinting, reuse of illustrations, recitation, broadcasting, reproduction on microfilms or in any other physical way, and transmission or information storage and retrieval, electronic adaptation, computer software, or by similar or dissimilar methodology now known or hereafter developed.

Trademarked names, logos, and images may appear in this book. Rather than use a trademark symbol with every occurrence of a trademarked name, logo, or image we use the names, logos, and images only in an editorial fashion and to the benefit of the trademark owner, with no intention of infringement of the trademark.

The use in this publication of trade names, trademarks, service marks, and similar terms, even if they are not identified as such, is not to be taken as an expression of opinion as to whether or not they are subject to proprietary rights.

While the advice and information in this book are believed to be true and accurate at the date of publication, neither the authors nor the editors nor the publisher can accept any legal responsibility for any errors or omissions that may be made. The publisher makes no warranty, express or implied, with respect to the material contained herein.

Managing Director, Apress LLC: Welmoed Spahr
Acquisitions Editor: Louise Corrigan
Development Editor: James Markham
Coordinating Editor: Nancy Chen

Cover designed by eStudioCalamar

Cover image designed by Freepik (www.freepik.com)

Distributed to the book trade worldwide by Springer Science+Business Media New York, 233 Spring Street, 6th Floor, New York, NY 10013. Phone 1-800-SPRINGER, fax (201) 348-4505, e-mail orders-ny@springer-sbm.com, or visit www.springeronline.com. Apress Media, LLC is a California LLC and the sole member (owner) is Springer Science + Business Media Finance Inc (SSBM Finance Inc). SSBM Finance Inc is a **Delaware** corporation.

For information on translations, please e-mail rights@apress.com, or visit http://www.apress.com/rights-permissions.

Apress titles may be purchased in bulk for academic, corporate, or promotional use. eBook versions and licenses are also available for most titles. For more information, reference our Print and eBook Bulk Sales web page at http://www.apress.com/bulk-sales.

Any source code or other supplementary material referenced by the author in this book is available to readers on GitHub via the book's product page, located at www.apress.com/9781484253120. For more detailed information, please visit http://www.apress.com/source-code.

Printed on acid-free paper

*This book is dedicated to the generous people that made
the Git community such an awesome environment to work within.
You have helped create one of the most useful tools in the tech world.
Thank you!*

Table of Contents

About the Author

Mariot Tsitoara is a Python and JavaScript developer with a passion for the Open Web and Data. He has been involved with Mozilla as a rep and a tech speaker since 2015 and has spoken extensively about Open Source and new technologies, including Rust, WebVR, and WebAssembly. Currently based in Bordeaux, he is constantly coding small, specialized tools for education. You can find him on Twitter @mariot_tsitoara.

About the Technical Reviewer

Alexander Chinedu Nnakwue has a background in Mechanical Engineering from the University of Ibadan, Nigeria, and has been a frontend developer for over 3 years working on both web and mobile technologies. He also has experience as a technical author, writer, and reviewer. He enjoys programming for the Web, and occasionally, you can also find him playing soccer. He was born in Benin City and is currently based in Lagos, Nigeria.

Acknowledgments

I'd like to thank my parents, Marie Jeanne and Tsitoara, for the amazing opportunities that they have given to me. Without their help and sacrifices, I would not be where I am today.

Thanks a lot also to my brothers and sisters, Alice, Elson, Thierry, Eliane, Annick, and Mamitiana, for being such amazing role models and for their constant support. To all my friends, Christino, Laza, Miandry, Mihaja, Miora, and Rindra, with whom I grew up and who taught me so much, I dedicate this book to you.

Almost everything I know about Git was taught to me by my coworkers. Thank you for being so helpful and a joy to work with.

This book wouldn't have seen the light of day if not for the amazing guidance of Nancy, Alexander, Louise, and Jim. Thank you so much!

Introduction

This book was written with a clear goal in mind: to be the book that I needed to read when I started my career in tech. Each chapter was crafted so that you will only be taught what you need to know as a beginner. It isn't a full reference book, but it can get you far enough to have a big impact on your career.

After reading this book, you will have the best tools for Version Control and Project Management.

Who is this book for

The targeted audience of this book is the absolute beginner with Git and GitHub and the people who have used them a little but want to know more. If you are searching for the best way to quick-start in the right direction, this book is for you.

How to use this book

Git is a very easy tool to learn, but you need to work with it to get the hang of it. The best way to learn is to directly use it on one of your real projects. Just reading the book and not doing any of the exercises will lengthen your learning curve.

PART I

Version Control with Git

CHAPTER 1

Version Control Systems

This is our first jump into Version Control Systems (VCSs). By the end of this chapter, you should know about Version Control, Git, and its history. The main objective is to know in which situations is Version Control needed and why Git is a safe choice.

What is Version Control?

As the name implies, Version Control is about the management of multiple versions of a project. To manage a version, each change (addition, edition, or removal) to the files in a project must be tracked. Version Control records each change made to a file (or a group of files) and offers a way to undo or roll back each change.

For an effective Version Control, you have to use tools called Version Control Systems. They help you navigate between changes and quickly let you go back to a previous version when something isn't right.

One of the most important advantages of using Version Control is teamwork. When more than one person is contributing to a project, tracking changes becomes a nightmare, and it greatly increases the probability of overwriting another person's changes. With Version Control, multiple people can work on their copy of the project (called branches) and only merge those changes to the main project when they (or the other team members) are satisfied with the work.

Note This book was written from a developer point of view, but everything in it applies to any text files, not just code. Version Control Systems can even track changes to many non-text files like images or Photoshop files.

© Mariot Tsitoara 2020
M. Tsitoara, *Beginning Git and GitHub*, https://doi.org/10.1007/978-1-4842-5313-7_1

Why do you need one?

Have you ever worked on a text project or on a code that requires you to recall the specific changes made to each file? If yes, how did you manage and control each version? Maybe you tried to duplicate and rename the files with suffixes like "review," "fixed," or "final"? Figure 1-1 shows that kind of Version Control.

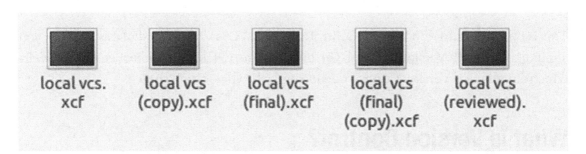

Figure 1-1. *Gimp files with suffixes like "final," "final (copy)," and "reviewed"*

The figure shows what many people do to deal with file changes. As you can see, this has the potential to go out of hands very quickly. It is very easy to forget which file is which and what has changed between them.

To track versions, one idea is to compress the files and append timestamps to the names so that the versions are arranged by date of creation. Figure 1-2 shows that kind to version tracking.

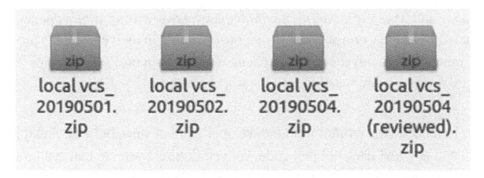

Figure 1-2. *Compressed version files sorted by dates*

The solution shown in Figure 1-2 appears to be the perfect system until you realize that even though the versions are tracked, there is no way to know what are the contents and descriptions of each version.

To remediate that situation, some developers use a solution like the one showed in Figure 1-3, which is to put the change summary of each version in a separate file.

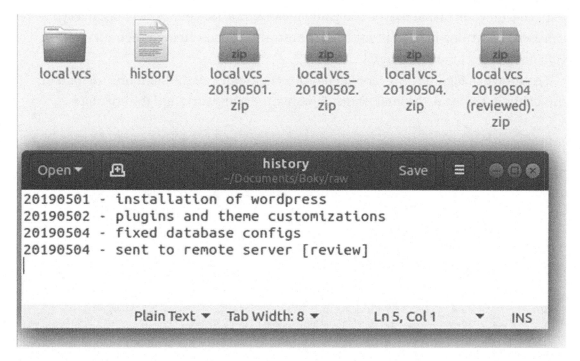

Figure 1-3. *A separate file where each version is tracked*

As Figure 1-3 shows, a separate file accompanies the project folder with a short description of the change made. Also note the many compressed files which contain the previous versions of the project.

That should do it, right? Not quite, you would still need a way to compare each version and every file change. There is no way to do this in that system; you just need to memorize everything you did. And if the project gets big, the folder just gets bigger with each version.

What happens when another developer or writer joins your team? Would you email each other the files or versions you edited? Or work on the same remote folder? In the last case, how would you know who is working on which file and what changed?

And lastly, have you ever felt the need to undo a change you made years ago without breaking everything in the process? An unlimited and all-powerful ctrl-z?

All those problems are solved by using a Version Control System or VCS. A VCS tracks each change you made to every file of your project and provides a simple way to compare and roll back those changes. Each version of the project is also accompanied by the description of the changes made along with a list of the new or edited files. When more people join the project, a VCS can show exactly who edited a particular file on a specific time. All of that makes you gain precious time for your project because you can focus on writing instead of spending time tracking each change. Figure 1-4 shows a versioned project managed by Git.

As shown in Figure 1-4, a versioned project combines all the solutions we tried in this chapter. There are the change descriptions, the teamwork, and the edit dates.

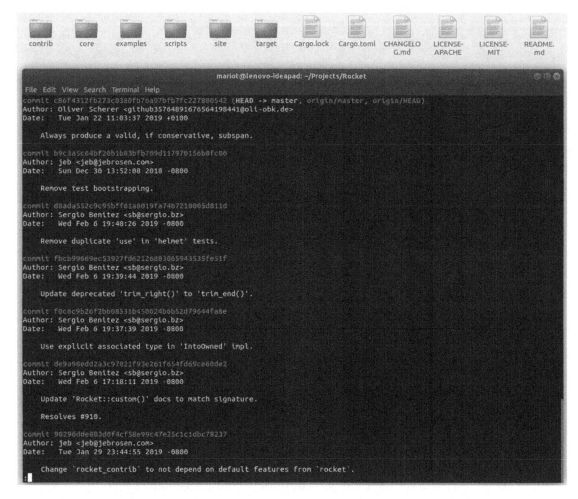

Figure 1-4. *A project versioned by Git*

Let's find out more about Version Control Systems.

What are the choices?

There are many flavors of Version Control Systems, each with their own advantages and shortcomings. A VCS can be local, centralized, or distributed.

Local Version Control Systems

These are the first VCSs created to manage source code. They worked by tracking the changes made to files in a single database that was stored locally. This means that all the changes were kept in a single computer and if there were problems, all the work were lost. This also means that working with a team was out of the question.

One of the most popular local VCSs was Source Code Control System or SCCS, which was free but closed source. Developed by AT&T, it was wildly used in the 1970s until Revision Control System or RCS was released. RCS became more popular than SCCS because it was Open Source, cross-platform, and much more effective. Released in 1982, RCS is currently maintained by the GNU Project. One of the drawbacks of these two local VCSs was that they only worked on a file at a time; there was no way to track an entire project with them.

To help you visualize how it works, here's Figure 1-5 which shows an illustration of a simple local VCS.

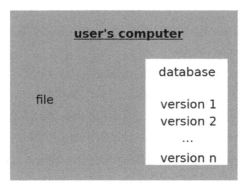

Figure 1-5. *How a local VCS works*

As you can see in Figure 1-5, everything is on the user's computer, and only one file is tracked. The versioning is stored in a database managed by the local VCS.

Centralized Version Control Systems

Centralized VCS (CVCS) works by storing the change history on a single server that the clients (authors) can connect to. This offers a way to work with a team and also a way to monitor the general pace of a project. They are still popular because the concept is so simple and it's very easy to set up.

The main problem was that, like local VCS, a server error can cost the team all their work. A network connection was also required since the main project was stored in a remote server.

You can see in Figure 1-6 how it works.

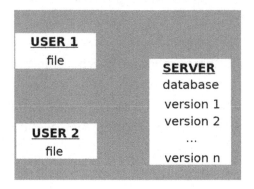

Figure 1-6. *How a centralized VCS works*

Figure 1-6 shows that a centralized VCS works similarly to a local VCS, but the database is stored in a remote server.

The main problem faced by team using a centralized VCS is that once a file is being used by someone, that file is locked and the other team members can't work on it. Thus, they had to coordinate between themselves just to modify a single file. This creates a lot of delays in development and is generally source to a lot of frustration for contributors. And the more members are on the team, the more problems arise.

In an effort to counter the problems of local VCS, Concurrent Version System or CVS was developed. It was Open Source and could track multiple sets of files instead of a single file. Many users could also work on the same file at the same time, hence the "concurrent" in the name. All the history was stored in a remote repository, and the users would keep up with the changes by checking out the server, meaning copying the contents of the remote database to their local computers.

Apache Subversion or SVN was developed in 2000 and could be everything that CVS could, with a bonus: it could track non-text files. One of the main advantages of SVN was that instead of tracking a group of files like the previous VCS, it tracks the entire project. So, it is essentially tracking the directory instead of files. That means that the renaming, adding and removing are also tracked. This made SVN, along with it being Open Source, a very popular VCS; and it is still wildly used today.

Distributed Version Control Systems

Distributed VCS works nearly the same as centralized VCS but with a big difference: there is no main server that holds all the history. Each client has a copy of the repository (along with the change history) instead of checking out a single server.

This greatly lowers the chance of losing everything as each client has a clone of the project. With a distributed VCS, the concept of having a "main server" gets blurred because each client essentially has all the power within their own repository. This greatly encouraged the concept of "forking" within the Open Source community. Forking is the act of cloning a repository to make your own changes and have a different take on the project. The main benefit of forking is that you could also pull changes from other repositories if you see fit (and others can do the same with your changes).

A distributed Version Control System is generally faster than the other types of VCS because it doesn't need a network access to a remote server. Nearly everything is done locally. There is also a slight difference with how it works: instead of tracking the changes between versions, it tracks all changes as "patches." This means that those patches can be freely exchanged between repositories, so there is no "main" repository to keep up with.

Figure 1-7 shows how a distributed VCS works.

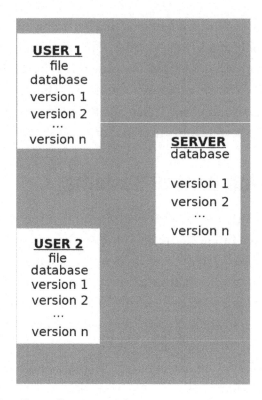

Figure 1-7. *How a distributed VCS works*

Note   By looking at Figure 1-7, it is tempting to conclude that there is a main server that the users are keeping up with. But it isn't the case with a distributed VCS, it is only a convention that many developers follow to have a better workflow.

BitKeeper SCM was a proprietary distributed VCS released in 2000 which, like SCCS in the 1970s, was closed source. It had a free "Community Version" that lacked many of the big features of BitKeeper SCM, but since it was one of the first distributed VCSs, it was pretty popular even in the Open Source community. This popularity of BitKeeper plays a big role in the creation of Git. It is now an Open Source software, after having its source code released under the Apache License in 2016. You can find the current BitKeeper project on `www.bitkeeper.org/`; the development has slowed down, but there is still a community contributing to it.

What is Git?

Remember the proprietary distributed Version Control System BitKeeper SCM from the last section? Well, the Linux kernel developers used it for their development. The decision to use it was wildly regarded as a bad move and made many people unhappy. Their fears were confirmed in 2005 when BitKeeper SCM stopped being free. Since it was closed source, the developers lost their favorite Version Control System. The community (led by Linus Torvalds) had to find another VCS, and since an alternative was not available, they decided to create their own. Thus, Git was born.

Since Git was made to replace BitKeeper SCM, it worked generally the same with a few tweaks. Like BitKeeper SCM, Git is a distributed Version Control System, but it is faster and works better with large projects. The Git community is very active, and there are many contributors involved in its development; you can find more about Git on `https://git-scm.com/`. The features of Git and how it works are explained later in this section.

What can Git do?

Remember all those problems we tried to solve at the beginning of this chapter? Well, Git can solve them all. It can even solve problems you didn't know you had!

First, it works great with tracking changes. You can

- Go back and forth between versions

- Review the differences between those versions

- Check the change history of a file

- Tag a specific version for quick referencing

Git is also a great tool for teamwork. You can

- Exchange "changesets" between repositories

- Review the changes made by others

One of the main features of Git is its Branching system. A branch is a copy of a project which you can work on without messing with the repository. This concept has been around for some time, but with Git, it is way faster and more efficient. Branching also comes along with Merging, which is the act of copying the changesets done in a branch back to the source. Generally, you create a branch to create or test a new feature and merge that branch back when you are satisfied with the work.

There is also a simple concept that you might use a lot: Stashing. Stashing is the act of safely putting away your current edits so that you have clean environment to work on something completely different. You might want to use stashing when you are playing around or testing a feature but need to work on a new feature in priority. So, you stash your changes away and begin to write that feature. After you are done, you can get your changes back and apply them to your current working environment.

As a little appetizer, here are some of the Git commands you will learn in this book:

```
$ git init      # Initialize a new git database
$ git clone     # Copy an existing database
$ git status    # Check the status of the local project
$ git diff      # Review the changes done to the project
$ git add       # Tell Git to track a changed file
$ git commit    # Save the current state of the project to database
$ git push      # Copy the local database to a remote server
$ git pull      # Copy a remote database to a local machine
$ git log       # Check the history of the project
$ git branch    # List, create or delete branches
$ git merge     # Merge the history of two branches together
$ git stash     # Keep the current changes stashed away to be used later
```

As you can see, the commands are pretty self-explanatory. Don't worry about knowing all of them by heart; you will retain them one by one when we will properly begin the learning. And you will not also use them all the time, you will mostly use git add and git commit. You will learn about each command, but we will focus on the commands that you will likely use in a professional setting. But before that, let's see the inner working of Git.

How does Git work?

Unlike many Version Control Systems, Git works with Snapshots, not Differences. This means that it does not track the difference between two versions of a file, but takes a picture of the current state of the project.

This is why Git is very fast compared to other distributed VCSs; it is also why switching between versions and branches is so fast and easy.

Remember how a centralized Version Control System works? Well, Git is the complete opposite. You don't need to communicate with a central server get work done. Since Git is a distributed VCS, every user has their own fully fledged repository with their own history and changesets. Thus, everything is done locally except the sharing of patches or changesets. Like previously said, a central server is not needed; but many developers use one as convention as it is easier to work that way.

Speaking of patch sharing, how does Git know which changesets are whose? When Git takes a snapshot, it performs a checksum on it; so, it knows which files were changed by comparing the checksums. This is why Git can track changes between files and directories easily, and it also checks for any file corruption.

The main feature of Git is its "Three States" system. The states are the working directory, the staging area, and the git directory:

- The working directory is just the current snapshot that you are working on.

- The staging area is where modified files are marked in their current version, ready to be stored in the database.

- The git directory is the database where the history is stored.

So, basically Git works as follows: you modify the files, add each file you want to include in the snapshot to the staging area (git add), then take the snapshot and add them to the database (git commit). For the terminology, we call a modified file added to the staging area "staged" and a file added to the database "committed." So, a file goes from "modified" to "staged" to "committed."

What is the typical Git workflow?

To help you visualize all that we talked about in this section, here is a little demo of what a typical workflow using Git is like. Don't worry if you don't understand everything right now; the next chapters will get you set up.

This is your first day of work. You are tasked to add your name to an existing project description file. Since this is your first day, a senior developer is there to review your code.

The first thing you should do is get the project's source code. Ask your manager for the server where the code is stored. For this demo, the server is GitHub, meaning that the

Git database is stored on a remote server hosted by GitHub and you can access it by URL or directly on the GitHub web site. Here, we are going to use the clone command to get the database, but you could also just download the project from the GitHub web site. You will get a zip file containing and the project files with all its history.

So, you clone the repository to get the source code by using the "clone" command.

```
git clone https://github.com/mariot/thebestwebsite.git
```

Git then downloads a copy of the repository in the current directory you are working from. After that, you can enter the new directory and check its contents as shown in Figure 1-8.

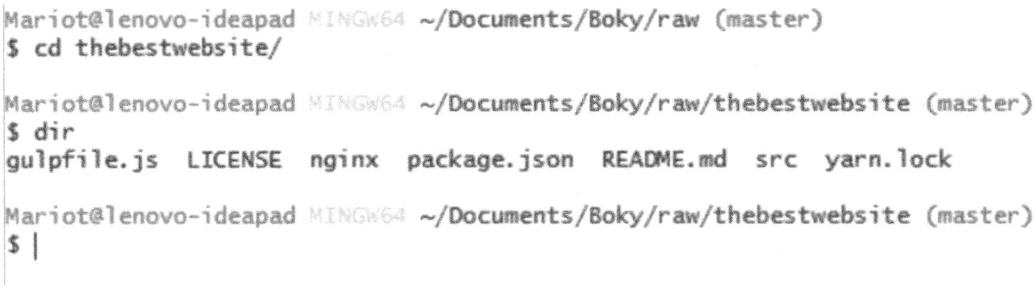

```
Mariot@lenovo-ideapad MINGW64 ~/Documents/Boky/raw (master)
$ cd thebestwebsite/

Mariot@lenovo-ideapad MINGW64 ~/Documents/Boky/raw/thebestwebsite (master)
$ dir
gulpfile.js  LICENSE  nginx  package.json  README.md  src  yarn.lock

Mariot@lenovo-ideapad MINGW64 ~/Documents/Boky/raw/thebestwebsite (master)
$ |
```

Figure 1-8. *The contents of the repository is shown*

If you want to check the recent changes made to the project, you can use the "log" command to show the history. Figure 1-9 shows an example of that.

```
Mariot@lenovo-ideapad MINGW64 ~/Documents/Boky/raw/thebestwe
$ git log
commit 0cc01f912449ed913c9f48673a4b450a66951f31 (HEAD -> mas
Author: Denys Vitali <denys@denv.it>
Date:    Fri Jan 18 17:44:45 2019 +0100

    Add Hugo Theme references

    Reference: https://github.com/hugomodo/hugomodo-best-mot

commit 033eb62a526e4ffd9c73257ab37e76c9d484cd74
Author: Denys Vitali <denys@denv.it>
Date:    Thu Jan 10 10:46:28 2019 +0100

    Fix #31, add inverted-contrast mode

commit 74452d4c8cacb2dcad4431532eb99ccac4b00eac
Merge: 13e4f7e 6c3ba31
Author: Denys Vitali <denys@denv.it>
Date:    Mon Nov 12 10:12:39 2018 +0100

    Merge pull request #30 from numbermaniac/patch-1

    create -> created

commit 6c3ba31b95190fdaecf95b9af2b9d2f5554d7203
Author: numbermaniac <numbermaniac@users.noreply.github.com>
Date:    Sun Nov 11 11:22:45 2018 +1100

    create -> created
```

Figure 1-9. *A typical Git history log*

Nice! Now you should create a new branch to work on so that you don't mess up with the project. You can create a new branch by using the "branch" command and checking it out with the "checkout" command.

```
git branch add-new-dev-name-to-readme
git checkout add-new-dev-name-to-readme
```

Now that the new branch is created, you can begin to modify the files. You can use whatever editor you want; Git will track all the changes via checksums. Now that you made the necessary changes, it is time to put them on the staging area. As a reminder, the staging area is where you put modified codes that are ready to be snapshotted. If we modified the "README.md" file, we can add it to the staging area by using the "add" command.

```
git add README.md
```

15

You don't have to add every file you modified to the staging area, only those which you want to be accounted in the snapshot. Now that the file is staged, it is time to "commit" it or putting its change in the database. We do this by using the command "commit" and attaching a little description with it.

```
git commit -m "Add Mariot to the list of developers"
```

And that's it! The changes you made are now in the database and safely stored. But only on your computer! The others can't see your work because you worked on your own repository and on a different branch. To show your work to others, you have to push your commits to the remote server. But you have to show the code to the senior dev first before making a push. If they are okay with it, you can merge your branch with the main snapshot of the project (called the master branch). So first you must navigate back to the master branch by using the "checkout" command.

```
git checkout master
```

You are now on the master branch, where all the team's work is stored. But the time you worked on your fix, the project may have changed, meaning that a team member may have changed some files. You should retrieve those changes before committing your own changes to master. This will limit the risk of "conflicts" which can happen when two or more contributors change the same file. To get the changes, you have to pull the project from the remote server (also called origin).

```
git pull origin master
```

Even if another coworker changed the same file as you, the risk of conflicts is low because you only modified a line. Conflicts only arise when the same line has been modified by multiple people. If you and your coworkers changed different parts of the file, everything is okay.

Now that we kept up with the current state of the project, it's time to commit our version to master. You can merge your branch with the "merge" command.

```
git merge add-new-dev-name-to-readme
```

Now that the commit has been merged back to master, it is time to push the changes to the main server. We do that by using to "push" command.

```
git push
```

Figure 1-10 shows the commands we used and the results.

```
Mariot@lenovo-ideapad MINGW64 ~/Documents/Boky/raw/thebestwebsite (add-new-dev-name-to-readme)
$ git commit -m "Add Mariot to the list of developers"
[add-new-dev-name-to-readme 4de128e] Add Mariot to the list of developers
 1 file changed, 1 insertion(+), 1 deletion(-)

Mariot@lenovo-ideapad MINGW64 ~/Documents/Boky/raw/thebestwebsite (add-new-dev-name-to-readme)
$ git checkout master
Switched to branch 'master'
Your branch is up to date with 'origin/master'.

Mariot@lenovo-ideapad MINGW64 ~/Documents/Boky/raw/thebestwebsite (master)
$ git merge add-new-dev-name-to-readme
Updating 0cc01f9..4de128e
Fast-forward
 README.md | 2 +
 1 file changed, 1 insertion(+), 1 deletion(-)

Mariot@lenovo-ideapad MINGW64 ~/Documents/Boky/raw/thebestwebsite (master)
$ git push
Enumerating objects: 5, done.
Counting objects: 100% (5/5), done.
Delta compression using up to 4 threads
Compressing objects: 100% (3/3), done.
Writing objects: 100% (3/3), 316 bytes | 316.00 KiB/s, done.
Total 3 (delta 2), reused 0 (delta 0)
remote: Resolving deltas: 100% (2/2), completed with 2 local objects.
To https://github.com/mariot/thebestwebsite.git
   0cc01f9..4de128e  master -> master
```

Figure 1-10. *A simple Git workflow*

It's that simple! And again, don't worry if you don't understand everything yet. This is just a little demo of how Git is usually used. It is also not very realistic: no manager would give a new recruit an all-access pass to their main repository like that.

Summary

This was only a sneak peek at Git; it has many more powerful features that you will learn along the way. But before anything else, here are some things that you should ask yourself before moving to the next step: "How will Git help me in my projects?", "which features are the most important?", and "will Git improve my workflow?"

The main takeaway for this chapter is the difference between distributed and centralized VCSs. The workflow of teams using CVCS is less organized and leaves too many developers unfulfilled. Thus, you need to learn more about distributed VCS to keep up with the times.

We've seen the typical workflow of a team using Git in this chapter; it's the workflow that most teams use in a professional environment and even in the Open Source community. Even if you plan to work alone, using the workflow will increase your productivity.

Don't worry about understanding all of Git right now; just focus on what it can do for you. You will get familiar with it after a couple chapters. But right now, let's task ourselves with how to install Git on your system.

CHAPTER 2

Installation and Setup

Now that you how what is Version Control and how Git works, we are going to learn how to install and set it up. This chapter is shorter compared to the others because it is so easy to set Git up.

Installation

The files necessary to install Git are on `https://git-scm.com/downloads` for all systems. Just follow the link and choose your Operating System.

You can also see in Figure 2-1 that there are GUI clients for Git also available there. Don't head out there before you complete this book's third part, Teamwork with Git. You need to familiarize yourself with Git commands before using GUI clients; if not, you will lose a lot of time trying to resolve a simple issue that would take seconds with simple Git commands.

© Mariot Tsitoara 2020
M. Tsitoara, *Beginning Git and GitHub*, https://doi.org/10.1007/978-1-4842-5313-7_2

Figure 2-1. The download section of git-scm.com as of May 2019

After you have familiarized yourself with Git commands, you can check out a GUI client and see for yourself. There is a chapter about GUI clients at the last part of this book. But please don't use any GUI client before that time; it will greatly lengthen your learning time.

Note   Git is bundled with two GUI tools: gitk to review history and git-gui for basic commands. You will learn to use them in the last part of this book, so the preceding advice still applies.

Windows

Installing Git on Windows systems is very easy. After opening the link (`https://git-scm.com/download/win`), the download should automatically begin, and you will arrive at the confirmation page shown in Figure 2-2. If not, just download the build that corresponds to your Windows flavor.

Figure 2-2. *The Git download screen for Windows*

Execute the download exe file to begin the installation. The first screen is the license declaration outlining the terms and conditions; you should read it until the end (yeah, right). Click next, and you will get to a component selection screen similar to the one shown in Figure 2-3. Here, you are prompted to select which components to install. I recommend to leave the default options on.

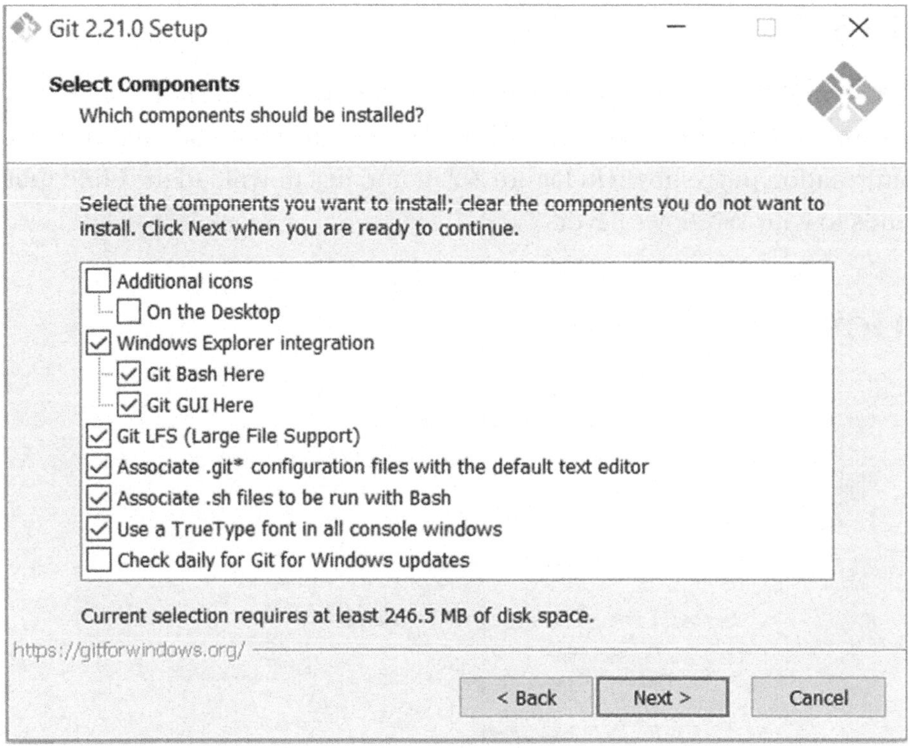

Figure 2-3. *Select the components to install*

You can see in Figure 2-3 that you just have to check the components to install them. It is a good idea to leave the Windows Explorer integration checked; that way you would just have to right-click a folder to find the options to start Git in the default GUI or the Bash (command window) in the context menu. All the other components are pretty self-explanatory so the decision is up to you.

Tip   If you didn't install the Windows Explorer integration and want to open the command window in a folder, you have to open the extended context menu with Shift + Right-click.

Click next after you made your choices, and you will see the default editor selection, shown in Figure 2-4. Git needs you to define a default editor because you need an editor to write out commit descriptions and comments.

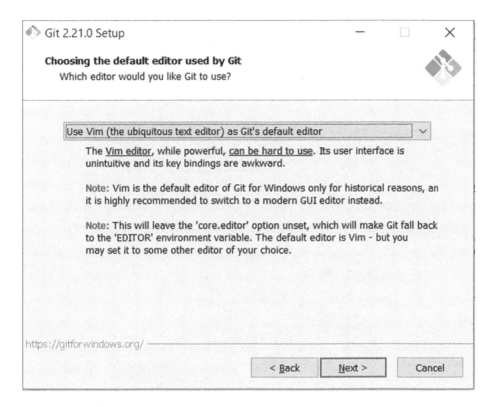

Figure 2-4. *Default editor selection*

As you can see in Figure 2-4, Vim is the default editor for Git for historical reason. Just pick your favorite text editor from the dropdown list. The first two, Nano and Vim, work in the console or command window, so you don't have to open another program. In the list, you can find many popular editors like Notepad++, Sublime Text, Atom and Visual Studio (VS) Code. If your editor isn't listed, you can choose the last option, and a new input will appear (shown in Figure 2-5) so you can provide a link to the editor's main executable file.

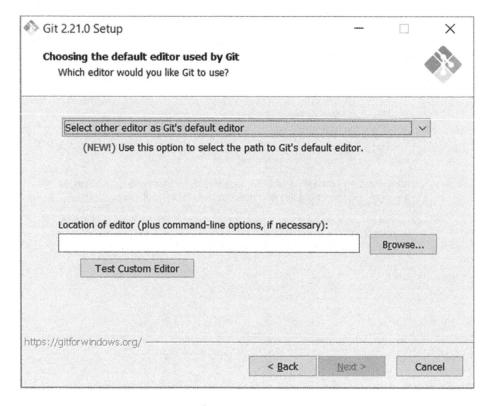

Figure 2-5. *Setting up a custom editor*

In Figure 2-5, you can see the screen where you can set up your custom editor if it isn't listed on the dropdown.

For this book, I decided to leave the default option and use Vim. It doesn't change anything in this book if you decide to use any other editor. But if you want to learn Vim (takes a bit of time), you can check out "vimtutor," which is a tutor program shipped with Vim, or learn through a fun video game on https://vim-adventures.com/. There is also www.vi-improved.org/vimusermanual.pdf which is more complete but is more than 300 pages!

And don't worry, this choice is not definitive, you can still change anytime you want. You will learn how at the last section of this chapter.

Caution   While online, never ever start or participate in an Editor War. Just choose your preferred text editor and never talk about it to anyone. I still bear scars from my old days in the "Emacs vs. Vim" war.

Once you chose your favorite editor, you can go to the next screen, which is the PATH environment adjustment, shown in Figure 2-6. The PATH environment is a variable that holds a list of directories where executable programs are located in their value. It's needed so you don't have to type in the full path to an executable when you want to execute it in the console; you just have to type its name. For example, to launch Visual Studio Code from the console, I should type C:\Program Files (x86)\Microsoft VS Code\bin\code. But since I have C:\Program Files (x86)\Microsoft VS Code\bin in my PATH, I just have to type "code" to launch it.

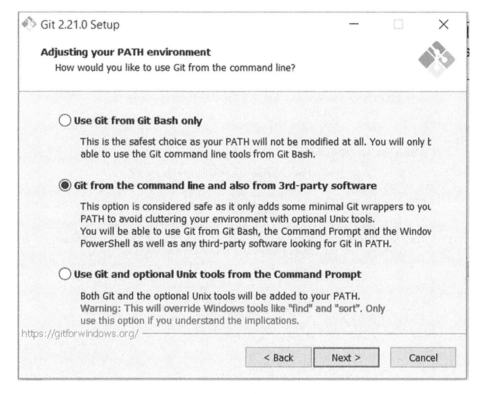

Figure 2-6. *Choosing to add Git to PATH or not*

The same could apply to Git if you want. If you don't want this and only want to use Git with its own isolated console "Git Bash," select the first option. So, to use Git, you would have to launch it from the Apps list or from the context menu of a folder (if you chose to install the Windows Explorer integration).

If you want to be able to use Git everywhere, leave the default option to add it to your PATH environment. That way, other tools can also use Git and you can work from any command window. I highly suggest this option.

The last option is a bit invasive. It will add many Git commands to your PATH and will overwrite some of Windows' default tools. Only choose this if you have a valid reason too; generally, you don't have such a reason.

Choose an option as shown in Figure 2-6 and proceed to the next step. You will arrive at a screen concerning HTTPS connections, shown in Figure 2-7. You will have to choose which library to use when sending data over HTTPS. Later in this book, you will have to connect to a remote server (since Git is a distributed VCS) to share your commits to other people, so all those connections must be encrypted to further secure your data and ensure they are not being stolen.

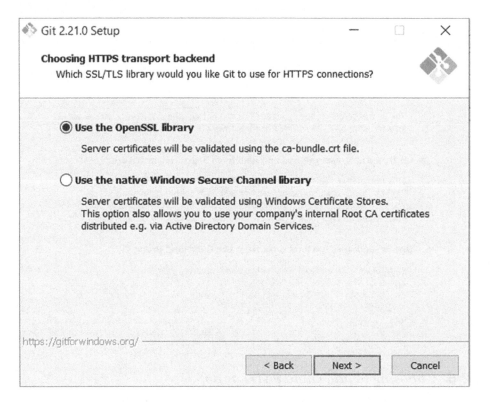

Figure 2-7. *Choosing the HTTPS transport*

Just use the default option unless you have a reason to (company policy or your own little security setup).

After this, go to the next step which is about line endings. Once again, it's a selection screen, so yours should look like the one shown in Figure 2-8. Different Operating Systems operate text files differently, especially when dealing with line endings. And odds are that the team you will be working with will be using different OS. So, Git needs to convert line endings to and from each ending style before sharing commits.

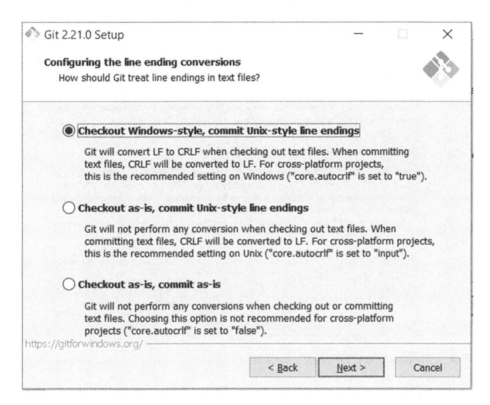

Figure 2-8. *Line ending conversions*

As you will be using Windows, you should check the default option. The other two options will do a lot of damage to your commits if you are not careful with line endings. You can go to next step after choosing the default option.

Caution   This step is important because Windows and MacOS use \r\n to end lines instead of Linux's \n. If you don't convert, your file will become very hard to read and Git will detect a lot of changes even if didn't make that many.

The next step is to choose a default terminal (or console) emulator. It's a simple selection screen like before, shown in Figure 2-9. Git Bash needs a console emulator to work, so you need to choose one. The default emulator is MinTTY, the other option being Windows' default console.

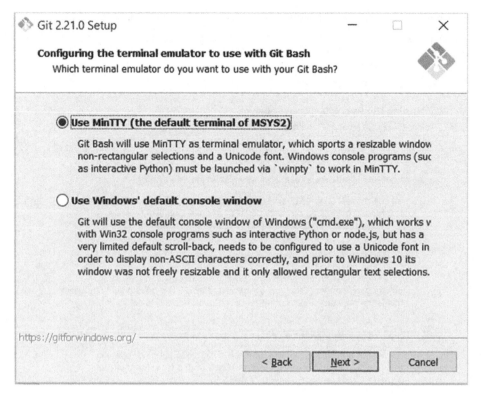

Figure 2-9. *Choosing a terminal emulator*

I suggest keeping the default option because MinTTY can do everything that the Windows console window can, but better in every way. Click next to proceed to the last step.

We are now in the endgame! This installation is nearly over. Just a few things to tweak in the extra options screen. This screen (shown in Figure 2-10) permits you to enable some extra features that will go great with your Git installation. For example, the Git Credential Manager will help you connect to remote servers securely and plays nicely with other Git tools.

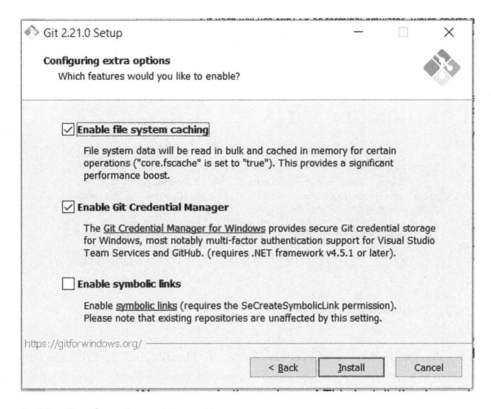

Figure 2-10. *Configuring extra options*

Just leave the default options unless you have a reason not to. After that, just launch the installation and let it finish. And that's it! Git is installed on your Windows system. But before using it, jump to the next section to properly set it up!

Mac

If you've already done some software development with Mac OS X, you probably already have Git because it's installed with XCode (`https://developer.apple.com/xcode/`). You can check if you have Git by running the command from your console:

```
$ git --version
```

It should give you the version of Git currently installed or if it's not installed prompt you to install XCode's Command Line Tools. If you choose install on that prompt, Git will be installed and you can skip the rest of this section.

To install Git on your Mac, you just have to go to the download link `https://git-scm.com/download/mac`, and the download should begin automatically, as shown in Figure 2-11. Execute the downloaded file and the installation will start; it's pretty easy.

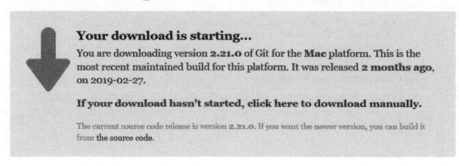

Downloading Git

Your download is starting...
You are downloading version **2.21.0** of Git for the **Mac** platform. This is the most recent maintained build for this platform. It was released **2 months ago**, on 2019-02-27.

If your download hasn't started, click here to download manually.

The current source code release is version **2.21.0**. If you want the newer version, you can build it from **the source code**.

Figure 2-11. *Download screen for Mac*

You can also use Homebrew (`https://brew.sh/`) to install it. Just run the command:

```
$ brew install git
```

This will install about half the universe, but it will eventually stop, and Git will be installed.

And that's it! For Mac OS X, installing Git is way easier and you probably already have it.

Linux

If you use Linux regularly, you probably know much about your distribution than me. So, installing Git with your package manager might be a piece of cake for you.

For Ubuntu- and Debian-flavored distributions, you use APT to install Git.

```
$ sudo apt-get install git
```

or

```
$ sudo apt install git (for newer systems)
```

For Fedora, you can use YUM or DNF.

```
$ sudo yum install git
```

or

```
$ sudo dnf install git (for newer systems)
```

If you have a different distribution, you can check https://git-scm.com/download/linux to have a list of commands on how to install Git for each popular distro. This list should be similar to the one shown in Figure 2-12, with more and more Linux flavors to come.

Download for Linux and Unix

It is easiest to install Git on Linux using the preferred package manager of your Linux distribution. If you prefer to build from source, you can find the tarballs on kernel.org.

Debian/Ubuntu

For the latest stable version for your release of Debian/Ubuntu

```
# apt-get install git
```
For Ubuntu, this PPA provides the latest stable upstream Git version

```
# add-apt-repository ppa:git-core/ppa  # apt update; apt install git
```

Fedora

```
# yum install git  (up to Fedora 21)
# dnf install git  (Fedora 22 and later)
```

Gentoo

```
# emerge --ask --verbose dev-vcs/git
```

Arch Linux

```
# pacman -S git
```

openSUSE

```
# zypper install git
```

Mageia

```
# urpmi git
```

Nix/NixOS

```
# nix-env -i git
```

FreeBSD

```
# pkg install git
```

Solaris 9/10/11 (OpenCSW)

```
# pkgutil -i git
```

Solaris 11 Express

```
# pkg install developer/versioning/git
```

OpenBSD

```
# pkg_add git
```

Alpine

```
$ apk add git
```

Red Hat Enterprise Linux, Oracle Linux, CentOS, Scientific Linux, et al.

RHEL and derivatives typically ship older versions of git. You can download a tarball and build from source, or use a 3rd-party repository such as the IUS Community Project to obtain a more recent version of git.

Slitaz

```
$ tazpkg get-install git
```

Figure 2-12. *How to install Git on Linux*

After you use the command corresponding to your distribution listed in Figure 2-12, Git is installed!

Caution   Just like Editor War, Distribution War is a big no-no online.

Setting up Git

Before beginning to use Git, you need a little bit of setup first. You will probably only do this once since all the setup is stored on an external global file, meaning that all your projects will share the same configs. There is also a way to configure projects one by one but we will see this later.

Since Git is a distributed Version Control System, you will one day need to connect to other remote repositories. To avoid making any identity mistake, it is necessary to tell Git a bit about yourself. Don't worry; it won't ask about a fun fact about you!

To set up Git, open Git Bash (for Windows systems) or the default console window (for Linux/MacOS or Windows systems that modified their PATH environment). In the command prompt, just tell Git your name and email address:

```
$ git config --global user.name "Mariot Tsitoara"
$ git config --global user.email "mariot.tsitoara@gmail.com"
```

Notice the "global" argument; it means that the setup is for all future Git repositories, so you don't have to set this up again in the future.

With the config command, you can also change your default editor. If you ever want to change your editor because you found a new one or uninstalled yours, the config command is there to help you. For example, to change the default editor to Nano, you would type

```
$ git config --global core.editor="nano"
```

You can find the file recording your Git configuration on your home folder. For Windows, you can find it in C:\Users\YourName\.gitconfig. For Linux and Mac OS, you can find it in /home/yourname/.gitconfig as shown in Figure 2-13.

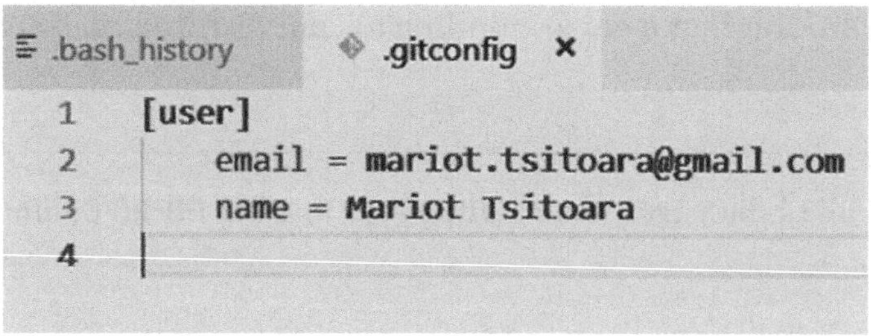

Figure 2-13. *My .gitconfig file*

Next to the .gitconfig file, you might find another file called .bash_history that records all the commands you type on the console. You can check this document if you want to check back on a command you forgot.

Summary

Let's review what we've learned so far! First, you should have had Git installed on your system by now. The installation process is very easy on Windows and easier on Mac and Linux. I suggest you keep all the default options (even if they aren't shown in the preceding screenshots) if you are not sure of what you need.

Next, there is the setup. You will only have to do this once in every system you install Git into. Git will use your name and email to sign every action you make so it's necessary to set them up before you using it.

And that's it! You are now ready to use Git with all its glory. Head to the next chapter to jump start with Git.

CHAPTER 3

Getting Started

You're finally ready to get started with Git! In this chapter, you'll be learning a few Git terminologies and concepts necessary for any project. Then, you'll be tasked to set up a project, make changes to it, review the changes, and finally navigate between versions. Let's go!

Repositories

A repository is a storage where all your project and all the changes made to it are kept. You can think of it as a "change database." But don't worry; it is only a normal folder on your system, so it is very easy to manipulate.

For each project you want to manage with Git, you have to set up a repository for it. Setting up a repository is very easy. Just navigate to the folder you want to track and tell Git to initiate a repository there.

So for each project you want to start, you should

- Create the directory containing your project

- Navigate into the directory

- Initialize a Git repository

See? It's very easy. Let's convert those statements into commands. But first, let's open a console to type our commands in. For Linux users, you just have to launch your favorite terminal (Ctrl-Alt-T for Debian like distros). For MacOS, you just have to use Cmd-Space to bring up Spotlight where you can search for the Terminal app. Windows users can open two consoles: cmd and powershell. Powershell is more modern and has UNIX-like commands. To open one of them, use Windows-R and type in the name (cmd or powershell). Note that you need to restart all these consoles on your first installation of Git if you had them open. Git for Windows also comes with a console emulator called Git Bash that provides a similar environment to Linux and Mac consoles. If you use

© Mariot Tsitoara 2020
M. Tsitoara, *Beginning Git and GitHub*, https://doi.org/10.1007/978-1-4842-5313-7_3

Windows, I highly suggest to use Git Bash so you can have the same experience as other people who use different OSs.

Open Git Bash (from the Apps list or the contextual menu), and type in those commands:

```
$ mkdir mynewproject
$ cd mynewproject/
$ git init
```

mkdir is a command used to create a directory; it is short for "make directory." *cd* is the command used to navigate between directories; it is short for "change directory." Finally, *git init* is short for "Git initialize."

After you initialize the repository, Git will tell you where the database was created like in Figure 3-1.

```
Mariot@lenovo-ideapad MINGW64 ~/Documents/Boky/raw (master)
$ mkdir mynewproject

Mariot@lenovo-ideapad MINGW64 ~/Documents/Boky/raw (master)
$ cd mynewproject/

Mariot@lenovo-ideapad MINGW64 ~/Documents/Boky/raw/mynewproject (master)
$ git init
Initialized empty Git repository in C:/Users/Mariot/Documents/Boky/raw/mynewproject/.git/
```

Figure 3-1. *Initialization of a new repository*

Note   mkdir and cd are system commands; they are managed by the OS, whereas init is a Git command. Every Git command begins with "git."

Git will create a directory called ".git" that will contain all your changesets and snapshots. If you want to check it out, you will have to show hidden files from your file explorer's settings. The repository looks like the directory shown in Figure 3-2.

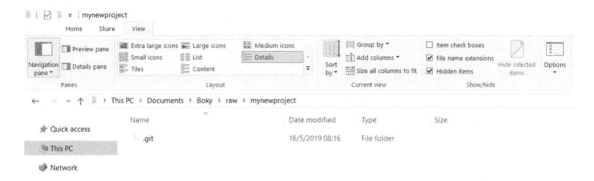

Figure 3-2. *An empty repository*

And if you open the .git directory, you will find many more items that are part of the Git database. Check Figure 3-3 for an example.

Name	Date modified	Type	Size
hooks	16/5/2019 08:16	File folder	
info	16/5/2019 08:16	File folder	
objects	16/5/2019 08:16	File folder	
refs	16/5/2019 08:16	File folder	
config	16/5/2019 08:16	File	1 KB
description	16/5/2019 08:16	File	1 KB
HEAD	16/5/2019 08:16	File	1 KB

Figure 3-3. *Inside the .git directory*

Remember Chapter 1 that said that instead of tracking changes between versions, Git takes snapshots? Well, all those snapshots are stored in the ".git" directory. Each snapshot is called "commit," and we'll look into that shortly after this section.

The HEAD file in this ".git" directory points to the current "branch" or subversion of the project that you are working on. The default branch is called "master," but it is just like any other branch; the name is just an old convention.

You should also know that initializing is the only way to get a repository. You can copy an entire repository with all its history and snapshots. It is called "cloning," and we will see that in another chapter.

EXERCISE: CREATE AN EMPTY REPOSITORY

Our first exercise isn't exactly rocket surgery. Just create an empty repository somewhere in your system. You can use the default console or Git Bash.

Working Directory

What about the empty area outside the ".git" directory? It is called the Working Directory, and the files you will be working on will be stored there. Generally, your most recent version will be on the Working Directory.

Each file you work on is on the Working Directory. There is nothing particular about this place except the fact that you will only manipulate the files here directly. Never modify the files inside the ".git" directory!

Git will detect any new file you will place in the Working Directory. And you check the status of the directory by using the Git command "status."

```
$ git status
```

For example, if we create a new file called README.md in the Working Directory, we will see that Git will know that the project has changed. Make sure that you place your new file alongside the .git directory like in Figure 3-4, not into it!

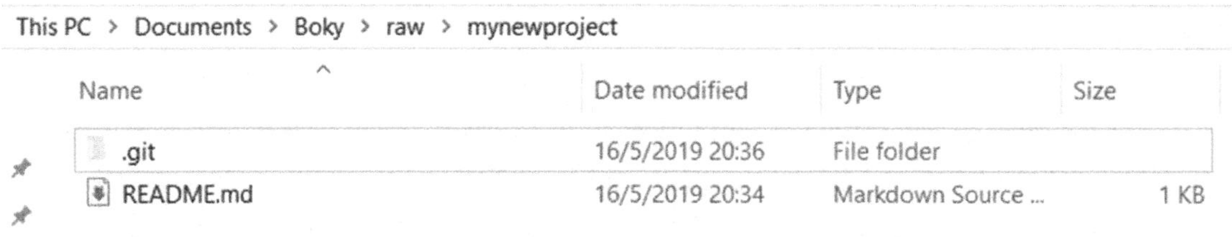

Name	Date modified	Type	Size
.git	16/5/2019 20:36	File folder	
README.md	16/5/2019 20:34	Markdown Source ...	1 KB

This PC > Documents > Boky > raw > mynewproject

Figure 3-4. *Creation of a new file in the Working Directory*

If we check the status of the Working Directory, we will get a result like the one shown in Figure 3-5.

As you can see in Figure 3-5, we don't have any commits yet; that's because we are still on the Working Directory and we haven't taken any snapshots yet. It also says that we are on the "master" branch; it is the default name for the only branch created on the repository initialization. Then we get the untracked files. Those are the files we modified (in this instance, created).

Figure 3-5. *The status of the Working Directory*

Essentially, that is the Working Directory: the area where you directly interact with your project files.

EXERCISE: CREATE SOME FILES FOR THE PROJECT

This exercise is again very easy. Just create some files within your project directory (repository) and check the Working Directory status.

Staging Area

The Staging Area is where your files go before the snapshots are taken. Not every file you modified on the Working Directory should be taken into account when taking a snapshot of the current state of the project. Only the files placed in the Staging Area will be snapshotted.

So, before taking a snapshot of the project, you select which changed files to take account of. A change in a file can be creating, deleting, or editing.

Think of it as designating which files get to be in the family photo. To add a file to the Staging Area, we use the Git command "add."

```
$ git add nameofthefile
```

It's that simple. If we wanted to stage the README.md that we created earlier, we would use "git add README.md." Or if you created multiple files, you can add them one after another or together like "git add file1 file2 file3."

Let's stage our new file by using the command:

```
$ git add README.md
```

Then let's check the status with git status command.

```
$ git status
```

Adding a file to the staging area won't produce any visible result, but checking the status will get you a result similar to Figure 3-6.

```
Mariot@lenovo-ideapad MINGW64 ~/Documents/Boky/raw/mynewsite (master)
$ git add README.md

Mariot@lenovo-ideapad MINGW64 ~/Documents/Boky/raw/mynewsite (master)
$ git status
On branch master

No commits yet

Changes to be committed:
  (use "git rm --cached <file>..." to unstage)

        new file:   README.md
```

Figure 3-6. *Staging a file*

If you check out Figure 3-6, you will notice that after staging the file, the Working Directory is clean again. That's because "git status" only keeps track on "unstaged" files (edited files that have not been marked for a snapshot).

As you can see in Figure 3-6 too, you can unstage a file using the Git command "git rm" with the option "--cached."

```
$ git rm --cached README.md
```

Caution   Don't forget the option "--cached" when unstaging a file. If you forget it, you could lose your file!

After you stage all the files that you want the changes to be taken into account, you are now ready to take your first snapshot!

EXERCISE: STAGE AND UNSTAGE YOUR FILES

Take the files you created on the previous exercise and stage them. Unstage one file and re-stage it. Check the Working Directory status after each stage/unstage.

Commits

Like we talked about in the section before this one, a commit is just a snapshot of the entire project at a certain time. Git doesn't record the individual changes done to the files; it takes a picture of the entire project.

In addition to the snapshot, a commit also contains information about the "author" of the content and the "commiter" or who put the changeset into the repository.

Note   "author" and "commiter" are usually the same person, unless the commiter took the changeset from another team member. Remember that Git commits are exchangeable since it is a distributed VCS.

Since a commit is a snapshot from the state of the project, the previous state of the project is another commit called "parent." The very first commit is created by Git when the repository is created, and it's the one commit that has no parents. All future commits are then linked to each other via parentage. The ensemble of those commits that are parents to each other is called "branch."

Note   If a commit has two parents, that means that it was created by merging two branches.

A commit is identified by its name, a 40-character string that is obtained by hashing the commit. It is a simple SHA1 hash so multiple commits with the same information will have the same name.

A reference to a specific commit is called "head," and it also has a name. And the head you are currently working on is called "HEAD" (see the previous section).

We can now commit the files we staged earlier. Before each commit, you should check the status of the Working Directory and the Staging Area. If all the files you want to commit are in the Staging Area (under the phrase "Changes to be committed"), you can commit. If not, you have to stage them with "git add."

To commit all the changes we made, we use "git commit." This will take a snapshot of our current state of the project.

```
$ git commit
```

If we execute this command, it will open our default editor (check Chapter 2 if you want to modify yours) and ask us for a commit message. A commit message is a short description of what has changed in the commit compared to the previous one.

My default editor is Vim, so if I execute the commit command, I will see a screen as shown in Figure 3-7.

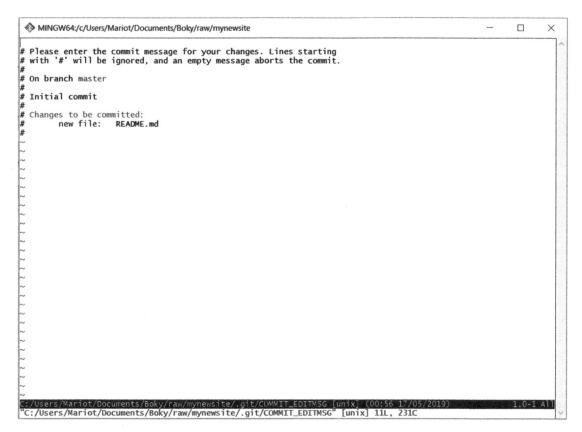

```
◈ MINGW64:/c/Users/Mariot/Documents/Boky/raw/mynewsite                    —    □    ×

# Please enter the commit message for your changes. Lines starting
# with '#' will be ignored, and an empty message aborts the commit.
#
# On branch master
#
# Initial commit
#
# Changes to be committed:
#       new file:    README.md
#
~
~
~
~
~
~
~
~
~
~
~
~
~
~
~
~
~
~
~
~
~
C:/Users/Mariot/Documents/Boky/raw/mynewsite/.git/COMMIT_EDITMSG [unix] (00:56 17/05/2019)          1,0-1 All
"C:/Users/Mariot/Documents/Boky/raw/mynewsite/.git/COMMIT_EDITMSG" [unix] 11L, 231C
```

Figure 3-7. *Git opens the default editor so you can edit the commit message*

You can see in Figure 3-7 that the first line of the file is empty; that's where you have
to write the commit message. The commit message should be written on one line, but
you can always add more lines of comments. Comments start with "#" and are ignored
by Git; they are only used to complete the commit message, to make it clearer. Also note
that Git puts automatically the list of changed files in the commit comments (the same
files you saw with "git status").

You will learn the proper way to write commit messages the right way in the later
chapters. But for now, just enter a simple message like "Add README.md to the project"
on the first blank line like in Figure 3-8.

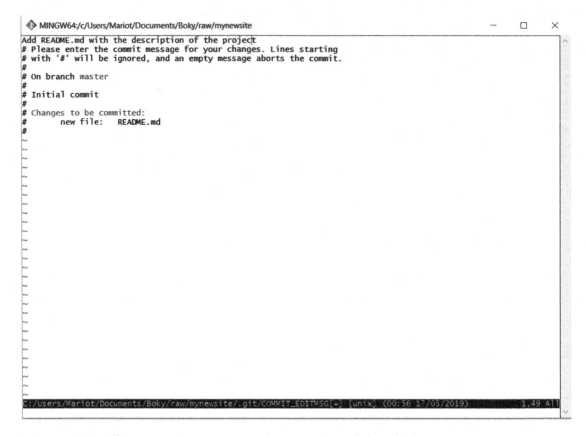

Figure 3-8. *The commit message written on top of the file*

After you wrote your commit message like in Figure 3-8, you can close the editor (after saving!). You will then get a summary of the commit like in Figure 3-9.

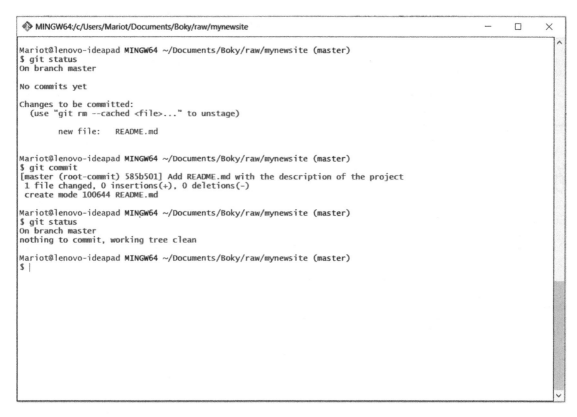

Figure 3-9. *Summary of the commit*

The summary of the commit will contain a lot of information:

- The current branch: master

- The name of the previous commit: root-commit because this is our first commit

- The name of the commit: the first seven letters of the commit hash

- The commit message

- The number of files changed: one file

- The operation done to each file: creation

We took our first snapshot! If you check the status of the repository, you can see that it is clean again, unless you left some files unstaged.

```
EXERCISE: COMMIT YOUR CHANGES
```

Take your staged files from the previous exercise and commit them. Then modify one of your tracked files, stage it again, and make a new commit. Compare the summary of each commit. What is different? In what way are those commits linked?

Quick start with Git

So, now that you are familiar with the basic concept of Git, we are going to apply them in a real project. Let's imagine you want to create a folder to hold your TODO list and want it to be versioned so you can check when each item was completed.

To get you more familiar with Git, you will be doing the next exercise without any help. If you get stuck, just check the previous sections for directions.

Just remember the basic principles of Git:

- You modify the files on the Working Directory.

- You put the files you want to record the current state on the Staging Area.

- You take a snapshot of the project with a commit.

Don't forget to put the files you modified on the Staging Area before committing or they won't be part of the snapshot. The modified files you didn't put on the Staging Area will just stay on the Working Directory until you decide to discard them or include them in a future commit.

Let's get started on the exercise! Please complete it until the end and don't move on to the next chapter until you understand clearly how Git works.

EXERCISE: A VERSIONED TODO APP

- Create a new repository.

- Create a file named TODO.txt in the directory and put in some text.

- Stage TODO.txt.

- Commit the project and put in a short commit message.

- Create two new files named DONE.txt and WORKING.txt.

- Stage and commit those files.

- Rename WORKING.txt to IN PROGRESS.txt.

- Add some text to DONE.txt.

- Check the directory status.

- Stage IN PROGRESS.txt and DONE.txt.

- Unstage DONE.txt.

- Commit the project.

- Check the directory status.

After you complete this exercise, close the book and try to explain those things to yourself in your own words:

- Working Directory

- Staging Area

- Commit

If you don't have too many problems understanding those concepts, you are ready for more Git commands and concepts.

Summary

This chapter is very important for your understanding of Git. The main takeaways are the three states that a file can be:

- Modified: You modified a file on the Working Directory.

- Staged: You added the file to the Staging Area so it could be snapshotted.

- Committed: You took a snapshot of the entire project (all the unmodified and staged files).

If a file was part of the previous commit and you didn't modify them, they will automatically be part of the next commit. A modified but unstaged file is considered as unmodified. You have to ask Git to track them by staging those files.

We also learned a little bit about committing and commit messages. Opening an external editor to write commit messages might be a little awkward at first, but you will eventually get the hang of it after some time.

In the next chapter, we will learn how to check the project history and navigate between versions. We will also learn about ignoring certain files and show the current changes done to the project since the last commit.

## CHAPTER 4

Diving into Git

Now that you are familiar with the basic commands of Git, we are diving deeper into the other features it has. You will discover in this chapter the features that I promised you in Chapter 1.

Ignoring files

Not everything in the working directory should be tracked by Git. There are certain files (configs, passwords, bad code) that are generally left untracked by authors or developers.

Those files (or directories) are listed in a simple file called ".gitignore." Notice the period before "gitignore"; it's important. To ignore files, create a file named .gitignore and list the files or folders to ignore in it.

Let's get back to our repository from the previous chapter, the TODO list. Let's imagine that you want to include a private, untracked file named PRIVATE.txt. You first have to create the .gitignore file using your favorite text editor and then write PRIVATE. txt in it like in Figure 4-1.

© Mariot Tsitoara 2020
M. Tsitoara, *Beginning Git and GitHub*, https://doi.org/10.1007/978-1-4842-5313-7_4

Figure 4-1. *The .gitignore file with PRIVATE.txt in it*

If you then create and modify the PRIVATE.txt file (like in Figure 4-2), it won't be taken into account by Git if you check the status.

Name		Date modified	Type	Size
⚙ .gitignore		2019-05-23 20:51	Git Ignore Source ...	1 KB
📄 DOING.txt		2019-05-23 20:17	Text Document	0 KB
📄 DONE.txt		2019-05-23 20:17	Text Document	1 KB
📄 PRIVATE.txt		2019-05-23 20:10	Text Document	0 KB
📄 TODO.txt		2019-05-23 20:15	Text Document	1 KB

Figure 4-2. *Adding PRIVATE.txt*

Let's try to check the status.

```
$ git status
```

You will get a similar result as shown in Figure 4-3.

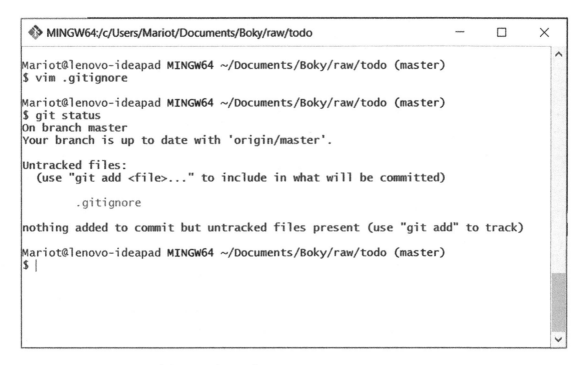

Figure 4-3. *Status of the working directory*

As you can see on the status shown in Figure 4-3, PRIVATE.txt is not tracked. You can also see that the .gitignore file IS tracked; so, you will have to add and commit it after you modify it.

```
$ git add .gitignore
$ git commit
```

As always, staging a file and then committing the project will result in a confirmation message summarizing the changes done (shown in Figure 4-4).

Figure 4-4. *Committing .gitignore*

Remember that the .gitignore global file should be placed at the root of your repository. If you put it in a directory, only the matching files in that directory will be ignored. Generally, having multiple .gitignore files in multiple directories is considered as a bad move unless your project is enormous. Prefer listing them into a single .gitignore file placed at the root of your repository.

You may ask yourself what kind of files to ignore when using Git. Well, the rule of thumb is to ignore all files generated by the project. For example, if your project is a software source code, you should ignore the compiled outputs (executable or translated files). Temporary files and logs should also be left out, along with big libraries (node_ modules). And don't forget to exclude all your personal configs and your text editor's temp files.

The .gitignore file doesn't only ignore files listed by name; you can also ignore directories and files matching a description. You will find in Table 4-1 a handy reminder of all the templates you can use.

Table 4-1. *.gitignore lines and what they do*

.gitignore line	What is ignored	Example
config.txt	config.txt in any directory	config.txt local/config.txt
build/	Any build directory and all files in it. But not a file named build	build/target.bin build/output.exe NOT output/build
build	Any build directory, all files in it, and any file named build	build/target.bin output/build
*.exe	All files with the extension .exe	target.exe output/res.exe
bin/*.exe	All files with the extension .exe in the bin/ directory	bin/output.exe
temp*	All files with name beginning by temp	Temp temp.bin temp_output.exe
**/configs	Any directory named configs	configs/prod.py local/configs/preprod.py
**/configs/local.py	Any file named local.py in any directory named configs	configs/local.py server/configs/local.py NOT configs/fr/local.py
output/**/result.exe	Any file named result.exe in any directory inside output	output/result.exe output/latest/result.exe output/1991/12/16/result.exe

Those are the most common lines used with .gitignore. There are others but they are only used in very specific situations and almost never used in common projects. If you are using a computer language or framework, you can go to `https://github.com/github/gitignore` to get a template of the .gitignore file you should use.

But what if you want to ignore all files matching a description except one? Well, you can tell Git to ignore all the files and then immediately make an exception. To exclude a file from the ignored list, you use "!." Per example, if you want to ignore all exe files except output.exe, you will write your .gitignore like in Figure 4-5.

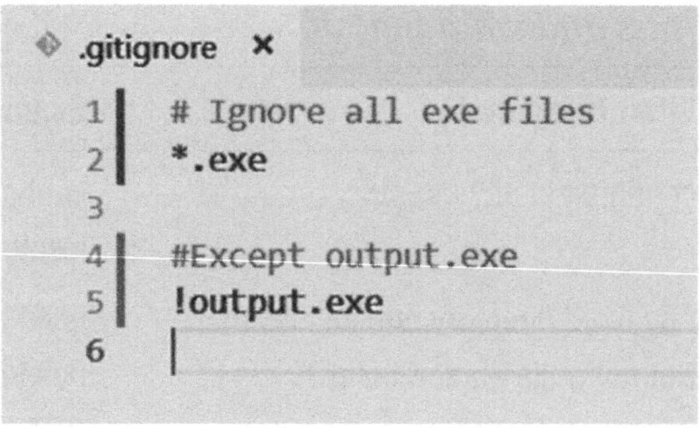

Figure 4-5. *How to make an exception*

Note the order of the lines. The exception comes AFTER the rule!

This exception marking only works for lines describing file names, though. You can't use it with lines ignoring directories. A .gitignore file as shown in Figure 4-6 won't work.

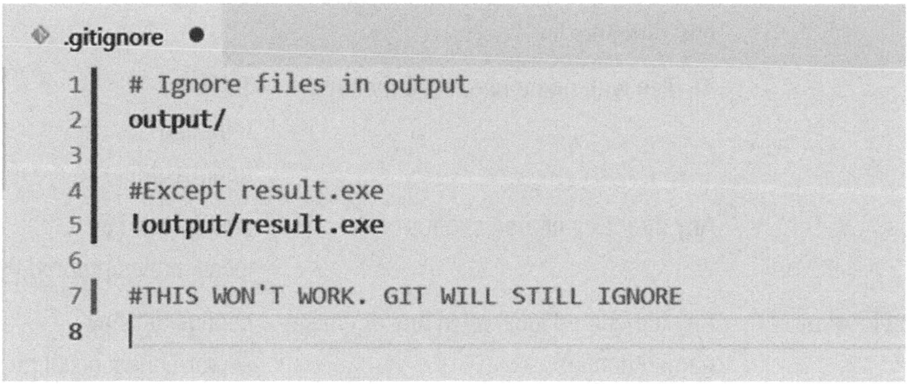

Figure 4-6. *Exception won't work with files ignored by directory matching*

EXERCISE: IGNORE FILES AND DIRECTORIES

Take your repository from the previous exercise and create multiple files and directories. Check Table 4-1 and try to ignore the files that you created using each line. Create as many files as you need and don't stop until you understand each pattern. No need to remember everything, but you should at least have an idea of when they should be used.

EXERCISE: WHAT DO THESE LINES IGNORE

Check out Figure 4-7. Without looking at the previous section, what do each line ignore?

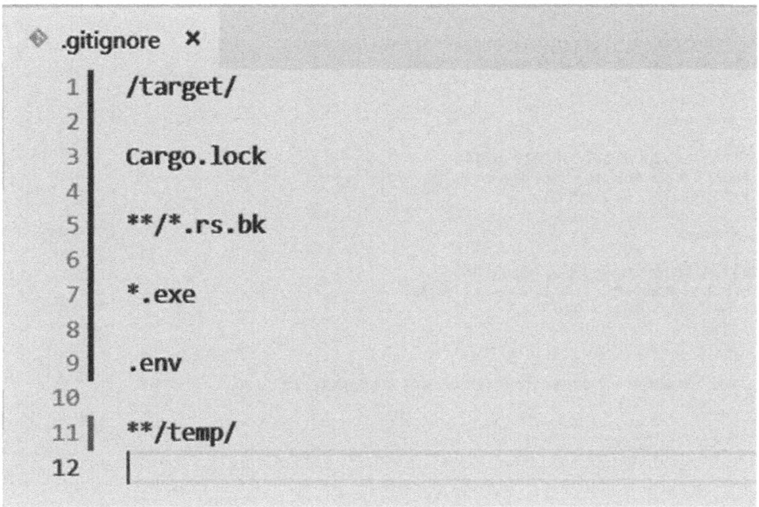

```
 .gitignore  ✕
  1  /target/
  2
  3  Cargo.lock
  4
  5  **/*.rs.bk
  6
  7  *.exe
  8
  9  .env
 10
 11  **/temp/
 12  |
```

Figure 4-7. *Guess what each line ignores*

And that's how you ignore files! It's almost as easy as ignoring your responsibilities! But remember: the .gitignore file is tracked and versioned, so don't forget to stage it before committing!

Checking logs and history

If you followed the exercises (as you should) or began to use Git for your own projects, you now have a little problem that I promised would be solved easily with Git: how to consult the history log.

This is one of the most used features of Git and also one of the easiest Git commands: git log

```
$ git log
```

Try it! Open your repository and run the command. You should see a view like the one shown in Figure 4-8.

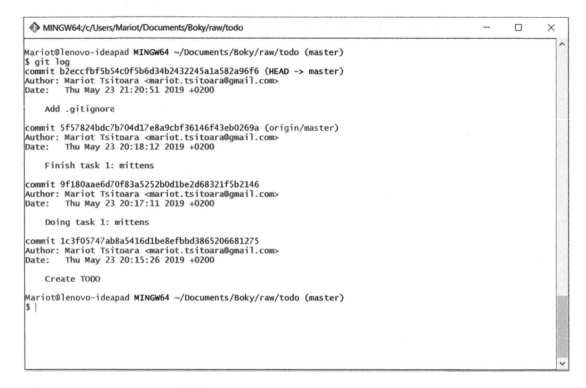

Figure 4-8. *The commit log*

The commit log will list (from the most recent to the oldest) all the snapshots you or other people committed. It also includes, for each commit

- The name (unique, obtained by hash)

- The author

- The date

- The description

Since the commit names are too long, we will only use the first five letters as the name. This will be important for the next section.

If your commit history is very long, you can use the keyboard and go

- Forward or backward one line: key up and down OR j and k

- Forward or backward one window: f and b

- At the end of the log: G

- At the beginning of the log: g

- Get help: h

- Quit the log: q

There are many parameters you can use with git log; Table 4-2 is presenting them to you.

Table 4-2. *The most common git log parameters*

Command	Use	Example
`git log --reverse`	Reverse the order of commits	
`git log -n <number>`	Limit the number of commits shown	`git log -n 10`
`git log --since=<date>` `git log –after=<date>`	Only show commits after a certain date	`git log --since=2018/11/11`
`git log --until=<date>` `git log --before=<date>`	Only show commits before a certain date	
`git log --author=<name>`	Show all commits from a specific author	`git log --author=Mariot`
`git log --stat`	Show change statistics	
`git log --graph`	Show commits in a simple graph	

EXERCISE: DISPLAYING HISTORY

This exercise is very simple. Just reopen your repository from the last exercise and check the history log:

- In reverse order

- From yesterday

- For the last two commits

Viewing previous versions

Now that you know how to check history and commit logs, it is time to check the files to see first what files were changed.

Remember those long names that are created with each commit? We are going to use those to navigate between commits or snapshots. To check how were your files on a specific snapshot, you just have to know its name. The best way to know the name of each commit is to check the history log like in Figure 4-9.

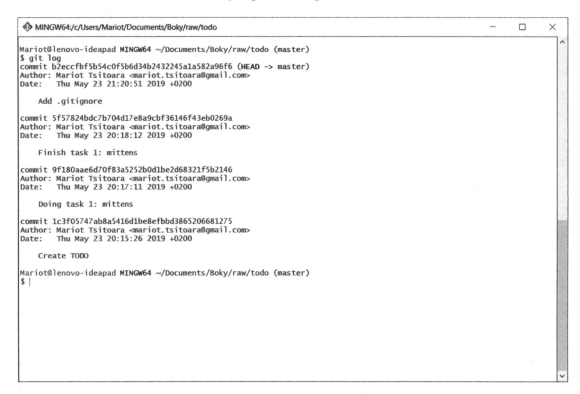

Figure 4-9. *History log of our TODO list*

To show and learn what changes have been done to your project, you just use the "git show" command followed by the name of the commit. You don't even need to write the full name, just the first seven letters.

```
$ git show <name>
```

Try with your repository! You should get a result as shown in Figure 4-10.

```
  MINGW64:/c/Users/Mariot/Documents/Boky/raw/todo

Mariot@lenovo-ideapad MINGW64 ~/Documents/Boky/raw/todo (master)
$ git show 9f180aa
commit 9f180aae6d70f83a5252b0d1be2d68321f5b2146
Author: Mariot Tsitoara <mariot.tsitoara@gmail.com>
Date:    Thu May 23 20:17:11 2019 +0200

    Doing task 1: mittens

diff --git a/DOING.txt b/DOING.txt
new file mode 100644
index 0000000..c6a584e
--- /dev/null
+++ b/DOING.txt
@@ -0,0 +1 @@
+-Put the mittens on the kittens
\ No newline at end of file
diff --git a/TODO.txt b/TODO.txt
index cb72b4b..02c3043 100644
--- a/TODO.txt
+++ b/TODO.txt
@@ -1,4 +1,3 @@
--Put the mittens on the kittens
 -Buy a hat for the bat
 -Clear the fogs for the frogs
 -Bring a box to the fox
\ No newline at end of file

Mariot@lenovo-ideapad MINGW64 ~/Documents/Boky/raw/todo (master)
$ |
```

Figure 4-10. *Result of git show*

As you can see, the commit is shown in a very detailed way. You will see the difference between the selected commit and the previous one. Additions are shown in green and deletions in red. You can show the details of any commit with the "git show" command.

EXERCISE: CHECK THE CHANGES YOU MADE TO YOUR PROJECT

List the commits you made to your project and check the changes for each one.

Reviewing the current changes

Checking previous versions is nice, but what if you only want to check the changes you just made? Checking differences between the last commit and the current working directory is an essential feature of Git. You will use it a lot! The command to check differences is simple: git diff.

```
$ git diff
```

Modify one or multiple files in your directory and then execute the command. You will get a result as shown in Figure 4-11, which is very similar to the result of the git show command from the previous section. They are actually the same view because the information shown is the same.

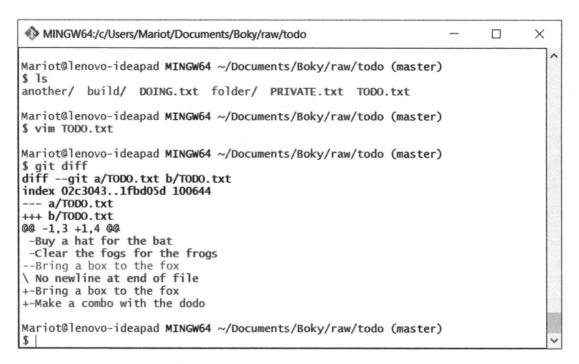

Figure 4-11. *Checking all the changes done in the working directory*

Most of the time, you will only need to check the changes made to a single file, not to the entire project. You can pass the name of the file as a parameter to review its differences compared to the last commit.

```
$ git diff TODO.txt
```

The main thing to remember is that git diff checks the changes made to the files in the working directory; it doesn't check staged files! To check changes made to staged files, you have to use the parameter "--staged."

```
$ git diff --staged
```

You should always check the diff in the staged files before committing a project, so you can do a final review. I know you will forget to do so one day, so go to the next chapter to learn how to undo or modify your commits.

This is the end of this chapter and we have learned a lot of things. Before going to the next chapter, please make sure you are comfortable with these features:

- Ignoring files

- Checking history logs

- Reviewing local and staged changes

If you are and you completed the exercises, congratulations! But we aren't finished with commits yet!

Summary

This chapter was all about the project history. We learned about checking logs with git log and git show but also learned to review the current changes with git diff. Git log and git diff will be particularly useful in the future, so make sure you understand them well. Git diff is about comparing the current modified files to the files in the last commit, while git log is just a list of all previous commits.

The ability to ignore files with .gitignore is also a nice skill to have so your git status isn't saturated with modified files that you aren't interested in committing. It's also a good way to ensure that a particular file (probably containing secret keys) isn't committed by accident.

We still have a lot to learn about commits in the next chapter. We will first review the three states of Git files, and then we will see how to bring back the previous versions into the working directory. And you will at least learn how to undo and modify commits. Hang tight!

## CHAPTER 5

Commits

The previous chapter taught you a little bit about the essential features of Git. You should know how to check the history log and see the changes made to the current version. But Git commits are a tough bone to bite, so we are going to talk about them more in this chapter. First, we will explore (again) the inner working of Git and its terminology. Then, we'll learn how to view and check previous versions. Let's go!

The three states of Git

Before talking about commits in detail, we have to go back to the basics and relearn about how Git works. You surely remember the three states that a file can find itself. If you don't, don't skip this chapter; it is essential for everything you will do with Git. If you remember, don't skip it either, because I spent a lot of time writing it.

As you saw on the last chapter, not all files are tracked by Git; some files are ignored (by the .gitignore file). And then there are also files that aren't ignored but not yet tracked by Git. They are the newly created files that have never been part of a snapshot (commit).

Tracked files can be in three states:

- Modified: You changed the file.

- Staged: You changed the file and prepared it to be snapshotted.

- Committed: You took a snapshot of the entire project and the file was in it.

Untracked files will stay as such until you decide to stage and commit them or explicitly ignore them.

Remember: Git doesn't track changes, it tracks snapshots. Each time you commit, the state of the entire project is saved, not just the little changes that were made.

Nerd fact: Git is fast because you always work on the last state of the project. When you want to see a previous commit, it just shows you the state of the project at that

© Mariot Tsitoara 2020
M. Tsitoara, *Beginning Git and GitHub*, https://doi.org/10.1007/978-1-4842-5313-7_5

specific time. Many VCSs stored each change done to a file, and when you wanted to go back at a previous state, they replayed the changes in reverse. When the project gets big, this causes many problems or speed and memory. Doesn't Git's way of thinking create super big databases? No, because when you take a snapshot and a file doesn't change, it is not stored again; instead, a reference to the file is used.

Let's go back to the three states again and see the relationship between them:

- You work on the working directory. It is just the directory that you created before initializing the repository. That's where you will read and edit your files.

- The staging area is where you put your changed files before taking a snapshot of the entire project. You can't take a snapshot if you don't stage your changed files. Only staged files (and unchanged files) will be taken into account in the snapshot. Unstaged files (tracked or untracked) and ignored files will just stay in the same state.

- The database or .git directory stores every snapshot you took. Those snapshots are called commits.

Remember: staging concerns only changed files you choose, while committing concerns the entire project. You stage a file; then commit the project.

Navigating between versions

Many times, you will want not only to know what has changed in your project but also to see in what state it was, to see the snapshot you took. It's easy with Git.

When you want to bring the previous state of the project to the working directory, we have to check out the commit with "git checkout." Since this changes the files on the working directory, you have to make sure not to have any unstaged files on there. Untracked files are fine since Git doesn't track their states yet.

To check a snapshot of the project, we use the "git checkout" command and pass the commit name as a parameter.

```
$ git checkout <name>
```

Let's try! Open your current project in a text editor and take a note of its contents. Now check out a previous commit like in Figure 5-1.

```
MINGW64:/c/Users/Mariot/Documents/Boky/raw/todo

Mariot@lenovo-ideapad MINGW64 ~/Documents/Boky/raw/todo (master)
$ git log
commit 8ba74a5546782e38d1c2d6dafd2386e814034c69 (HEAD -> master)
Author: Mariot Tsitoara <mariot.tsitoara@gmail.com>
Date:    Mon May 27 21:31:51 2019 +0200

    Rearrange .gitignore

commit b2eccfbf5b54c0f5b6d34b2432245a1a582a96f6
Author: Mariot Tsitoara <mariot.tsitoara@gmail.com>
Date:    Thu May 23 21:20:51 2019 +0200

    Add .gitignore

commit 5f57824bdc7b704d17e8a9cbf36146f43eb0269a
Author: Mariot Tsitoara <mariot.tsitoara@gmail.com>
Date:    Thu May 23 20:18:12 2019 +0200

    Finish task 1: mittens

commit 9f180aae6d70f83a5252b0d1be2d68321f5b2146
Author: Mariot Tsitoara <mariot.tsitoara@gmail.com>
Date:    Thu May 23 20:17:11 2019 +0200

    Doing task 1: mittens

commit 1c3f05747ab8a5416d1be8efbbd3865206681275
Author: Mariot Tsitoara <mariot.tsitoara@gmail.com>
Date:    Thu May 23 20:15:26 2019 +0200

    Create TODO

Mariot@lenovo-ideapad MINGW64 ~/Documents/Boky/raw/todo (master)
$ git checkout 9f180aa
Note: checking out '9f180aa'.

You are in 'detached HEAD' state. You can look around, make experimental
changes and commit them, and you can discard any commits you make in this
state without impacting any branches by performing another checkout.

If you want to create a new branch to retain commits you create, you may
do so (now or later) by using -b with the checkout command again. Example:

  git checkout -b <new-branch-name>

HEAD is now at 9f180aa Doing task 1: mittens

Mariot@lenovo-ideapad MINGW64 ~/Documents/Boky/raw/todo ((9f180aa...))
$ |
```

Figure 5-1. *Checking out older commits*

Caution   You can't check out any other commit if your Working Directory isn't clean! Make sure to commit your changes before switching snapshots.

Be careful not to change anything when checking out previous commits. Just like in the movies, changing the past is a very bad idea!

If you check your text editor, you will notice that the project is now just like it was when you took the snapshot. That is what's best with Git. Nothing you took a snapshot of is ever lost!

Now let's learn some Git terminology. First is "head." "head" is just a reference to a commit. Instead of saying "name," when talking about commits, we say "head."

When switching between different commits, we need a way to know which "head" are we on. The current head (the one being checked out) is just called "HEAD."

And that's it! A head is a reference to a commit (there can be multiple heads in a repository), and the head pointing to the currently checked-out commit is called HEAD.

EXERCISE: MOVE AROUND IN YOUR HISTORY

Move from one commit to another using "git checkout." Make sure not to change anything.

But how to return to the normal, current Working Directory? Since we didn't make any big change to our repository, returning to the Working Directory is just checking out the only branch that we have. By convention, that branch is called "master."

```
$ git checkout master
```

Try it out! And remember the two golden laws of time travel:

- Only travel back in time when the present is clean (nothing unstaged in the working directory).

- Don't change the past (until you have more experience).

Don't forget to check out the current branch (master) after navigating between versions.

Undo a commit

The time will come when you will stage and commit files but change your mind later. It happens to everyone. But with traditional methods (without versioning), it is very difficult to roll back changes especially if the changes were ages ago. With Git, it is just a single command: git revert.

Why not just delete the commit? Because of the time traveling rule from the previous section: never change the past. Whatever changes committed must stay so, for the sake of history; changing what has happened in the past is very dangerous and counterintuitive. Instead, you will use git revert to create a new commit that contains the exact opposite of the commit you are trying to undo.

So, undoing a commit is just committing its exact opposite. It's that simple! To use it, you have to pass the name of the commit to be undone as a parameter.

```
$ git revert <commit name>
```

You can revert any commit; just make sure to work on a clean working directory. So, don't forget to stage and commit your files before reverting a commit. Let's try it!

First, make sure that the working directory is clean like in Figure 5-2.

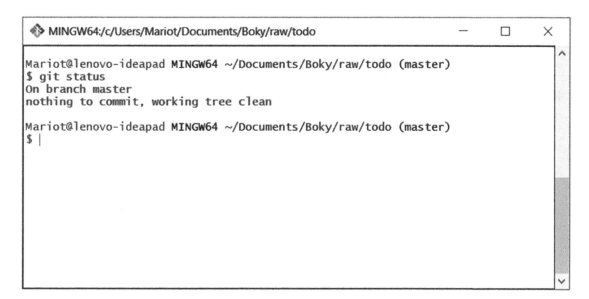

Figure 5-2. *Using git status to check the working directory*

Perfect. Now that we know that the working directory is clean, it's time to check the history to know which commit to undo. We should get a result like the one shown in Figure 5-3.

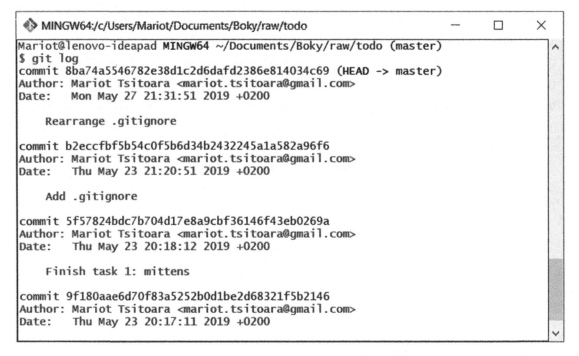

Figure 5-3. *Checking commit history with git log*

Note   If you don't like the way the commit history is shown, you can pass the "--oneline" parameter to reduce the information shown. Check Figure 5-4 for an example.

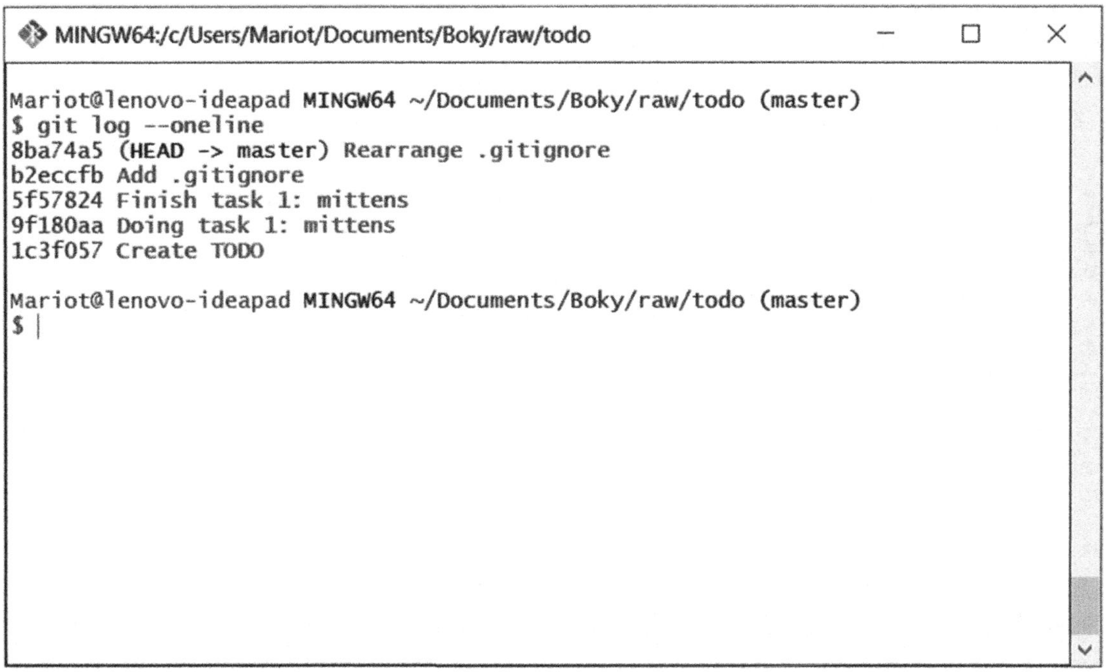
MINGW64:/c/Users/Mariot/Documents/Boky/raw/todo
Mariot@lenovo-ideapad MINGW64 ~/Documents/Boky/raw/todo (master)
$ git log --oneline
8ba74a5 (HEAD -> master) Rearrange .gitignore
b2eccfb Add .gitignore
5f57824 Finish task 1: mittens
9f180aa Doing task 1: mittens
1c3f057 Create TODO
Mariot@lenovo-ideapad MINGW64 ~/Documents/Boky/raw/todo (master)
$

Figure 5-4. *A prettier git log output*

Let's revert the third commit! We just use git revert followed by the commit name.

```
$ git revert 5f57824
```

Since git revert only creates a new commit containing opposite changes, the rest of the procedure is the same as any new commit. As shown in Figure 5-5, you will be asked to describe your new commit. I suggest always keeping the default commit description as it makes it easy to identify.

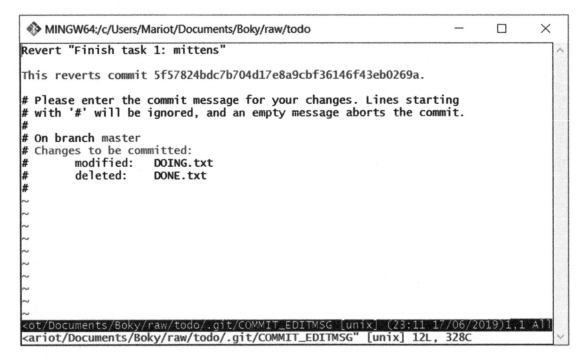

Figure 5-5. *The new commit description*

After you save the commit description (like on all commits), you are presented with a summary of the snapshot content. Figure 5-6 shows the result you will get after running the commands and saving the commit description.

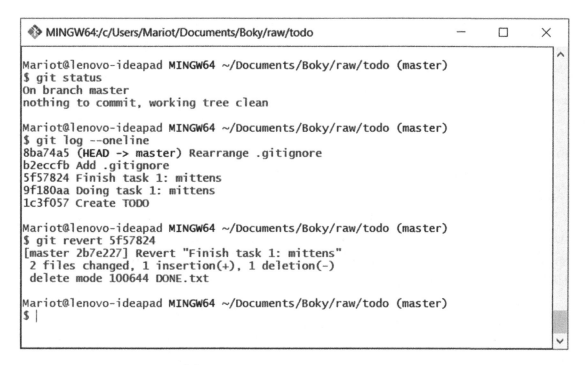

```
 MINGW64:/c/Users/Mariot/Documents/Boky/raw/todo          —    □    ✕

Mariot@lenovo-ideapad MINGW64 ~/Documents/Boky/raw/todo (master)
$ git status
On branch master
nothing to commit, working tree clean

Mariot@lenovo-ideapad MINGW64 ~/Documents/Boky/raw/todo (master)
$ git log --oneline
8ba74a5 (HEAD -> master) Rearrange .gitignore
b2eccfb Add .gitignore
5f57824 Finish task 1: mittens
9f180aa Doing task 1: mittens
1c3f057 Create TODO

Mariot@lenovo-ideapad MINGW64 ~/Documents/Boky/raw/todo (master)
$ git revert 5f57824
[master 2b7e227] Revert "Finish task 1: mittens"
 2 files changed, 1 insertion(+), 1 deletion(-)
 delete mode 100644 DONE.txt

Mariot@lenovo-ideapad MINGW64 ~/Documents/Boky/raw/todo (master)
$ |
```

Figure 5-6. *Summary of the revert*

As you can see, undoing changes is very easy with Git. The thing to remember is git revert only creates a new commit containing opposite changes. That means you can revert a revert! Reverting a revert will just reapply your original commit, and the two "reverts" will cancel each other. The commits will, however, stay on your history log as you can't change the past.

Note   Actually, you can change the past. But never ever do it. It's a very bad idea, and it will only bring more problems your way.

Modifying a commit

As I promised you in the last chapter, you will learn how to modify a commit in this chapter. This is to be used when you forgot to stage a file or you want to change the commit message. This should not be used to modify a lot of files as this is counterintuitive. The next chapter will discuss in detail when and where to use this. And I'll say it again: don't ever try to change the past.

To modify a commit, you have to use the git commit command but with "--amend" as a parameter. It will open your default text editor like a normal commit but with the staged files and commit message already there.

```
$ git commit --amend
```

You then just save and close the text editor like for every commit. The "modify" word that I used is a bit misleading because you are not modifying a commit; you are creating a new commit and replacing the current one. So, from now on, I will use the word "amend."

Amending a commit takes everything in the staged area and makes a new commit with it. So, if you want to add a new file to the commit or remove a file from it, you can stage and unstage them at will. Reminder: to unstage a file, you have to use git reset HEAD <file>. Here's a little example.

Let's use our TODO app again. Edit an existing file; then create two new files named filenottocommit.txt and fileforgotten.txt like in Figure 5-7.

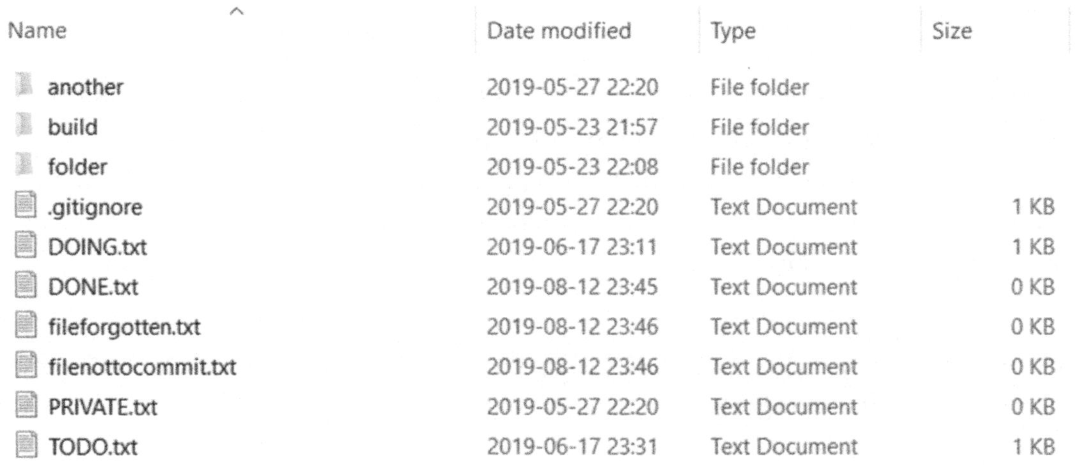

Name	Date modified	Type	Size
another	2019-05-27 22:20	File folder	
build	2019-05-23 21:57	File folder	
folder	2019-05-23 22:08	File folder	
.gitignore	2019-05-27 22:20	Text Document	1 KB
DOING.txt	2019-06-17 23:11	Text Document	1 KB
DONE.txt	2019-08-12 23:45	Text Document	0 KB
fileforgotten.txt	2019-08-12 23:46	Text Document	0 KB
filenottocommit.txt	2019-08-12 23:46	Text Document	0 KB
PRIVATE.txt	2019-05-27 22:20	Text Document	0 KB
TODO.txt	2019-06-17 23:31	Text Document	1 KB

Figure 5-7. *All the files in our Working Directory*

You can check the current state of the project by executing the git status command:

```
$ git status
```

Depending on how many files you added to the project before, you might have a slightly different result but still similar to Figure 5-8.

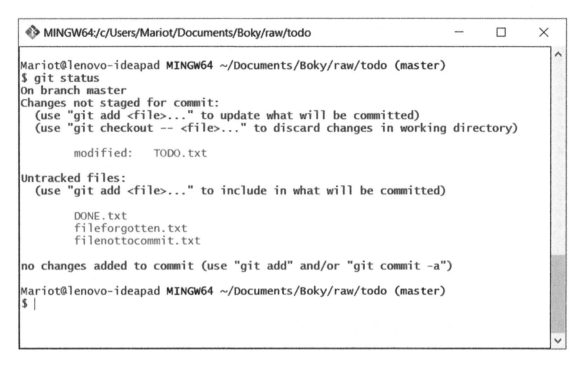

```
MINGW64:/c/Users/Mariot/Documents/Boky/raw/todo                —    □    ×

Mariot@lenovo-ideapad MINGW64 ~/Documents/Boky/raw/todo (master)
$ git status
On branch master
Changes not staged for commit:
  (use "git add <file>..." to update what will be committed)
  (use "git checkout -- <file>..." to discard changes in working directory)

        modified:   TODO.txt

Untracked files:
  (use "git add <file>..." to include in what will be committed)

        DONE.txt
        fileforgotten.txt
        filenottocommit.txt

no changes added to commit (use "git add" and/or "git commit -a")

Mariot@lenovo-ideapad MINGW64 ~/Documents/Boky/raw/todo (master)
$ |
```

Figure 5-8. *The modified and untracked files are highlighted*

The next thing we have to do is to stage the files to be part of the commit. Add the changed files and filenottocommit.txt.

```
$ git add TODO.txt DONE.txt filenottocommit.txt
```

You know from the last chapter that you should always check what you staged with "git diff --staged" before committing. But let's pretend you forgot to check and commit immediately.

```
$ git commit
```

Even then, you will arrive at the commit message screen that outlines the changes to be committed like in Figure 5-9.

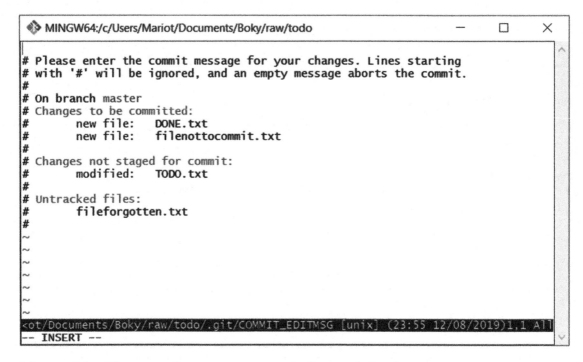

Figure 5-9. *The commit message screen is the last failsafe*

As you can see, the changes to be committed and the untracked files are outlined and highlighted. It's pretty difficult to miss them, but let's pretend to and write a simple commit message, save, and then close the editor. You will get the usual summary shown in Figure 5-10.

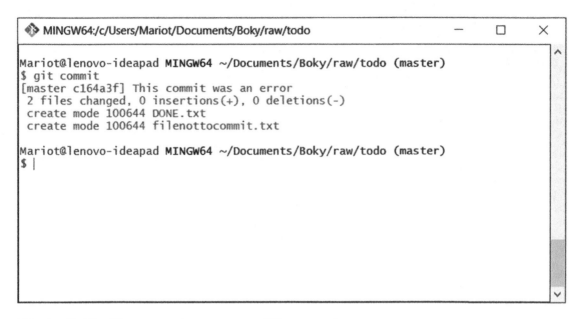

Figure 5-10. *The commit summary. We messed up*

Now that you read the commit summary, you notice that you committed the wrong file and forgot to commit another.

First, you should remove the last commit from your project with git reset. We will use the "--soft" option so that the edits we made stay on the working directory. HEAD~1 means the previous commit as HEAD is a reference to the current one.

```
$ git reset --soft HEAD~1
```

After this, you can unstage the file with git reset again:

```
$ git reset HEAD filenottocommit.txt
```

Check if the commands worked as intended by reviewing the current status of the project.

```
$ git status
```

You will get a result like the one shown in Figure 5-11.

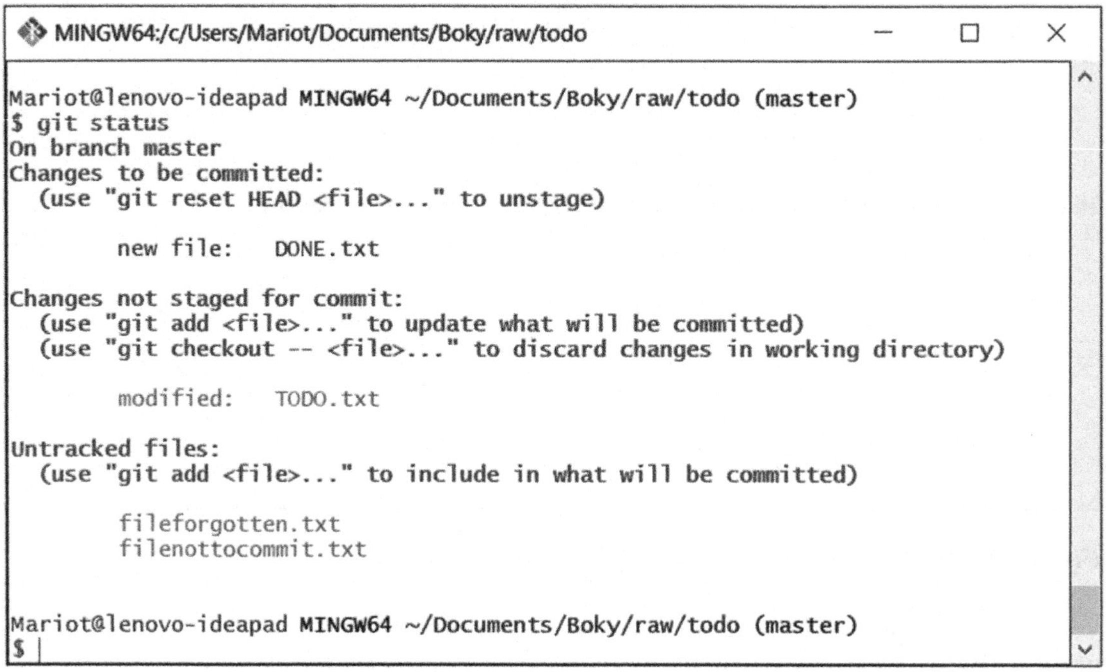

```
MINGW64:/c/Users/Mariot/Documents/Boky/raw/todo                    —    □    ×

Mariot@lenovo-ideapad MINGW64 ~/Documents/Boky/raw/todo (master)
$ git status
On branch master
Changes to be committed:
  (use "git reset HEAD <file>..." to unstage)

        new file:   DONE.txt

Changes not staged for commit:
  (use "git add <file>..." to update what will be committed)
  (use "git checkout -- <file>..." to discard changes in working directory)

        modified:   TODO.txt

Untracked files:
  (use "git add <file>..." to include in what will be committed)

        fileforgotten.txt
        filenottocommit.txt


Mariot@lenovo-ideapad MINGW64 ~/Documents/Boky/raw/todo (master)
$ |
```

Figure 5-11. *Status of the project after resetting*

As you can see, filenottocommit.txt is untracked now, because we removed it from the staging area. Naturally, fileforgotten.txt is also untracked because we didn't stage it. Only DONE.txt remains on the staging area because we haven't touched it after the commit.

Caution   Be careful when you use the reset command. It's very dangerous. Make sure to double check what you write.

Then stage the correct one.

```
$ git add fileforgotten.txt
```

Now that you staged the correct files, you can commit the project.

```
$ git commit
```

Put a grammatical error in the commit message so you can see another feature of Git.

Amending a commit

For simple mistakes like an error in the commit message, there is no need to modify the entire commit. You just need to amend it. Let's try with our project!

```
$ git commit --amend
```

The amend process looks just like a normal commit, but instead the commit message is already written, as you can see in Figure 5-12.

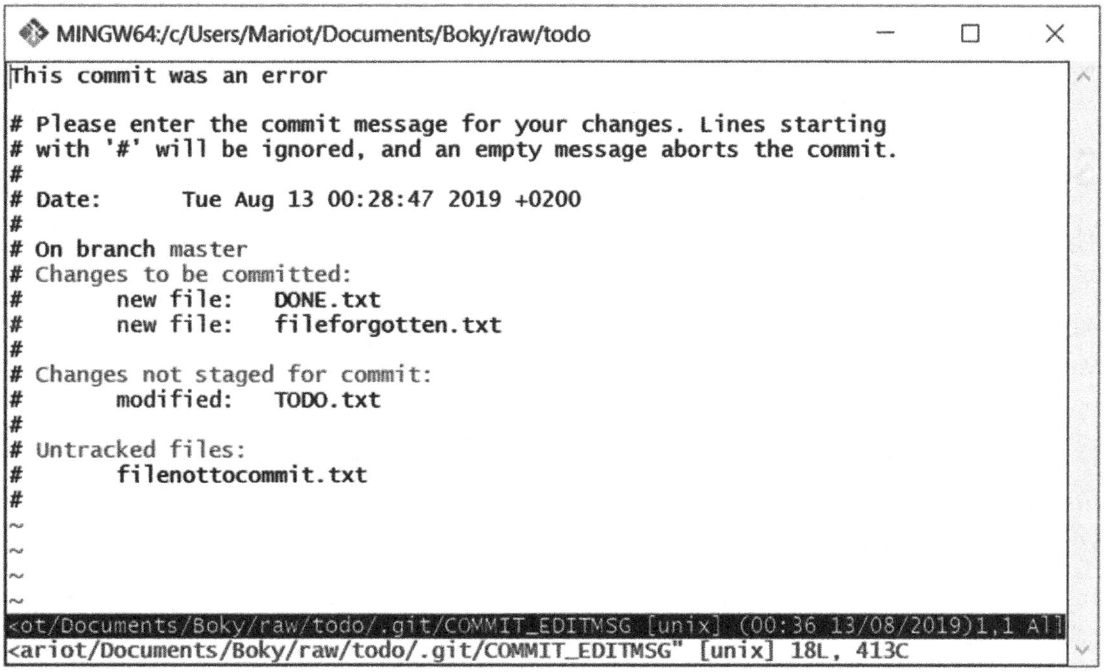

Figure 5-12. *Editing a commit message*

You can change the commit message at will and then save and close the editor like always.

It's that simple! Take a look at the new commit's name and compare it to the old one. You'll notice that they are different. That's because the commit name is a hash of the information in the snapshot. So different states of the project result in different names.

A parting note about modifying commits: don't abuse it! Yes, making errors is not ideal when writing code, and most of the time we want to correct them immediately. But errors also help us be better; and keeping tracks of our mistakes is a great way to learn.

EXERCISE: CLEANLY AMEND A COMMIT

Get back to your TODO project. The goal of this exercise is to cleanly amend a commit.

- Edit some files and stage them.

- Commit them and make a grammatical error in your commit message.

- Unstage a file.

- Stage another.

- Amend the commit with the correct message.

Summary

This chapter mainly dealt with navigating, undoing, and amending versions of your project. You should have no problem now with small corrections in your commits. Make sure to reread the first section of this chapter as it's essential for everything you do in Git. You should know the differences between the three states of Git by heart.

The next chapter is a small one as we will only talk about theory. You will learn how to write a nice commit message, what to include and ignore in commits, and what are the common errors beginners do. Be sure to read the next chapter carefully because it will help you and your team greatly. Let's go!

## CHAPTER 6

Git Best Practices

The previous chapter was one of the most important ones in this book. Make sure to come back to it every time you have doubts about commits. After reading it, you should be able to make, review, and amend project snapshots without any problems. Now that you know the basic features of Git, it's time for you to learn the best practices to make your life (and your teammates') easier. These are the stuff that I wish I knew when I first used Git. We'll cover commit messages, the dos and don'ts of Git, and a list of the most common mistakes beginners do. Then we'll finish with a little reminder of how Git works.

Commit messages

Commit messages are one of the most important aspects of Version Control and one of the most overlooked. Those messages are there to help you (and others) understand what changes were made in the commit and, most importantly, why were those changes made. Clean and readable commit messages are essential for a better Git experience. Let's begin by identifying the problem.

The most common problem faced with Git is that commit messages are often void of sense and don't convey any meaningful information. And most of the time, the messages get less and less clear with each commit. This is because of a misunderstanding of Git concepts: each commit must stand by itself; if a commit needs other commits to make sense, it shouldn't exist. You should never commit a project that is half-done. If a task is getting too big, split it in several logical chunks, where each part makes sense by itself. A good way to know if you are in the wrong path when splitting tasks is to check the possible commit message: if you think about using a very similar commit message, you probably made an error when splitting the task. For example, if your task is to make many small corrections in a big web site, it would make sense to divide it into smaller tasks like a commit for each page or a commit for each page category. So remember: your commits must be independent, atomic and complete.

© Mariot Tsitoara 2020
M. Tsitoara, *Beginning Git and GitHub*, https://doi.org/10.1007/978-1-4842-5313-7_6

One problem many beginners also have is passing too much information in the commit message, thus clogging most screens with unnecessary details. A commit message must be concise and straight to the point. You don't need to tell everything that has changed, you just need to explain why those changes were made. If someone wanted to see what has changed, they would use the git show command, which shows a complete recap of the changed files in the commit.

Remember that you are not the only one who will read your code or text. You have to invest a little bit of time to explain the context of the changes and why were they done. Saying to yourself "I'll remember it" is a lie and should never be practiced. For every commit, you should ask yourself: "If another person looks at my project, will they understand the timeline of changes in the project just by looking at my commit messages?" And also remember that that other person might be you in a few months; codes are easily forgotten.

The bottom line is that your Git message should tell WHY the changes were made. If someone wants to see WHAT has changed, they would look into the Git diff.

Git commit best practices

For a better commit message and to avoid the problems listed earlier, here are some tips that you should follow from now on. Those tips will help your coworkers, and most likely, in the future, you have a clear view of why a commit was made. As the project goes, we tend to forget our previous steps, so having a good history log is imperative in a fast-paced development.

- Commit messages should be easy on the eye.

When you use git log, there are no newlines formed when the messages are too long; so the user would have to scroll to view everything. This is not ideal because you should be able to search and retrieve commits easily.

- You should not write messages longer than 50 characters.

- Begin the message by a capital letter.

- Don't end the message with a period.

- Use the present time and ditch unnecessary articles.

- Commit messages should be consistent.

Since Git messages are fundamental in any project, they should be consistent and should not be subject to brutal changes. You should always use the same language for every commit and follow its internal logics. Changing writing styles mid-project will make it very difficult to search commits.

- The messages must be clear and contextualized.

Context is key in big projects when many writers work on different parts. For example, many developers begin their commit messages by the context or area of the project touched by the changes; but this only concerns very big projects.

Unclear or vague messages such as "change CSS," "fix tests," "hot fix," "little fixes," and "updates" should be avoided at all cost. They are often misleading and force the user to look at diffs. Always make sure to include why the changes were made. And never force users to look at your code changes to understand the commit.

- Don't go crazy on the details.

You can expand your commit message in the body, but don't make the error of giving too much information. The only thing you have to explain is WHY the changes were made, not WHAT.

Remember: your commit message should say what will happen to the project if it is applied. So you should always use a clear, present-time, and imperative language. The best commit messages are usually short, straight to the point, and clear.

There's no better way than examples to make it clearer so let's do so. Table 6-1 is a handy tool to point you in the right direction.

Table 6-1. *Some examples of the best and worst commit messages*

Best	Bad	Worst
[login] Fix typo in DB call	Fixed typo in DB call	Fix typo
Refactor login function for reuse	Changing login function by moving declarations to parameters	Code refactoring
Add new API for user program check	Adding a new API for user program check	New user API

The examples presented in Table 6-1 should indicate if you are in the good direction when writing a commit message.

Note that those are recommended actions and are not written in stone. If you REALLY have to, you can ignore some of them if that makes the message clearer.

What to do

Let's begin by enumerating the good practices that you should always remember when using Git. It is essential to your success as it will save you some serious time down the line.

The most important thing to remember is that a commit is a change in the project that should stand on its own. You should always keep the commits small and independent. A commit's role is (most of the time) to introduce a feature or fix a bug; it is not for keeping track of every change you made. If a feature or bugfix requires big independent steps, separate them in multiple commits. For example, a feature needs an API endpoint and a frontend call. There is no need to make all those changes in a single commit because they are independent and are not linked in any logic. If you make an error in the backend code, you can revert the changes without disturbing the frontend code. Separating them by multiple commits will also make the history log more readable and the commit message clearer.

We've already talked about this earlier, but since it is very important, let's go back at it. Each commit message must answer the question "why?" Why was the commit created? What problem does it solve? Remember that in Git, the commits can be exchanged between many users. So, the commit message must answer the question: if I pick and apply this commit, what will it do? That's why the commit tense should be in the present form. It is difficult to shake the need to write it in past tense, but after a few weeks, you should be comfortable with it.

And that's it! The list of things to do is very small with Git. Just make sure to write clear messages for your small, independent commits. The list of things not to do, on the other hand, are as follows.

What not to do

This list is a bit longer than the previous one. That is because Git is a very powerful tool that doesn't limit the things that you can do. So, it's very easy to make mistakes, especially when you think that it will save you time. It won't. Bad practices will always serve you more problems along the way. It is best to avoid doing those things altogether.

One common error most beginners tend to make is to solve multiple problems in one commit. For example, they are in the process of fixing a bug when they spot another one. They solve both problems and then commit the project. This seems fine until it is discovered that the commit introduced many problems in the codebase. Since there's only one commit, they don't know which changes introduced the problems. That is only one facet of the problem with clogged commits. Another one is that it makes it difficult to write coherent and clear commit messages. If you find yourself committing many changes from different contexts, consider splitting the commits into smaller ones.

Another mistake akin to the previous one is to combine commits that don't have anything in common. For example, code refactoring shouldn't be in the same commit as bugfixes or new features but in a commit of its own. This, again, is to facilitate bug chasing and to make the history log cleaner.

The next mistake comes from a fundamental misuse of Git and the demands of some companies. It is the error of using Git as a backup system. Since Git is a distributed Version Control System, the repository can be stored in a remote server. This prompts some developers to commit their changes each end of the day, whether it makes sense or not. This is also caused by the need to show your daily progression because some companies look at the number of lines of code produced to measure productivity. This is a very counterintuitive way to work as it creates many commits that are trying to resolve the same problem. It will also lead to confusing commit messages that are less and less clear as the time goes by. Avoid this at all cost. You should commit when the work is ready, not because you have to. If you need to commit because you are tasked to work on something else, you will have the occasion to do so with the help of concepts like branching or stashing. You will learn those after a few chapters.

Another abused feature of Git is the amend command. Avoid amending commits to introduce big changes to it. Amending should only be used to correct typos and add forgotten files or very small changes. If the changes are so big that you feel the need to update the commit message, just do another commit. But doesn't that leave my mistakes in the codebase? Yes, but Git is there to track the versions and show what has changed. You will need to keep track of your errors too, as they're easy to forget. Don't be ashamed of your mistakes. Trying to erase them will help no one, and it will save you lots of time when confronted with the same problem again.

This last common mistake has already been talked about in this book and in countless movies: never try to change history. It is very tempting to go back in the previous versions and change things. This is a very bad idea and one of the most dangerous things you can do. Your coworkers will hate you if you do this and you will probably mess up the entire repository. The correct way to change something is to make a new commit. The past is the past. Let it go.

Note   Later in this book, you will be taught how to go back in time and change history. I trust you to never do this.

How Git works (again)

I know, I know. We've been through this already. But I want to make sure that you are completely comfortable with this before we move on to the second part of this book.

Remember the three states of Git? They are also referred at as the Three Trees (in fact it is the official appellation in the docs). Let's review them once again. Figure 6-1 will help you quickly identify the trees.

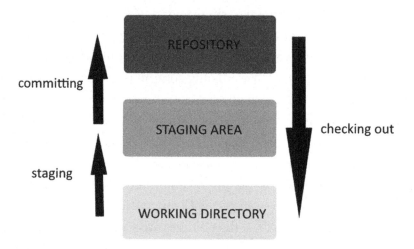

Figure 6-1.   *The relationship between the three states of Git*

As you can see in Figure 6-1, there's nothing new here, just a reminder. To track changes in a project, you need to take a snapshot of the entirety of it. Git doesn't track changes; it tracks versions.

You will only interact with the Working Directory because that's where your files can be freely edited. There is nothing in particular to say about it: it's just the current state of your files.

The Staging Area is where you put your files when you are ready to take a snapshot of your project. Any changed files that haven't been put on the Staging Area (or Staging Index) will not be part of the snapshot. The changes will still be available on the Working

Directory, though. So, it's necessary to check the state of the Working Directory before and after adding files to the Staging Index to make sure everything is okay.

The Repository is the database of the Git architecture. You will find there all your commits and history log. You can find it in the ".git" folder (which you should never touch, unless to adjust configs). The act of committing takes everything in the Staging Area and takes a snapshot of it. That's why we say "commit a project," not "commit a file" or "commit changes." Unchanged files that have been committed in the past are already in the Staging Area. That's why you don't have to stage everything, just the edited files. Remember to stage new or deleted files too!

Lastly, checking out brings back the state of a project to a previous one. The Working Directory will change to reflect the changes, so make sure to not have any uncommitted files lying around.

So the basic steps when using Git are

- Make changes (in the Working Directory)

- Stage every changed file (in the Staging Index)

- Commit the project (in the Repository)

It's that simple but please make sure to understand the relationship between those states before proceeding to the next chapter. Every section after this one assumes that you are familiar with those.

But how do the commits look inside the Repository? It's simple: they look like linked lists. A commit contains many information: the contents and the metadata. The contents are just the project files (changed files and references to unchanged files). The metadata contains other data that are also very important: date of commit, committer identity, and Git messages. Another metadata present in the commit is the parent pointer or reference. It is just the name of the previous commit; and if it's empty, it means that the commit is the first one. So, each commit is linked to the next with a parent-child relationship.

Caution   Since the name of a commit is obtained by hashing its contents and metadata, changing one of them will result in a change of name. And if the name changes, the next commit will point to nothing as a parent as it has the parent reference in its metadata. That's why it's very dangerous to change history. Never do it.

Summary

This has been a chapter full of concepts and terminologies. It's not as technical as the others but it's essential to your success with Git. You should now know when is the correct time to commit and how to write a useful commit message. Remember: your goal is to make it easier to follow the project changes. The commit message should be clear enough to answer the question: what does the commit bring? Don't forget that the history log may also be read by a non-developer team member.

The main thing to remember is that commits are the brick and mortar of your project, so, each one must be stable and independent. Your commit message should always explain the reason why a commit exist and not what was done.

This chapter also has many tips on the dos and don'ts of Git. Try to remember those as it will save you countless hours of debugging.

This also concludes the first part of this book. We are going to learn about a very useful tool: GitHub. We can at least share and track our project. You might wonder about the Git features that I promised you earlier. Don't worry; they will come later after this part. I know you are excited to get started so let's go!

CHAPTER 7

Remote Git

Congratulations on completing the first part of this book! Now, the fun begins. The first part taught you the basic features of Git. You should be comfortable at making change and tracking them with Git. Writing meaningful commit messages is a little bit hard, but you will get better with each commit if you follow the last chapter's advices. You should also be able to peek at a previous version and view the history logs; those are very important features needed for all further chapters.

You are now ready to tackle a brand-new challenge: leave your local repository and play with remote repositories. In this chapter, you will learn why it is important to work on remote and, most importantly, how does it work. You will also be introduced to typical teamworking workflow and how to correctly use remote repositories. Since the concept of remote Git is a little bit challenging, you will be presented to an easy tool that will help you greatly along the way (hint: it's in the name of this book). Let's go online!

Why work on remote

Since the beginning of this book, we've only worked alone on our local repository. But Git is a great teamworking tool; it would be a shame to use it only on a local repository. We are going to see in this section what is remote Git and why would anyone want to use it.

In the beginning of this book, I said that Git was a distributed Version Control System. That means that the repositories are not stored in a single server, but in many local repositories. Each client has its own local repository with their own commits and history. Those commits can be freely exchanged, and all files are always ready to be edited at any time. That's how Git manages to support teamworking.

Since teamworking is based on commit exchange, a way to ensure that all commits must be available at all time must be found. It will be very inconvenient to wait for your coworkers to arrive at work and start up their computers before having access to their commits. The obvious solution is to have a server host the repository and everyone just push and pull the commits from it. But isn't that dangerously close to a central VCS

© Mariot Tsitoara 2020
M. Tsitoara, *Beginning Git and GitHub*, https://doi.org/10.1007/978-1-4842-5313-7_7

workflow? Not at all (well, a little bit). As we previously discussed, distributed VCSs were created to avoid the problems caused by having a central repository. Each client has their own repository and they can work on it at any desired time; almost all Git actions are done locally. A remote server is just designated as a client that has a repository where everyone pushes their commits. That way, all the changes are available to everyone at any time. This way of working is just used to facilitate the commit exchange; it is not built into Git. For Git, all repositories are created equal. Developers just decided that some repositories are more equal than others.

Note   It is possible to share commits without the need of an intermediate server. But it is such a bad idea that we won't even teach it in this book.

Even if you work alone, it is still a good idea to have remote repository in addition to your local one. That way, you have a backup of your project with all its history in a safe location. You can also access your project anytime, provided that you have network access to the server holding the repository.

Caution   As we said in the last chapter, just because Git can be used as a backup system doesn't make it one. Using it for this sole purpose is not a good idea.

So, are you interested in that remote repository yet? Of course you are, it's amazing! Let's see how it all works.

How does it work

Using a remote server is just having a computer holding a copy of your project and its history. You don't have to push all your commits into it, you just push the commits you want to share. Your coworkers then pull the commits that interest them and apply them to their own repositories. And that's basically it! You work with a remote server to copy repositories and to push and pull changes. Let's see in detail how it all works.

To set up a remote repository, you will first need a server capable of running the Git software. Any computer worth its salt can run Git as it is a very small software. You won't also need a lot of firepower to run it properly. Even a very small computer like the Raspberry Pi is more than enough for Git.

Now that you have the server, you have to find a way to communicate with it. A network access to the server is necessary so that multiple clients can push and pull to and from the same repository. This communication with the server should be very secured. It would be extremely disappointing if anyone with an access to the server could read and edit the repository. To be able to interact with the repository, the users must authenticate themselves with each Git operation. A login/password HTTPS type of authentication can be used, but since the authentication must precede each operation, it would get tiring very fast. A solution to this is to use SSH authentication. The principle of SSH authentication is simple: only the clients that have been predetermined can access the repository.

And that's basically it! Setting up a remote Git server is a very easy task. Maintaining and securing it, on the other hand...

Note   Just like earlier, Git doesn't make any difference between "server" and "client." They are just social constructs enforced by the developers.

Using your own server to host your Git projects is a good idea if you work alone or want to keep them private. However, it becomes a pain when you work with a team. Each team member must have access to the Git server via a network, so you need to set up a local network if your team is the same working space. The server should also run 24/7 so that there is no delay in Git operations.

What happens if some of your coworkers are in remote or in a different working space? Well, you need to hook your server up to the Internet. Thus, you will also need to ramp up your security game. The more coworker you will have, the more authentication exception you will have to manage.

Another problem of using your own Git server is that you will need to deal with permissions. As seen in Chapter 1, not all developers should have writing access to the repository. Junior members, for example, need their commits reviewed by senior members before pushing to the repository. Given them direct access to the project is a bad idea (due to their insatiable need to change history).

Those are the problems that come with maintaining your own Git server. If only there was a tool that we could use that takes care of those for us...

The easy way

Guess what? There is a tool that takes care of all those things for us! And its name is GitHub! GitHub is the tool of choice when dealing with remote repositories; you can think of GitHub as a code hosting server for projects using Git. It works just like your own Git server but with less headaches.

It was created in 2008 to host Git projects and is now a subsidiary of Microsoft, which has been investing a lot in Open Source Communities. Figure 7-1 shows their homepage at github.com.

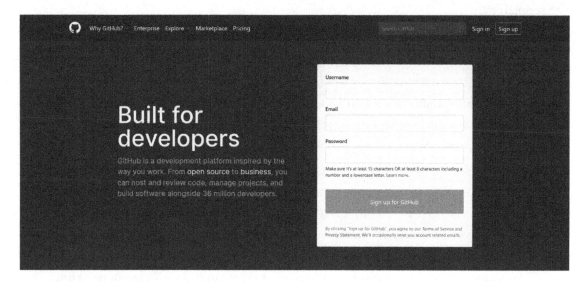

Figure 7-1. *GitHub homepage*

Now let's talk about the numbers. GitHub houses more than 100 million repositories built by more than 36 million users. As you can see in Figure 7-2, they are very proud of those numbers.

...whether you're making your first commit or sending a Rover to Mars, there's room for you here, too.

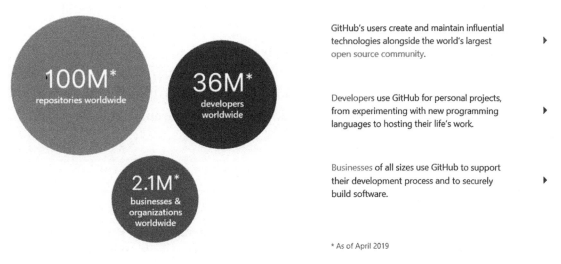

Figure 7-2. *The users of GitHub*

GitHub covers nearly every need of developers, be it Open Source developers that want to share their software or professional teams that want to work in private without the hassle of using their own server.

Almost like a social media, GitHub also provides a space for developers to build, share, and document their projects. No need for external tools or web site anymore. GitHub is also a very important tool for Open Source projects, because it is designed to facilitate developer relations and code release. User can review and propose change to each other's projects. You can even follow and contribute to your favorite repositories!

And it's not limited to Open Source projects! Companies and developers can also create private repositories, which are only accessible by them. They benefit from the usual features of Git, but also so much more. That's why GitHub is so popular: there is something for everyone!

There are also many software companies that offer services very similar to GitHub, and the most popular are GitLab and BitBucket.

GitLab is very similar to GitHub in most of its features and comes in two editions: Community and Enterprise. GitLab Community Edition is Open Source and so similar to GitHub that you can follow almost the entirety of this book without any problem. GitLab is also highly regarded in DevOps circles, so if you are interested in that career path, you should definitely check it out.

Originally created to host Mercurial projects, BitBucket has since 2011 added a support for Git projects. Developed by Atlassian, its business model is very similar to Git and it offers the same enterprise benefits.

Using a local server has its pros and cons; but the number of cons is so much higher that we are going to choose the easy way in this book. However, you are expected to at least know how a remote repository works and why is it needed. If you still want to use your own server, there is a guide on how to do that in one of the annexes of this book. Have fun ☺

Summary

This chapter was just a very simple presentation of remote repositories. Working locally is fun but teamwork requires sharing your carefully crafted commits. You can host your Git repositories on remote servers of your choice, but the easiest way is to use a service like GitHub that specializes in code hosting.

But GitHub does so much more than all that! In the next chapter, we will discuss in details what are its big features and how can we take advantage of them. We are going to learn about bug tracking, access control, feature requests, and so much more. Let's move on!

PART II

Project Management with GitHub

CHAPTER 8

GitHub Primer

In the last chapter, we did an initial discovery of remote repositories and why they are important. You should have a basic understanding of how they work too and, most importantly, what are the benefits of using one. Now, we are going to talk about the most famous of code hosting platforms: GitHub.

First, we are going to present a short history of GitHub, just to know it better. Then, we will talk about the kind of people who use GitHub and what they are using it for.

GitHub overview

Slapping a definition of GitHub is really difficult, because it does so many things at the same time. So, I'll use its own words: "GitHub is a development platform inspired by the way you work. From Open Source to business, you can host and review code, manage projects, and build software alongside 36 million developers."

GitHub is thus not only a code hosting platform but a development platform. What does that mean? It means that you don't just use GitHub to store your code; you use it to plan and track its evolution. We'll see all its features on the next section, but the main thing to remember is that GitHub is there to help you build and release your project.

If you only need one reason to use GitHub, it's the development workflow it offers. Long gone are the days when the project manager wrote all the pending tasks on a whiteboard and team members sent emails to each other to keep track of whom were doing what. No need for long chains of back and forth emails to check a task's progress either. All of that is managed by GitHub.

© Mariot Tsitoara 2020
M. Tsitoara, *Beginning Git and GitHub*, https://doi.org/10.1007/978-1-4842-5313-7_8

GitHub and Open Source

GitHub has always been a close ally of Open Source projects; in fact, GitHub is home to the largest Open Source community in the world. Since developers need a convenient place to build and share their projects, GitHub is an obvious choice. That way, all of the decisions and discussions concerning the projects can be consulted and joined by anyone; and that is the beauty of Open Source.

With GitHub, the best thing you can do to an Open Source project is now easier than ever: contributing. When you spot a project that you like, you can follow it like on social media and see its progress. If you want to work on a new feature or fix a bug, you just have to make a clone of the project and work on it. That process is called "Forking," and it's the backbone of Open Source projects. When you've made all the changes to your copy of the project, you can submit a Pull Request (PR) to the maintainer of the project. That means that you are requesting that the changes that you made be pulled and merged into the project. Other contributors will then review your changes and may request some additional changes. Instead of communicating by email or instant messaging, all of this is done on GitHub. After all the parties are in agreement about the changes, the Pull Request is accepted and your changes are now part of the project!

Of course, Open Source projects are more than code; they need docs, translators, community managers, maintainers, and so much more. You can contribute to projects by writing documentations and providing translations or even reviewing the changes that other contributors made. Projects also need testers and people that can provide insights about the final products. They are projects that have millions of contributors, so community managers are needed. They are responsible for the wellbeing of the community and are expected to enforce the internal code of conduct of the community. Some contributors are tasked with welcoming and tutoring beginners, which is difficult but very necessary for any project.

GitHub was chosen by millions of Open Source projects because the workflow from idea to release is so easy and accessible. The concept of forking a project to contribute to it is the main driving force of any Open Source project. And if you like a project but don't like the direction it's going; you can fork it and start your own flavor of the project. You will then be the maintainer of the new project, and others can submit Pull Requests to you if they want to contribute. Thus, anyone is happy!

As previously established, Open Source projects need documentation and tutorials for beginners. For small projects, a text file (called README by convention) is enough. The README file should present the project and convey which problems does it solve.

It should also tell users how to install and use it and also how to contribute to it. You can check Figure 8-1 for an example of a README file (that you can also check on `https://github.com/git/git`).

Git - fast, scalable, distributed revision control system

Git is a fast, scalable, distributed revision control system with an unusually rich command set that provides both high-level operations and full access to internals.

Git is an Open Source project covered by the GNU General Public License version 2 (some parts of it are under different licenses, compatible with the GPLv2). It was originally written by Linus Torvalds with help of a group of hackers around the net.

Please read the file INSTALL for installation instructions.

Many Git online resources are accessible from https://git-scm.com/ including full documentation and Git related tools.

See Documentation/gittutorial.txt to get started, then see Documentation/giteveryday.txt for a useful minimum set of commands, and Documentation/git-.txt for documentation of each command. If git has been correctly installed, then the tutorial can also be read with `man gittutorial` or `git help tutorial`, and the documentation of each command with `man git-<commandname>` or `git help <commandname>`.

CVS users may also want to read Documentation/gitcvs-migration.txt (`man gitcvs-migration` or `git help cvs-migration` if git is installed).

The user discussion and development of Git take place on the Git mailing list -- everyone is welcome to post bug reports, feature requests, comments and patches to git@vger.kernel.org (read Documentation/SubmittingPatches for instructions on patch submission). To subscribe to the list, send an email with just "subscribe git" in the body to majordomo@vger.kernel.org. The mailing list archives are available at https://public-inbox.org/git/, http://marc.info/?l=git and other archival sites.

Issues which are security relevant should be disclosed privately to the Git Security mailing list git-security@googlegroups.com.

The maintainer frequently sends the "What's cooking" reports that list the current status of various development topics to the mailing list. The discussion following them give a good reference for project status, development direction and remaining tasks.

The name "git" was given by Linus Torvalds when he wrote the very first version. He described the tool as "the stupid content tracker" and the name as (depending on your mood):

- random three-letter combination that is pronounceable, and not actually used by any common UNIX command. The fact that it is a mispronunciation of "get" may or may not be relevant.
- stupid. contemptible and despicable. simple. Take your pick from the dictionary of slang.
- "global information tracker": you're in a good mood, and it actually works for you. Angels sing, and a light suddenly fills the room.
- "goddamn idiotic truckload of sh*t": when it breaks

Figure 8-1. *The README file of Git*

As you can see in Figure 8-1, README files can have basic text formatting and links. They can also include images and code examples.

Big projects need more than README files because they need to be properly presented and documented. GitHub projects have a section called "wiki" specifically tailored for those needs. Just like all wikis (it was modeled from Wikipedia), GitHub wikis are there to help newcomers understand how the project works. Many wikis also have a section called Frequently Asked Questions where the most common user queries are answered. Generally, wikis are used by projects where the documentation and the tutorials are too lengthy to fit in a README file. You can see in Figure 8-2 an example of a wiki page that you can also find at `https://github.com/Dash-Industry-Forum/dash.js/wiki`; notice the sidebar where all the links are presented.

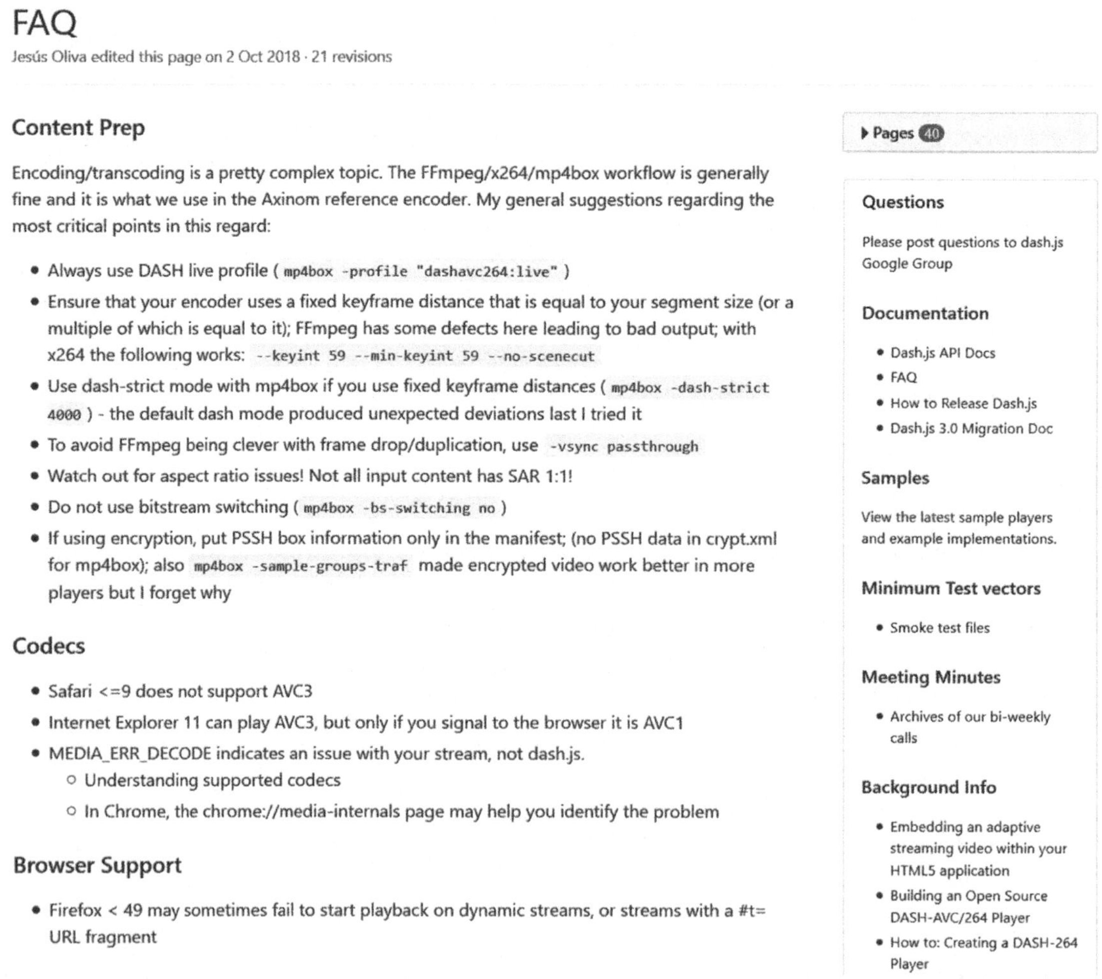

FAQ

Jesús Oliva edited this page on 2 Oct 2018 · 21 revisions

Content Prep

Encoding/transcoding is a pretty complex topic. The FFmpeg/x264/mp4box workflow is generally fine and it is what we use in the Axinom reference encoder. My general suggestions regarding the most critical points in this regard:

- Always use DASH live profile (`mp4box -profile "dashavc264:live"`)
- Ensure that your encoder uses a fixed keyframe distance that is equal to your segment size (or a multiple of which is equal to it); FFmpeg has some defects here leading to bad output; with x264 the following works: `--keyint 59 --min-keyint 59 --no-scenecut`
- Use dash-strict mode with mp4box if you use fixed keyframe distances (`mp4box -dash-strict 4000`) - the default dash mode produced unexpected deviations last I tried it
- To avoid FFmpeg being clever with frame drop/duplication, use `-vsync passthrough`
- Watch out for aspect ratio issues! Not all input content has SAR 1:1!
- Do not use bitstream switching (`mp4box -bs-switching no`)
- If using encryption, put PSSH box information only in the manifest; (no PSSH data in crypt.xml for mp4box); also `mp4box -sample-groups-traf` made encrypted video work better in more players but I forget why

Codecs

- Safari <=9 does not support AVC3
- Internet Explorer 11 can play AVC3, but only if you signal to the browser it is AVC1
- MEDIA_ERR_DECODE indicates an issue with your stream, not dash.js.
  - Understanding supported codecs
  - In Chrome, the chrome://media-internals page may help you identify the problem

Browser Support

- Firefox < 49 may sometimes fail to start playback on dynamic streams, or streams with a #t= URL fragment

▶ Pages 40

Questions

Please post questions to dash.js Google Group

Documentation

- Dash.js API Docs
- FAQ
- How to Release Dash.js
- Dash.js 3.0 Migration Doc

Samples

View the latest sample players and example implementations.

Minimum Test vectors

- Smoke test files

Meeting Minutes

- Archives of our bi-weekly calls

Background Info

- Embedding an adaptive streaming video within your HTML5 application
- Building an Open Source DASH-AVC/264 Player
- How to: Creating a DASH-264 Player

Figure 8-2. *A wiki providing documentation*

Since documentations are very important in Open Source projects, it is many contributors' job to write and keep it updated. Remember that wikis are also Git repositories, so the changes made to it are also tracked just like any repository. This is done to separate the development workflow from the documentation workflow.

And as a cherry on the top, README files and wikis are written in a Markup language called Markdown. It's a very simple language that can render simple formatting and linking. You can see an example of it in Figure 8-3. But you can also choose to write everything in HTML than convert it to Markdown. And you will also find a Markdown cheat sheet in the Appendix of this book!

Headers

```
# This is an <h1> tag
## This is an <h2> tag
###### This is an <h6> tag
```

Emphasis

```
*This text will be italic*
_This will also be italic_

**This text will be bold**
__This will also be bold__

_You **can** combine them_
```

Lists

Unordered

```
* Item 1
* Item 2
  * Item 2a
  * Item 2b
```

Ordered

```
1. Item 1
1. Item 2
1. Item 3
   1. Item 3a
   1. Item 3b
```

Figure 8-3. *Markdown example*

One little thing that Open Source projects also need to prosper: marketing. Yes, README files and wikis are great resources for developers, but end users might not find them too helpful. That's why many projects have a web site that is dedicated to attract users to their product. Web sites are also a good way to make a name for themselves and put themselves out there. If a project doesn't have a web presence or is not referenced by search engines, it will have little chance of being discovered by end users. All of that being said, maintaining and hosting a web site is not an easy task; it can even be expensive money-wise. And many Open Source projects don't have the kind of resources that are necessary for a good marketing campaign; they mostly rely on search engine hits and word-of-mouths. That's why GitHub Pages exists. GitHub Pages is just a web site hosted directly on your repository; you can use it to present your product, provide tutorials, or anything you want, really. It gets rid of the hassle of creating a web site and getting it hosted. But doesn't that interfere with code? Not at all, like wikis, GitHub pages live in other parts of the repository; so they can have different contributors. You can check Figure 8-4 for an example of a GitHub page hosted on `https://scd-aix-marseille-universite.github.io/latexamu/`. As you can see, it is just a simple web site but hosted directly on GitHub. And it's not limited to simple presentation web sites; you can build blogs and similar web sites too. You will see in the Appendix how to build a GitHub page. ☺

Figure 8-4. *A GitHub page example*

As you can see, GitHub has a lot to offer to the Open Source community. And all of that is free of charge! But now, let's see what GitHub has to offer you, personally.

Personal use

Yes, Open Source is great, but what is it's not you jam? Or when you have a project that you want to keep to yourself? GitHub has you covered as well!

You don't have to make all your GitHub repositories public; there is also an option to make them private. That way, only you and a few collaborators (that you choose) can have access to it. You can create an unlimited number of public and private repositories on GitHub; the only limit is your creativity and time. There is, however, a limit of the number of contributors you can have on private repositories: 3. If you want to work with more contributors, you can sign up for GitHub Pro, which is a paid plan. But for almost everybody, a Free plan is more than enough.

Having a personal GitHub account to showcase your work is also a good way to market yourself. That way, people can check the Open Source or personal projects you contribute to and even check your code. Many developers also use GitHub Pages to render their resumé or showcase their portfolio. You can check Figure 8-5 for an example of that.

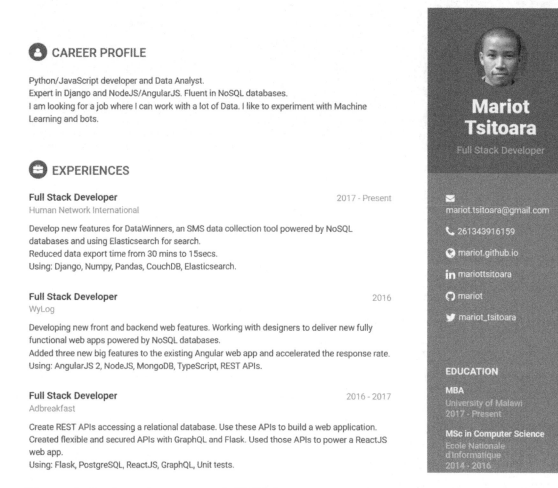

Figure 8-5. *A random person's GitHub page*

And since there are 36 million developers on GitHub, you might want to connect with some of them. One way to connect is to follow a particular project. When the project moves along, you will receive updates and can check out the changes. Note that you will automatically follow a repository you contribute to. Another way to show your appreciation for a project is also to "star" it. It's akin to liking a content on social media.

Hence, the more stars a repository has, the more users are happy with it. GitHub also offers a News Feed that are news and notifications from specific projects. Those projects are chosen because you contribute to them or "starred" them. They are also tailored by analyzing your most used language or tools. You can check Figure 8-6 for an example of it. It's a good way to have a clear vision of what happen around you.

Figure 8-6. GitHub Explore

Before we go to the next section, there is a cool thing that you can check out with GitHub: your contribution activity. Every commit you push on GitHub is registered as a contribution, even to your personal or private repositories if you enable the option. Those activities are rendered in a nice illustration like the one shown in Figure 8-7. They show your contributions throughout the year and indicate your achievements to your profile's visitors.

Figure 8-7. My contribution history in 2018

GitHub for businesses

GitHub is not just for personal projects or Open Source communities; businesses have their place there too. Many businesses now invest in Open Source for some of their products, and which better place to find quality developers than GitHub?

There is an Enterprise plan in GitHub that incorporates all the benefits of a paid plan, but with many additional features. Those features range from the choice of hosting, to security, to online support. All of those features may be very attractive to businesses, but for us, a simple Free plan is enough for now.

Summary

This chapter presented the users of GitHub and some small features. You should now have some ideas about what are you going to use it with. In the next chapter, GitHub's main features will be presented along with some tips on how to use it to work with teammates. We'll talk about Project Management, Code Reviews, and so much more. And to finish in beauty, we will quick start with GitHub with our first repositories! You'll be back in action in the next chapter, so make sure to review the previous exercises to stay sharp. Let's begin!

## CHAPTER 9

Quick Start with GitHub

So far, we only talked about what is GitHub and who needs it. Now, we are going to see what it can do exactly and what its main features are. The most important features of GitHub are its Project Management tools; combined with the right development workflow, it is a sure way to get a project moving.

For this section of the book, nothing better than good old-fashioned exercises! I could tell you all the advantages of GitHub, but you'll understand better if you are doing the exploration yourself. Let's begin by creating a GitHub account and starting a project.

Project management

The ability to manage a project while following a well-established path is one of the most admired features of GitHub. You are going to follow along with me in this section. It's very important that you do so because you'll have a better understanding of the features.

Since we are going to manage our project with Git and GitHub, our very first step is to create an account. It's very straightforward, and you don't need any more information more than your name and email just like in Figure 9-1.

© Mariot Tsitoara 2020
M. Tsitoara, *Beginning Git and GitHub*, https://doi.org/10.1007/978-1-4842-5313-7_9

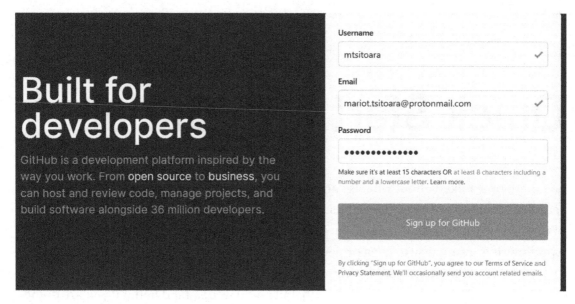

Figure 9-1. *GitHub signup page*

After signing up, you'll receive a confirmation link in your email client and following the provided link will conclude the inscription. You will then arrive at the main GitHub page which should look like in Figure 9-2.

Figure 9-2. *GitHub homepage*

You GitHub homepage is pretty empty but we're working on filling it with cool projects. At the right side of the page, you'll see some trending repositories or news story; but we won't go there yet.

As you can see in Figure 9-2, there are three links that you can follow to create a new repository: one on the left side, one in the middle, and the last one in the navigation bar. Click one of them so we can create our repository.

The repository creation form is also very simple, as you can see in Figure 9-3. You only need to fill out the form with a name and a short description of the project. That description is optional, but you should try to make it as simple as possible so that users who visit your repository know what's up.

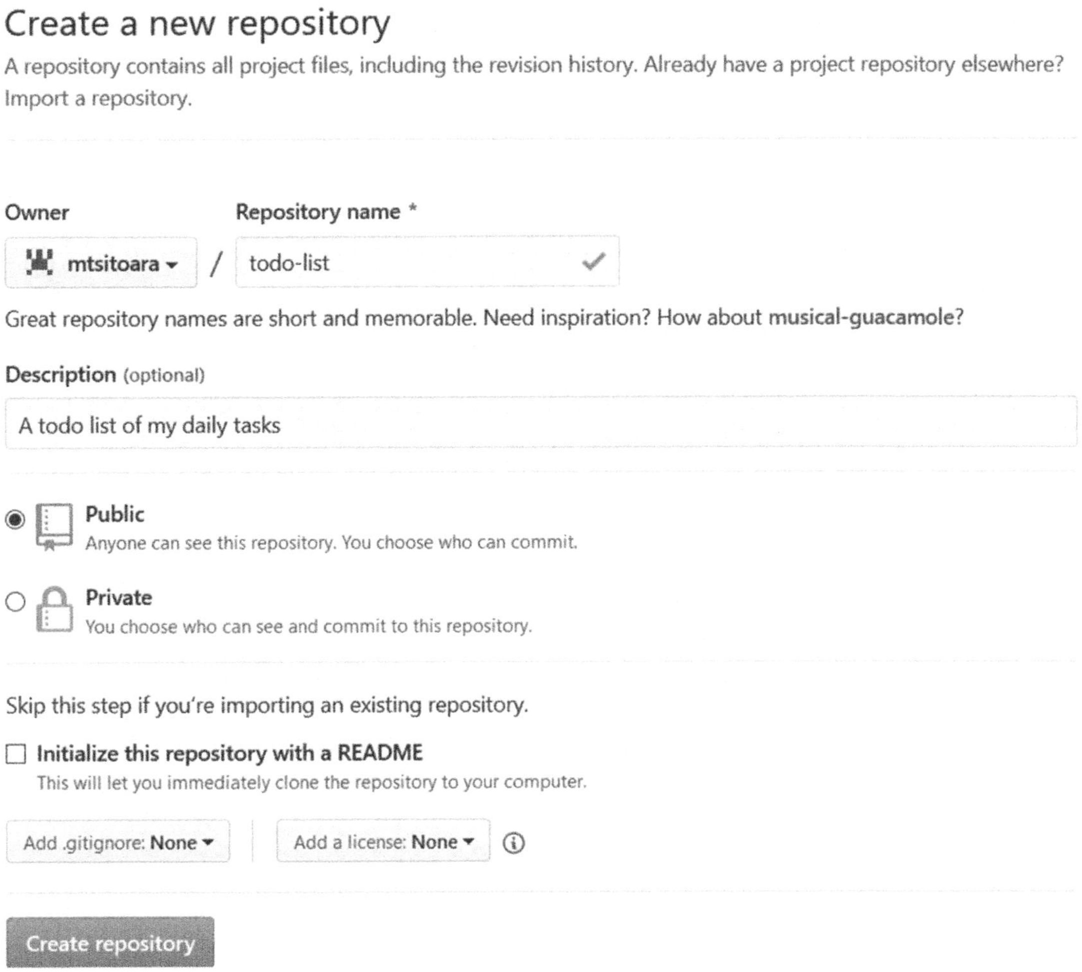

Create a new repository

A repository contains all project files, including the revision history. Already have a project repository elsewhere? Import a repository.

Owner   Repository name *

🏛 mtsitoara ▾   /   todo-list   ✓

Great repository names are short and memorable. Need inspiration? How about **musical-guacamole**?

Description (optional)

A todo list of my daily tasks

◉ 📖 **Public**
    Anyone can see this repository. You choose who can commit.

○ 🔒 **Private**
    You choose who can see and commit to this repository.

Skip this step if you're importing an existing repository.

☐ **Initialize this repository with a README**
    This will let you immediately clone the repository to your computer.

Add .gitignore: **None ▾**   Add a license: **None ▾**   ⓘ

Create repository

Figure 9-3. *Creation of a new repository*

You can choose to make the repository private, if you like; nobody but you will have access to it. A public repository doesn't mean that anyone can edit it; it just means that anyone can read it and logged in users can propose changes to it. You will still be the maintainer of the project and the owner of the repository.

Then, you have the choice to initialize the repository with a README file. Ignore this for now because we are aiming to create a repository from scratch; and we will add README, .gitignore, and license files later.

After all is done, click the Submit button to create your first GitHub repository! It's that simple! You will then be redirected to your project page, which is a unique link to your repository. The link looks like this: `https://github.com/your_username/your_repository`; for example, the new repository I created is accessible through the following link: `https://github.com/mtsitoara/todo-list`. Thus, you can't create two repositories with the same name. Your project page should be similar to the one shown in Figure 9-4.

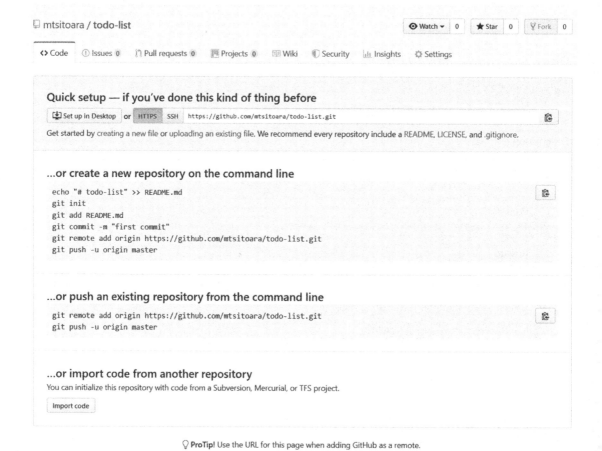

Figure 9-4. Your brand-new repository

As you can see in Figure 9-4, there are some instructions on how to get started whether you want to create a new repository or push an existing one. Since we are building our repository from scratch, we will go with the first option. The second option would have worked for us too because we already have a local repository, but we are going to ignore that from now.

So, we created our first repository and are ready to push our project on it. But let's look into the magic box and see what exactly has just happened.

How remote repositories work

Remember Chapter 7 about remote Git and how we decided to use GitHub as a remote repository store? This section is a logical extension of that chapter because we are going to learn how remote repositories managed with GitHub works.

When we created our repository using the GitHub web site, we were giving instructions to GitHub servers and asked them to initialize an empty repository. And if you remember Chapter 2, initializing a repository is very simple: go to any directory and execute git init. That's exactly what happened here, except not on your computer but to a server hosted by GitHub.

So, it's as if we executed the following commands on a faraway server which has git installed

```
$ mkdir todo-list
$ cd todo-list
$ git init
```

It's the same commands that we will use to create our local repository. So now, there is a remote repository in GitHub's servers that we will use to share our project.

Remote repositories are used so you don't have to use your own computer to share your project. In the case of GitHub, the remote repositories are accessible by anyone but only the owner can edit them. We will discuss teamwork in a later section.

The main takeaway is that a remote repository is where you can publish your project to make it available to everyone. And anyone can clone your repository, so they can follow your advancements to get the latest changes.

Publishing your local repository to a remote one is called "pushing," and getting the latest commits from a remote repository to a local one is called "pulling." Push and pull are maybe the most used commands you'll use in Git.

But how can I tell GitHub which remote repository I want to be linked with my local one? That's where the unique link to your repository is needed. You'll use the link to push your local changes or pull the commits you don't already have.

In conclusion, GitHub created an empty remote repository which can only be modified by you but can be seen by everyone. What we need to do now is create a local repository and link it to the remote one.

Linking repositories

Now that GitHub has created the remote repository for us, it's time to create our own local repository and link it to the remote one.

As we've done in the previous chapters, we're going to create a repository with the git init command. The repository names can differ between local and remote, but it would be a good idea to use a unique name so you don't get confused. For this particular project, the commands will be

```
$ mkdir todo-list
$ cd todo-list
$ git init
```

Note   If you prefer to work with the repository that you created earlier in this chapter instead of a new one, you can just skip the initialization part and go straight to linking.

Nothing new here; and you should get the same result as shown in Figure 9-5.

Figure 9-5. *Initialization of a Git repository*

Now that we have our local repository, it's time to link it to the remote! To list, add, or remove remotes, we will use the git remote command. For example, let's link our current remotes using this command:

```
$ git remote
```

You shouldn't get any result because it's a brand-new repository and we haven't linked any remote to it. Let's add one now.

Note   If you see remotes in your results, you can remove them by using git remote rm [remote_name]. Anyway, you shouldn't see any remote if it's a new repository.

You will need the unique link to your repository to be able to link a local repository to it; so, grab yours from the previous section. Mine is https://github.com/mtsitoara/ todo-list.git. Don't forget the .git at the end!

You will also need to create a name for your remote repository. That way, you can have multiple remotes within a single project. It may be necessary in the case where the test and production remotes are different for each other. The default name is "origin" per convention. Although you can choose any name, it is recommended to use origin as the name of the remote where teammates share their work.

The command to add a link to a remote is simple. It's

```
git remote add [name] [link]
```

So, to add a link to the newly created repository, you'll have to execute this command:

```
$ git remote add origin https://github.com/mtsitoara/todo-list.git
```

That's it! You can check if the remote has been added by executing git remote or git remote -v to get more information. You should get a result similar to the screen shown in Figure 9-6.

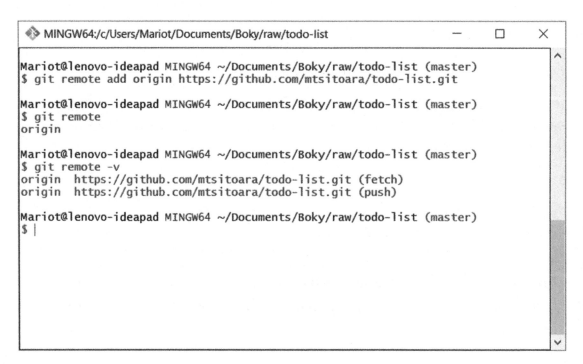

Figure 9-6. *Adding a new remote*

And that's it! Adding a new remote is a simple, straightforward task. Now that we got that cleared, let's push the project to GitHub!

Pushing to remote repositories

We finally got our local and remote repositories linked. It's time to push our project to GitHub so we can share our work.

Pushing commits to a remote repository is very simple; but first, let's create some commits to push. In your working directory, create a file called README.md and put in the description of your project in Markdown. For example, here is my README.md file:

```
# TODO list
A simple app to manage your daily tasks

## Features
* List of daily tasks
```

Now, let's add the newly created file to the staging area by using git add.

```
$ git add README.md
```

Now is the time to commit our project with git commit. As commit message, many developers choose "Initial commit" when it's the first. It's not a rule and you can change it if you want to.

```
$ git commit
```

Since we've done these many times already, you should be comfortable with staging and committing by now. After the commit, you should have a result similar to Figure 9-7.

113

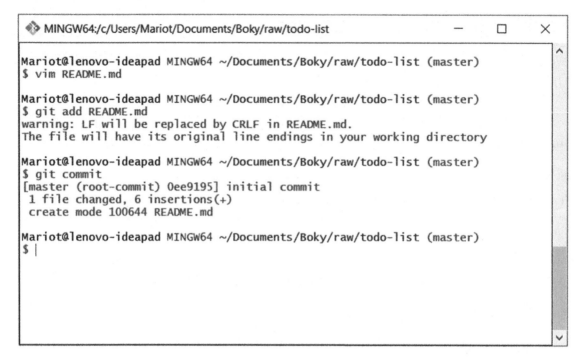

Figure 9-7. *Creating, staging of a new file*

So, we have our first commit! Now, we can push those changes to the remote repository. The command to push changes to remote is simple; you just need the name of the remote repository and the branch to be pushed. Since we haven't created any branch yet (we'll learn about branches in a later section), our only branch is called "master." The git push command is

```
git push <remote_name> <branch_name>
```

So, in our case, the command will be

```
$ git push origin master
```

With a little bit of luck, everything goes well; but it's not always the case. If you use a password manager or used different configs (name and email) from the ones you provided to GitHub, you'll get an authentication problem. For example, I am denied access to my repository because I used a password manager and it tried to log me in with my old credentials. You can check an example of authentication error in Figure 9-8.

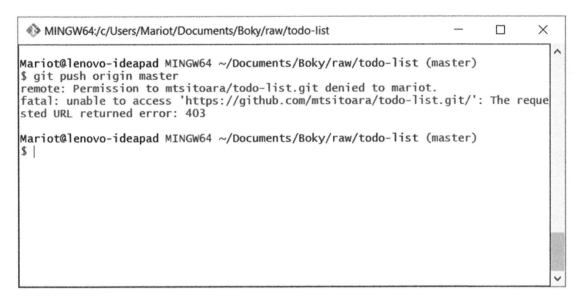

Figure 9-8. *Authentication error*

To resolve these kinds of problems, we have to configure Git again, with the correct information. You can see in Figure 9-9 that I changed my email in the global configs, that is, on every repository on my computer.

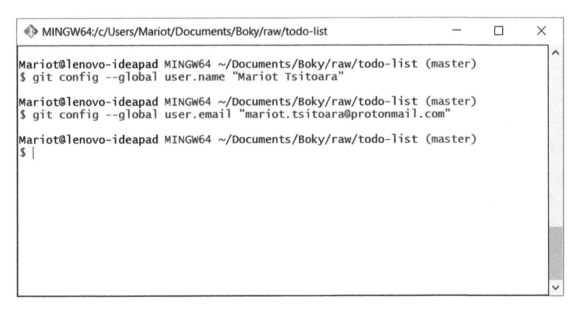

Figure 9-9. *Reconfiguration of Git*

Now, we have to make sure to remove any link to a password manager in this repository. For my case, I use credential helpers (password managers) in other repositories on this computer; so I will not set a global config but a local one.

```
$ git config --local credential.helper ""
```

This should resolve our problem and we can resume our push. After you execute the git push command, you will be asked for your username and password. Then, you'll get a result similar to Figure 9-10.

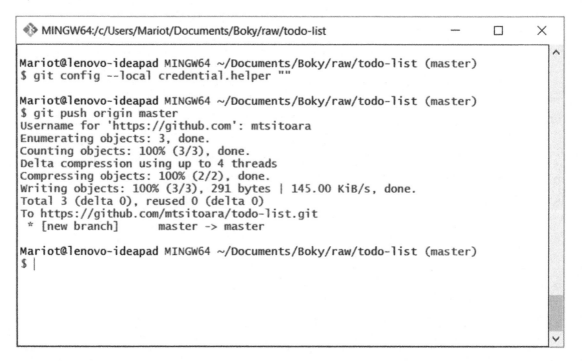

Figure 9-10. *Successful git push*

Tip   Since we are using HTTPS to push and pull changes, we will need to provide our username and password each time. It gets tiring real fast, so if you want to use a password manager or stop using passwords altogether, check the lessons in the Appendix of this book.

Now, our project is visible on GitHub by everyone! Let's check it out on its project page. If we refresh the project page, we should get a page like the one shown in Figure 9-11.

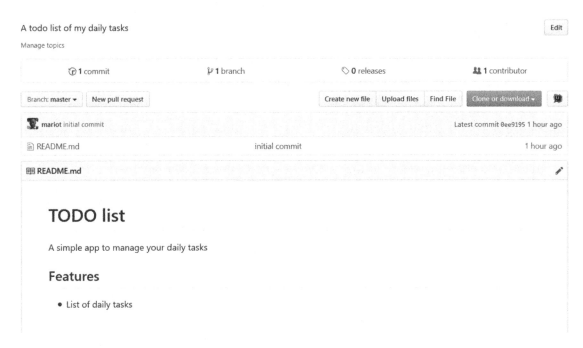

Figure 9-11. *The updated project page*

As you can see in Figure 9-11, the repository page now displays many intel:

- The number of commits

- The last commit name and its committer

- A list of all project files

- A preview of README.md

What we just did is the basis of code sharing: pushing changes. You will be using this command over and over again when working with remote repositories. It is a very simple feature, but it is imperative that you understand completely what it does. Pushing just means to copy all your current commits (in a specific branch) to a remote branch in a remote repository. All history logs are also copied.

Before you go to the next chapter, ask yourself these questions: where are the remote repositories stored? Who has a read-only access to them? Who can edit them? Also make sure to understand the basis of remote and local repositories linking and why is it necessary.

Summary

In this chapter, we had our very first interaction with remote Git repositories. As we've already established, they are just normal repositories that are stored in a remote server instead of your local machine. We saw how to create and link local and remote repositories, a feature that we will use a lot of times. And the main command we learned was git push, which copies the state of your local repository to a distant one.

In the next chapter, we are going to dive deep into Project Management and see what other features GitHub has to offer. We will also learn to pull changes from the remote repository as well as resolve push and pull issues. Let's go!

## CHAPTER 10

Beginning Project Management: Issues

Last chapter, we did a quick peek at using GitHub to host and share our code. But that doesn't even begin to describe what GitHub can do for you; there are so many features that can help your project mature. In this chapter, we are going to begin to learn about how to manage projects with GitHub. Thus, we are going to begin with the basic form of GitHub project management: Issues.

Overview on issues

To successfully manage a project, any project, you have to plan in advance; just reacting to new inputs and generally do whatever you feel like doing is a perfect recipe for disaster. A GitHub project is no different; you have to keep track of your actions before even thinking about doing them. That's why GitHub has an awesome feature called Issues. We are going to discuss them in this section and learn how to manage them properly.

During all the chapters in this book, you are both the developer and the project manager; but in a big project, you might not be included in the planning phases. But for now, you are temporarily promoted to project manager and lead developer (in addition to being the only developer), congratulations! One of the duties of the project manager is to plan in advance all the tasks that need to be done. The plans don't need to be very precise yet (in the real world they never are), but it is necessary to have a list of all the tasks that need to be done. Those tasks can be either new features, bugfixing, or just a team discussion. In GitHub, those tasks are called Issues.

An issue is used to track new feature development, bugfixing, or new ideas that a team member suggested. They are the brick and mortar of GitHub project management; in theory, no action should be done with an issue being attached to it. The aim of each action you take should be the resolving of an issue.

© Mariot Tsitoara 2020
M. Tsitoara, *Beginning Git and GitHub*, https://doi.org/10.1007/978-1-4842-5313-7_10

Long gone are the days where planning the next steps was done by boring team meetings; now you know exactly what will be your next steps and most importantly what is everybody else doing. Suggesting new ideas to your coworkers is easier than ever; just open an issue to discuss it with your team without using another app of email client. The biggest plus for using issues is that the history is kept forever—each feature, each bug, and each discussion.

Creating an Issue

The best way to learn about issues is to directly interact with them; so, let's go back to our GitHub project page and deal with them.

When you open your GitHub project page, you directly arrive on the "Code" part of the project. It is the part where your project files are shown. For now, your project page should look like mine, shown in Figure 10-1.

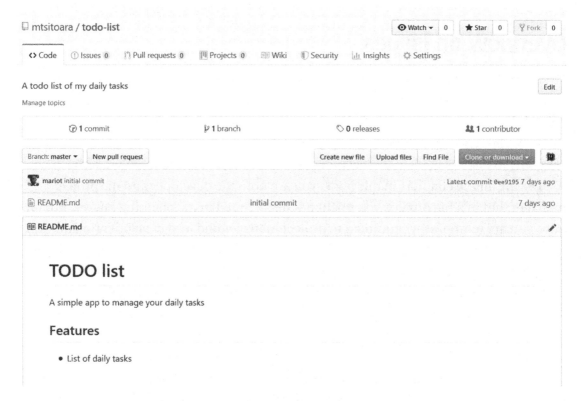

Figure 10-1. *Project page open on the "code" section*

Just below the project name, there are many tabs that show all the sections of your project. You will mostly work on "Code," "Issues," "Pull Requests," and "Projects." But for now, let's focus on Issues. Go ahead and click it to begin. You should arrive at an empty section like the one shown in Figure 10-2 because your project has no issues yet.

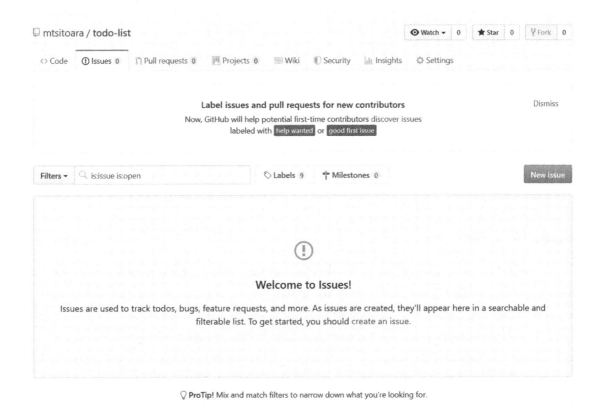

Figure 10-2. *The Issues section*

There are many calls to action there about creating a new issue. Click one of them, and you will see a form similar to mine as shown in Figure 10-3.

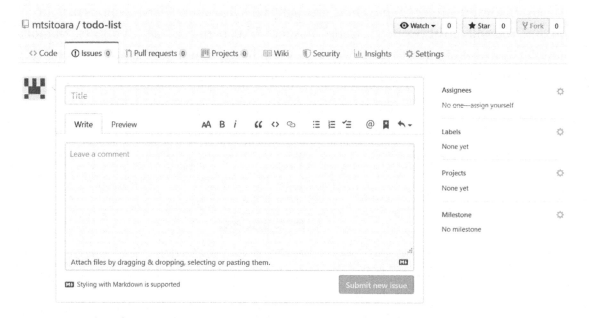

Figure 10-3. *New issue form*

The form is pretty simple; and only the title is mandatory. There is also a comment section below the title if you need more room to explain. Let's go ahead and fill our first issue with the basic stuff; don't change the values on the right side just yet.

For our first issue, we are starting a discussion about the technology we will use for our product. Issues aren't needed for features and bug tracking only; they are also used to start a discussion and share ideas. Go ahead and fill your first issue like mine as shown in Figure 10-4; I titled mine "Choose the technologies to be used for the app" because it's the first step for any project.

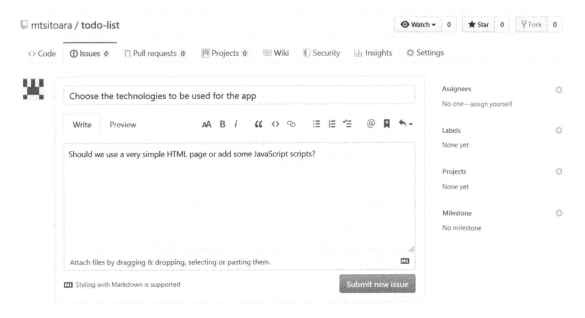

Figure 10-4. *Our first issue*

Now that we filled out the basic info about the issue, submit it. You will then be redirected to the detailed view of your new issue. It should be similar to my issue shown in Figure 10-5.

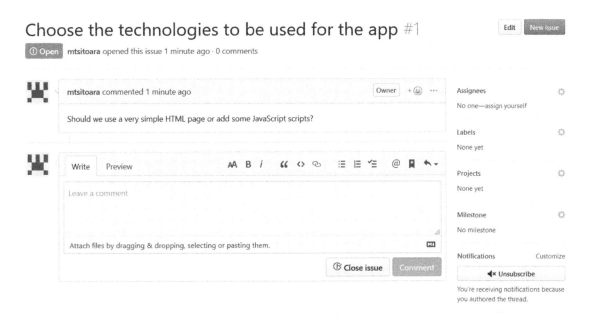

Figure 10-5. *Details of an issue*

The first thing to notice is that your issue has been given a number. Each issue has a unique number, and those numbers are not recycled, meaning that even if you delete an issue, its number will never be reused. This number is important, as you will see in this section.

The details page also includes a comment section where team members can discuss the idea. It even includes a limited number of emojis that you can use as a substitute to commenting. For example, if you agree with someone, giving them a thumbs-up is better than commenting or writing "me too"! It would clog the communication and stall the conversation.

In the bottom right side of the page, you can see a subscribe button. If you choose to subscribe to an issue, you will receive notifications about the changes done to it. You will also receive new comments and news about milestones reached.

Since you are the only member of the team, you won't do much discussion. Just add a comment or a reaction image and close the issue. Closing the issue won't delete it; it will just mark it as completed. Deleting issues is not advised because keeping a history of the project is needed, and issues are the best way to keep track of changes. And remember: if your repository is public, anyone can read your comments; so please be kind and rewind any unpleasantries that might arise.

After commenting and closing the issue, you will go back to the issue details page, and it will look similar to mine as shown in Figure 10-6.

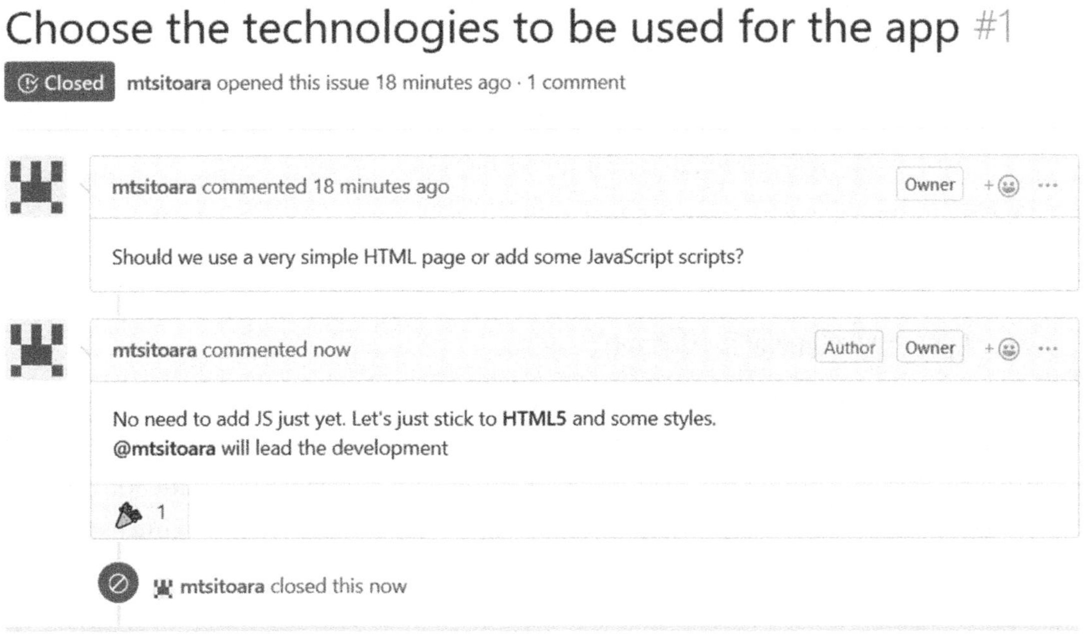

Figure 10-6. *A closed issue*

You can continue to comment on a closed issue, but it is discouraged as everyone has considered the issue complete and moved on. An issue can also be locked and nobody can comment on it anymore; this is considered as a last effort way to keep the peace. We all have our opinions, and discussing them on the Internet is never easy, especially on an open forum. But try to be professional at all times because everything you say will be visible to anyone.

Interacting with an issue

We've successfully created and closed an issue, but we haven't been involved in them too much. What good is an issue if it doesn't have any impact on the project? In this section, we will directly interact with issues on GitHub and in our code.

For the first part of this section, you will keep your Project Manager hat because we are going to need to plan our project. Up until this moment, our TODO list app was just multiple text files next to each other. Then we decided to use HTML5 to present them in a better way. To code this, we need a plan of action; and it is your job as a Project Manager to dress up this plan.

Since it's a simple HTML5 app, we aren't going to need a very big plan, just some necessary bullet points. So, to create this app, we will need to

- Write the skeleton of the app with HTML5

- Add some styles to make it prettier with CSS3

- Describe the app in README.md

- Document the code

- Create a web page for the app

Those are some basic steps that we will need to do to accomplish our goal: ship a TODO app.

Since you already know how to create issues, I will let you create an issue for each of these bullet points. After you are done, your Issues page should look like mine as shown in Figure 10-7.

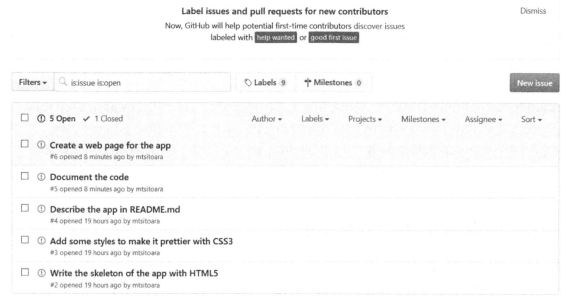

Figure 10-7. *All open tasks*

As you can see, the tasks are shown in the order they were introduced. There's also no way to distinguish them except for their numbers, and it's very easy to get lost if there are too many issues. So, to have a clearer look at all our tasks, we are going to use Labels.

Labels

Labels are exactly what you expect them to be: texts to help you quickly filter through your issues. Let's use them directly so you can get familiar with the concept.

As you can see in Figure 10-7, there is a search bar in the Issues page, and you can use it to filter through the issues. But since we don't have any labels yet, we can't do any filtering; just basic search. Click the Labels button next to the search bar to show all the labels available. You will then see a list of the default labels that you can use; check Figure 10-8 for an example of this.

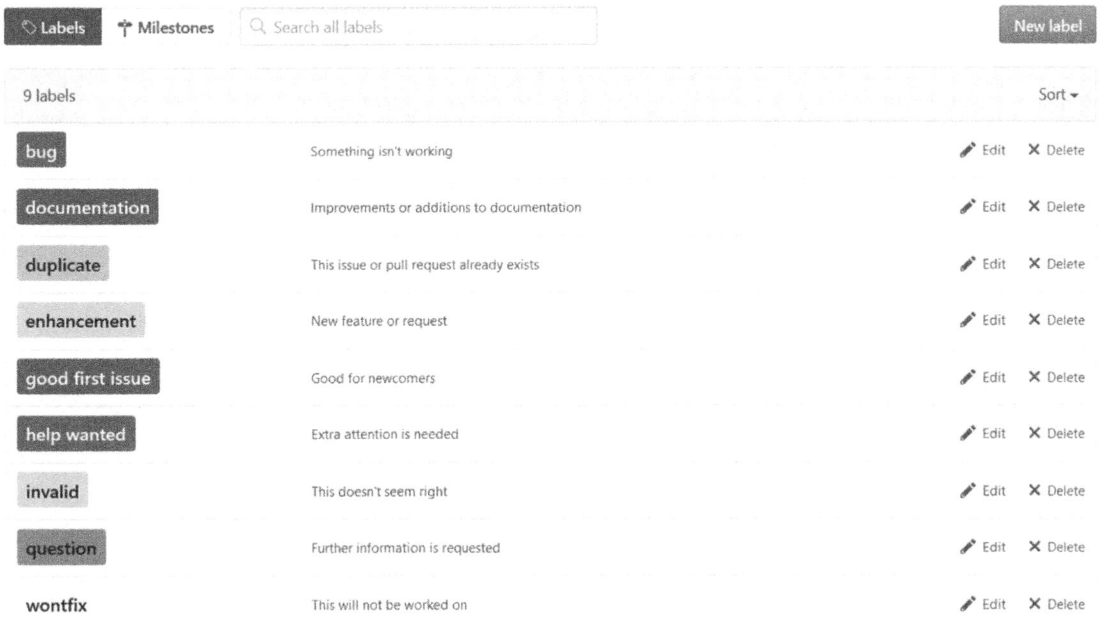

Figure 10-8. *List of the default labels*

Those are the most commonly used labels in the developers' community. But that doesn't mean than they are mandatory or immutable; you can change them at your pleasure and need. Only when you are working on an Open Source project is it ill advised to change them because most developers are so used to them.

But since it's your personal project and you are the project manager, you can add, edit, or remove any label you want. For example, the label "help wanted" will be useless if you work alone in a private setting. You can also use labels to tag the severity of the issue; many projects use labels like "urgent" or "breaking" if the issue is severe. Labels can also be used to differentiate the origin of the issue if the project is big enough. A big project can use the labels "frontend," "backend," or "database" to separate issues into groups.

After you made your changes to the labels (although I recommend to only add the new that you need and leave the default ones), get back to your issues and open the details page. Then, apply one or more labels on each one of them by clicking the Labels button. You can check Figure 10-9 for an example.

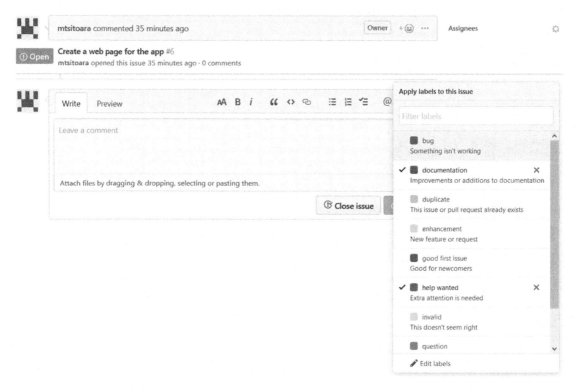

Figure 10-9. *Adding a label to an issue*

After you add the labels, a notification will appear on the comment section of the Issues page; you can check Figure 10-10 for an example.

Figure 10-10. *Notification about the newly added labels*

Now, go through each one of your issues and apply some labels on them. Then, when you have finished, go back to the Issues page. It should look like mine as shown in Figure 10-11.

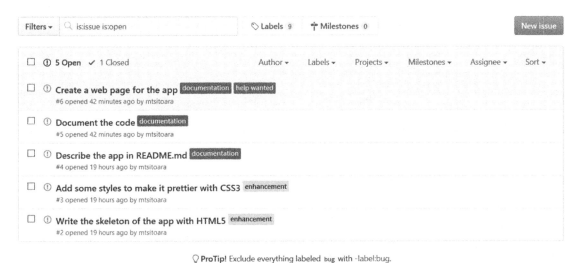

Figure 10-11. *Labeled issues*

Perfect! Now that we put labels on the issues, we can filter through them. For example, to see every issue labeled "enhancement," just click Filter (shown in Figure 10-12), and you will get a result similar to mine as shown in Figure 10-13.

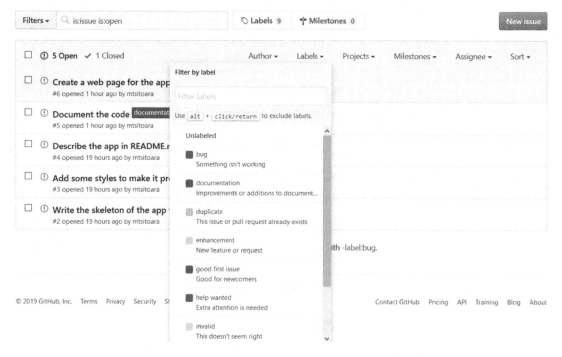

Figure 10-12. *Filtering by label*

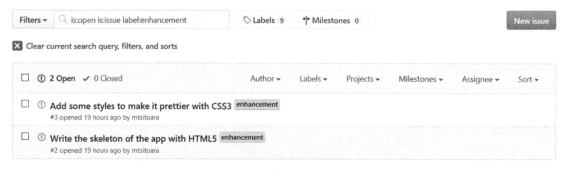

Figure 10-13. *Filtered issues*

Isn't filtering fun?! But you know what is even more fun? Assign issue to others!
Let's do it.

Assignees

Now that our issues are correctly labeled, it is time to assign them to a developer. It's fairly an easy task and it's not so different from labels.

You can assign an issue to up to ten members of your team. But since you're the only one right now, you can only assign yourself. Let's do it! Navigate to the issues titled "Write the skeleton of the app with HTML5" and "Add some styles to make it prettier with CSS3" and assign them to yourself. Assigning an issue to a team member works exactly like adding labels. You can check Figure 10-14 for an example.

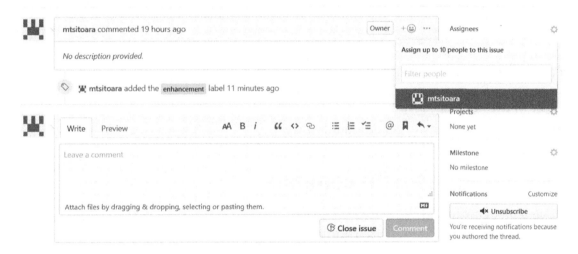

Figure 10-14. *Assigning an issue*

After you assigned those two issues to yourself, you will get a result like mine as shown in Figure 10-15 on your Issues page. You can now filter through your issues by labels and assignees.

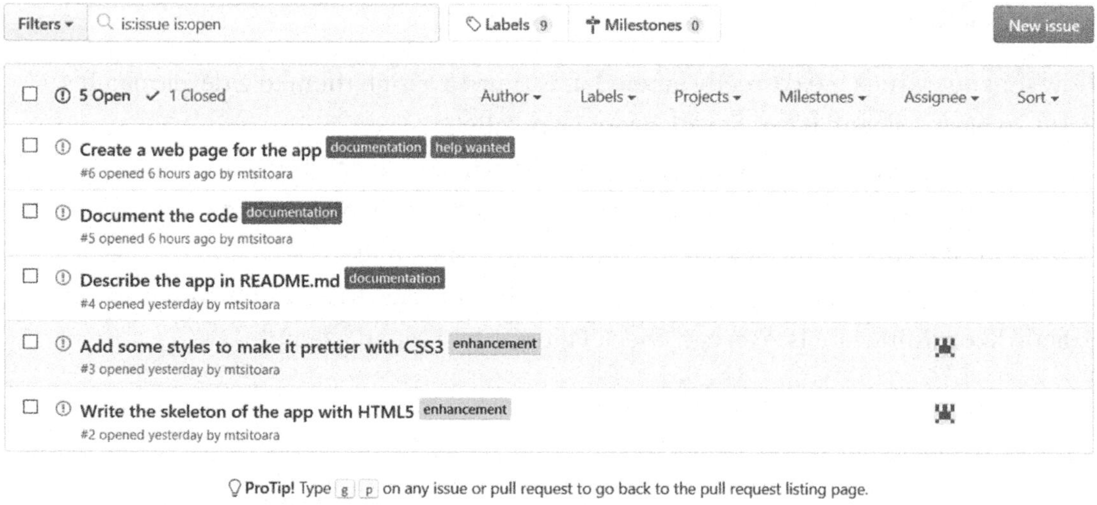

Figure 10-15. *A complete issues list*

Now that the issues are assigned to you, take off your manager hat and put on your developer one. It's time to get our hands dirty!

Linking issues with commits

As we said in the beginning of this chapter, each action you take with Git should have the resolving of an issue as its goal. Most of the time, when using Git, you will work with commits; so, each of these commits should be tied to an issue. In this section, we are going to learn how to link our commits to issues.

First, let's decide which issues we will be working on. As we saw in Figure 10-15, there are two issues assigned to us: "Write the skeleton of the app with HTML5" and "Add some styles to make it prettier with CSS3." We are going to work on writing the skeleton first because it makes so much sense to begin by that. So open up the details page of this issue and take note of its number. As you can see in Figure 10-16, mine is issue number 2.

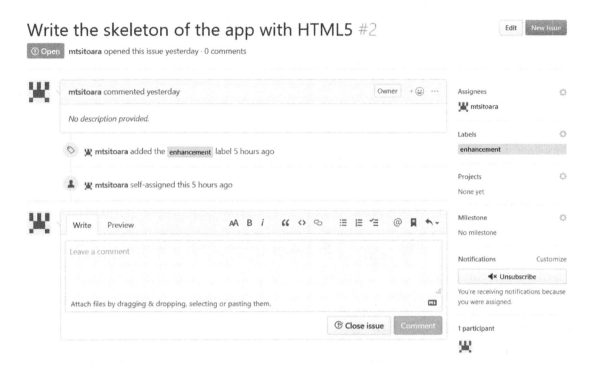

Figure 10-16. *Issue number 2 details page*

Working on the commit

Now that we have an issue to resolve and its number, it's time to prepare the commit. Since we decided to use simple HTML5 for this app, we only need a single file for the skeleton. So, create a file named index.html in your working directory and paste in this code:

```
<!doctype html>
<html>
    <head>
        <meta charset="utf-8">
        <title>TODO list</title>
    </head>
    <body>
        <h1>TODO list</h1>

        <h3>Todo</h3>
        <ul>
```

```
        <li>Buy a hat for the bat</li>
        <li>Clear the fogs for the frogs</li>
        <li>Bring a box to the fox</li>
    </ul>

    <h3>Done</h3>
    <ul>
        <li>Put the mittens on the kittens</li>
    </ul>
    </body>
</html>
```

Now, I'll let you stage the newly created file, but don't commit it yet; we have to talk about the commit message.

Referencing an issue

We are ready to commit the project in its current state, but we have to tweak the commit message so that the commit can be linked to an issue. The most common way to link a commit to an issue is to mention the issue number in the commit message.

Until the point, we only used very short commit messages as we tried to keep them under one line. But since we need room for a more elaborate way to describe our commits, we are going to structure our commit messages this way from now on: a title, a body, and a footer separated by a blank line. To help you understand, you can find an illustration of it in Figure 10-17.

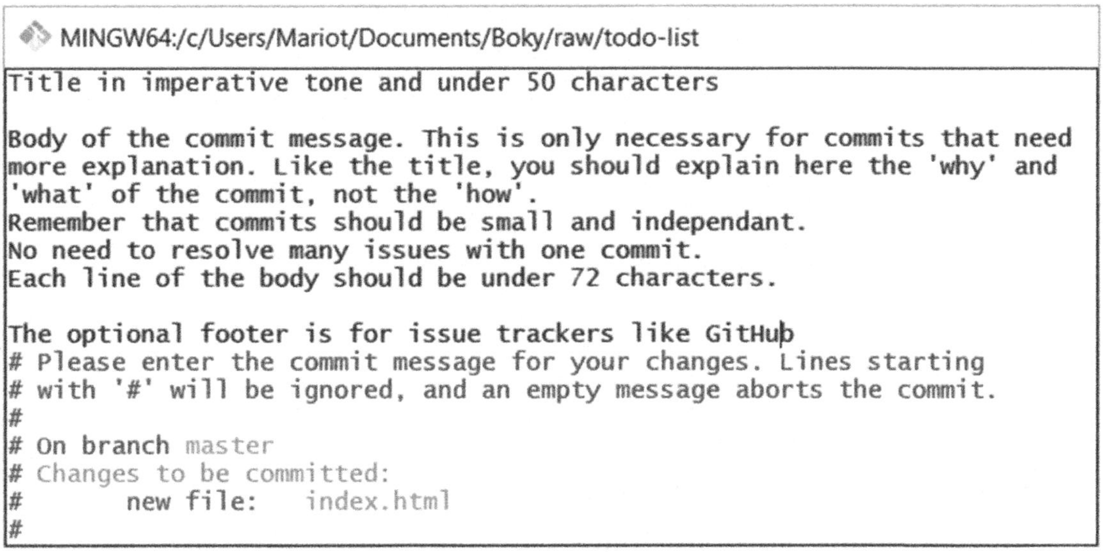

```
MINGW64:/c/Users/Mariot/Documents/Boky/raw/todo-list

Title in imperative tone and under 50 characters

Body of the commit message. This is only necessary for commits that need
more explanation. Like the title, you should explain here the 'why' and
'what' of the commit, not the 'how'.
Remember that commits should be small and independant.
No need to resolve many issues with one commit.
Each line of the body should be under 72 characters.

The optional footer is for issue trackers like GitHub
# Please enter the commit message for your changes. Lines starting
# with '#' will be ignored, and an empty message aborts the commit.
#
# On branch master
# Changes to be committed:
#       new file:   index.html
#
```

Figure 10-17. *The commit message structure*

Caution   Don't forget the blank line between each part of the commit message. They are really important.

The body and the footer are optional; only use them when necessary, especially the body. People are lazy; they will probably only read the title and move on, so make it extra clear even without the body.

The footer is what interests us right now; it's the section reserved for issue trackers like GitHub. We use the footer to make references to issues using their numbers. For example, to make a reference to the issue we're working on, we're just going to put its number in the footer preceded by "#." When GitHub sees this, it immediately links the commit with the issue referenced.

Note   We can put the references to the issues anywhere in the commit message, even in the title. But this practice is very ugly and should be discouraged.

Combining all of that, let's make our commit with a proper commit message. Take for example my commit shown in Figure 10-18.

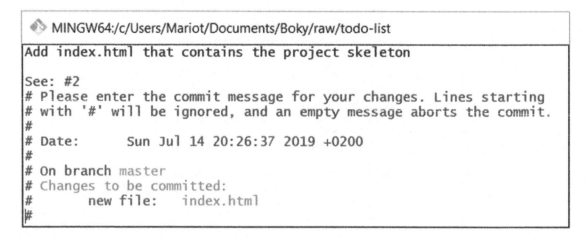

Figure 10-18. *Commit message linked to issue #2*

In my commit message, I skipped the body part because it was unnecessary. I only needed to link this commit to issue #2 so I put that number in the footer.

Now, push it! Take a look at the previous chapter if you forgot how (hint: git push origin master).

Now let's go back to the details page of our issue. First thing you will notice is that a new comment has been added to it: that's the reference to our commit. It should look like mine depicted in Figure 10-19.

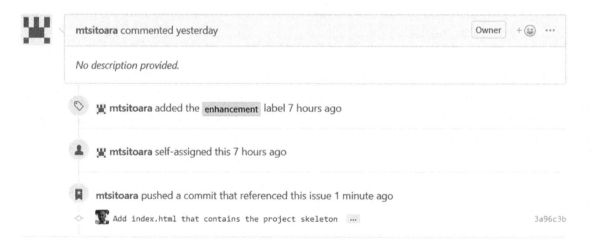

Figure 10-19. *A reference to our last commit*

This is a very useful feature of GitHub that you will certainly use a lot: show all the commits linked to a particular issue. That's why no commit should be pushed without being tied to an issue; it's better for the management of the project.

If you click the title of the commit shown on the reference (see Figure 10-19), you will see a familiar screen. I'll let you discover by yourself which screen is depicted in Figure 10-20.

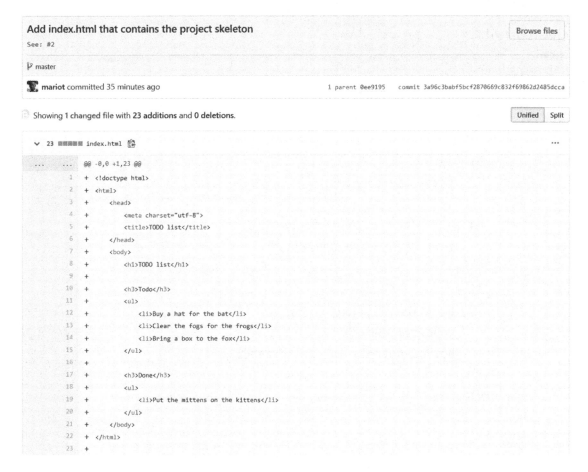

Figure 10-20. *A detailed view of a commit*

That's right! It's the "git show" view. No need to get lost in Git commands to see what a commit does, you can directly see it in GitHub!

Now that we successfully resolved the issue, get back to its details page and close it. Let's resolve the next one!

Closing an issue using keywords

It was nice to work on an issue and close it, right? Well, there is still something even more fun: closing an issue by using keywords in commit message!

First, we have to decide which issue to resolve. Our next issue is "Add some styles to make it prettier with CSS3" which has the number 3. Let's resolve it! Open index.html and change the contents to this:

```
<!doctype html>
<html>
    <head>
        <meta charset="utf-8">
        <title>TODO list</title>
        <style>
            h1 {
                text-align:center;
            }
            h3 {
                text-transform: uppercase;
            }
            li {
                overflow: hidden;
                padding: 20px 0;
                border-bottom: 1px solid #eee;
            }
        </style>
    </head>
    <body>
        <h1>TODO list</h1>

        <h3>Todo</h3>
        <ul>
            <li>Buy a hat for the bat</li>
            <li>Clear the fogs for the frogs</li>
            <li>Bring a box to the fox</li>
        </ul>

        <h3>Done</h3>
```

```
    <ul>
        <li>Put the mittens on the kittens</li>
    </ul>
  </body>
</html>
```

Stage the file but don't commit yet. The keywords to close an issue are

- close

- closes

- closed

- fix

- fixes

- fixed

- resolve

- resolves

- resolved

Using one of these words followed by an issue number will mark it as resolved and close it. Our commit will resolve issue #3 so we will put that in the commit message footer. Your commit message should then look like mine as shown in Figure 10-21.

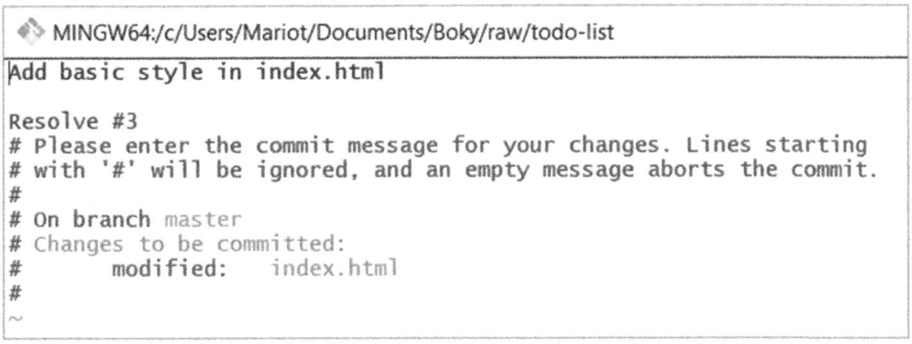

```
 MINGW64:/c/Users/Mariot/Documents/Boky/raw/todo-list

Add basic style in index.html

Resolve #3
# Please enter the commit message for your changes. Lines starting
# with '#' will be ignored, and an empty message aborts the commit.
#
# On branch master
# Changes to be committed:
#       modified:   index.html
#
~
```

Figure 10-21. *Resolving an issue by commit message*

Just like commit messages, the issue references should use the imperative tone; so it is preferred to use "resolve" instead of "resolved." Now, it's time to push our commit and see for ourselves!

Navigate to the issue you worked on (you won't find it in the open issues, use the filter to see the closed issues) and open the details page. You should see a new comment on it just like mine as shown in Figure 10-22.

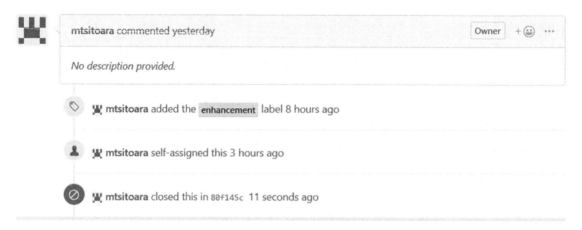

Figure 10-22. *Issue closed by keywords*

If you click the commit name, you will again see the "git show" view of the commit.

The little feature of GitHub is useful but be very careful when using it. Only close an issue when you are perfectly sure that it was resolved. Closing and reopening issues confuse people and generate a lot of notifications. And don't close a different issue by mistake! 83% of all workplace violence is due to Issues closing mistakes. And just because I just invented this statistic doesn't mean that you should take it seriously!

Summary

Oof! That chapter was a little bit long, wasn't it? We learned a lot about issues but, most importantly, how to link them to commits. Always remember to put all your actions into issues before acting on them. And don't forget to triage them with labels and assignees.

That concludes our chapter on basic project management. You should know how to plan your next moves in GitHub by now. But project management isn't only planning tasks beforehand; you should also have a clear view of what happened in the past and which milestones were reached. Thus, we will jump into "proper" project management with Projects; this section also includes a very short summary of most form of GitHub workflow. Let's go!

CHAPTER 11

Diving into Project Management: Branches

Last chapter, we discovered Issues and used them to plan our project. We also learned how to link our commits to issues, so that we can follow each change in our project. Our way of work was simple: choose an issue, make a commit that can resolve it, and push to GitHub. The issue was then resolved and closed. But this way of work is not very adapted in most real-world projects; the potential of screw-ups is too high.

What if you need more than one commit to resolve an issue? What if other team members pushed a commit that contained changes to the same files you were working on? How to make sure that the pushed commits really resolve the issue? All of these are part of the reasons why making direct changes to the project is not advised, even if you work alone.

As we said in the last chapter, closing an issue by keywords in the commit message is cool, but you should be very careful with it. Only you have seen your work, and it might not resolve the issue. or it might introduce new bugs in the project. That's why it is better for someone else to review your code before accepting the changes.

It's that part that we are going to talk about in this chapter. First, you will be introduced to the most common GitHub workflow (how most teams work on GitHub), and then we are going to learn about the concept of Branches.

But before we begin this chapter, here's a little thing that you should always remember: "You will make mistakes. A lot of the time. So you must make sure to use as many safeguards as possible." Let's go!

© Mariot Tsitoara 2020
M. Tsitoara, *Beginning Git and GitHub*, https://doi.org/10.1007/978-1-4842-5313-7_11

GitHub workflow

In this section, we will talk about the most common way that developers use GitHub. Keep in mind that each team has its own way of doing things, but each of these ways of working is inspired by the basic workflow that we are going to present.

Remember the little fact about making mistakes? This omnipresent possibility of mistakes is why you need to follow this GitHub workflow, so even if mistakes happen, you isolate its repercussion in a controlled manner. Our way of work from the previous chapter was to commit everything directly to the main project, and this is very dangerous. The main project is most of the time the "production" line, the version that the clients see and use. So, this version must be very clean and should be always exploitable. If any error makes its way to the main version, the clients will experience bugs and it will disrupt every team member.

One way to resolve this issue is to create a copy of the main project and work on this clone. Each change you make to this copy will not affect the main project, so none of your mistakes can impact clients. And when you (and other people) are perfectly sure that the changes to made resolve the issue, you can reproduce those changes in the main version.

Those copies of the main project are called Branches, and the concept of reproducing changes into another branch is called Merging. You can make as many branches as you like, and you can trade commits between them. When you first create a repository, Git creates a new branch for you; it's called "master." Most developers put their main or production version in master and only recreate changes there when they are absolutely sure that it's okay to do so.

Just like tree branches, Git branch can have many ramifications, meaning that you can even create new branches from branches other than master, even it's difficult to maintain such architecture. Most of the time, you will create a branch when working on an issue and delete it after the issue was resolved.

To put all this into perspective, we are going to learn about the default or common GitHub workflow. As you know, everything should begin by an issue. We already covered this last chapter so you are already familiar with this. So, we are going to talk about each of the next steps of the workflow.

When you are going to resolve an issue by making code changes, you should first make a copy of the current working version of the project: create a new branch.

Then, as usual, you make your changes and commit the state of the project. You can make any number of commits as you need; it won't affect the main branch. You can also push your commits to GitHub so your code can be seen.

Then, you link your branch to the master one, so others can compare the changes and review your code. This link is called a Pull Request: you are requesting that your commits be applied to the master branch.

Other team members can then review your code and make comments about it on GitHub. You then push more commits addressing those comments until all problems are solved.

If every party (developers, managers, testers, or clients) agrees that your changes are okay and resolve the issue at hand, the pull request is accepted. This means that every commit you made on your branch will be applied to the master branch. You can then delete the branch you created.

And that's it! You might wonder how is it different from directly pushing in master. It's very different because mistakes and omissions are caught before applying the changes to the production version; this means that the number of production bugs is reduced to a minimum. It also makes it possible for various members of your team to review to changes before they are applied, which is the standard way of work in most tech companies. Bundling the changes into one pull request also solve the problem about multiple people pushing commits solving different issues at the same time. It keeps the history log clean.

You might be tempted to open pull requests only when you feel that you are done with your work. Unless the work you did was very small and straightforward, don't wait long before opening a PR. By working a PR early in your development, you can receive feedback before making too many changes. It is very useful for beginners especially because following the wrong path from the start will take a long time to correct and you would wish that you were told the correct way earlier. Opening a pull request doesn't mean that the work is done; it just means that you are thinking about applying commits from a branch to another.

Note   As previously established, you can create branches from any branch and open pull requests to it. It's not only reserved for the master.

To summarize all these steps, you can find a little illustration in Figure 11-1.

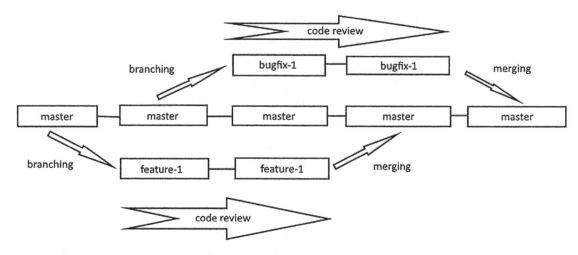

Figure 11-1. *Basic Git workflow*

As you can see, we can create branch from any branch in our project. Git created a branch called master for us at the initialization of the repository. We then can create more branches (e.g. a bugfix branch or a feature branch) to introduce changes in the master branch.

Branches

As we said earlier, branches are the main feature behind code reviews. You have to work on your own branch before publishing your work, so that it won't be bothered by other people's changes. Put simply, a branch is just your own independent copy of the project at a certain time. Let's see how they work and let's create and delete some.

The logic behind branches is simple: take the current state of the project and make a copy of it. In this copy, you can make your changes without impacting other people. You can use branches to have distinct channels of distributions or just to try new things with the project.

When creating a repository, you get a branch by default: master. When working on very small projects, this branch is enough; but most projects need more branches to get the best results. First, they need a production branch, where clients can get the last stable version of the software; this is the master branch. The production branch is only updated when the project is sure to be stable as this is the release branch. Then, there is the development branch, where all the progress is recorded and all the commits tested. You will mostly work on the development branch as it is where most of the fun is. Finally, there is the short-lived patching branches which you will create to hold your commits before merging them to the development branch. Those patching branches live and die with a pull request; you create one when you are solving an issue and delete it afterward.

To summarize a little bit, you will (most of the time) have three sorts of branches:

- Production branch, where you will release stable versions of your project

- Development branch, where you will test your latest version

- Patching branch, where you will work on your issues

Unless there is a VERY urgent major problem that needs solving immediately, you will never commit directly to the production or the development branch. To update those branches, you will use pull requests so that the changes will be reviewed and tested. There are some companies where every developer just commits directly to the development branch, but this is very counterintuitive because if a bug is discovered, they won't know which commit introduced it. Also, it forces the developer to push "one-do-it-all" commits, which is an anti-pattern. Do-it-all commits are commits that try to resolve many issues at the same time, for example, a commit that fixes a bug and introduces a new feature at the same time. This practice is often caused by the laziness of developers as they don't want to create a new branch for another issue. This creates very bad pull requests and makes it difficult to track the progress of the project. It also creates a big challenge for the testers as they don't know which version is the stable one. It's an all-around bad idea; don't do it even with your small projects. It may seem tiring to create and delete branches all the time, but it is the best workflow when working with Git.

The one thing to remember about Git branches is that they just are simple references to commits; that's why creating and deleting them is so fast. Remember when we talked about how Git stores its commits in chained links? Well, a branch is just a reference to one of those commits. A commit contains information about the author, the date, the snapshot, and, most importantly, the name of the previous commit. The name of the previous commit is called parent and every commit except the first one has at least a parent. Thus, each commit is linked to the previous one so that we can recreate the change history of the project.

For now, you only have the default branch called master and it references the last commit of your project. To create a new commit, Git checks where is the reference and uses the info in that commit to build the link between the new commit and the previous referenced one. So, each time you commit, the reference moves to the new commit and the cycle continues. Thus, a branch is just a reference to a commit that is designed to be the parent of the next one.

But how does Git know on which branch are we one? Well, it uses another reference called HEAD that references the current commit. If you are on a branch, HEAD references the last commit of that branch. But if you are checking out a previous version (like we did when we used "git checkout <commit_name>"), the HEAD references that commit, and you are in a state called "detached HEAD."

Caution   Just like human bodies, never be in a state of "detached HEAD" if you can avoid it. It is a very dangerous situation to find oneself in.

For most situation, you can think of HEAD as the reference to the current branch, and every commit you create will use the last commit in that branch as a parent.

When you merge a branch into another, a new commit is created that has two parents: one parent from each branch. So you can recognize the commit type by its number of parents:

- No parents: The very first commit

- One parent: Normal commit in a branch

- Multiple parents: A commit created by the merge of branches

Creating a branch

Now that you know a lot about branches, let's create one! It's very easy; you just need to use the "git branch" command followed by the branch name. Keep in mind that the branch name should only contain alphanumeric values and dashes or underscores; no spaces allowed.

```
$ git branch <name>
```

For example, let's create a development branch for our project. Let's name it "develop." Here's how to do it:

```
$ git branch develop
```

After you execute that command, you will notice that nothing has changed in your project. That's because creating a branch is just about creating a reference to the last commit of the current branch and nothing else. To begin working with a branch, you have to switch to it.

Switching to another branch

We created our development branch and now it's time to switch to it. But here's the problem: I've forgot the name I gave to the branch. Now, someone might suggest that we could turn back and look at the previous section to look at the name. But I have a better idea: list all our current branches. To do so, just execute the git branch command without any parameters.

```
$ git branch
```

This command will give you the list branches you currently have and will put a little star next to the one you're currently on (the HEAD). Check out Figure 11-2 for an example of branches list.

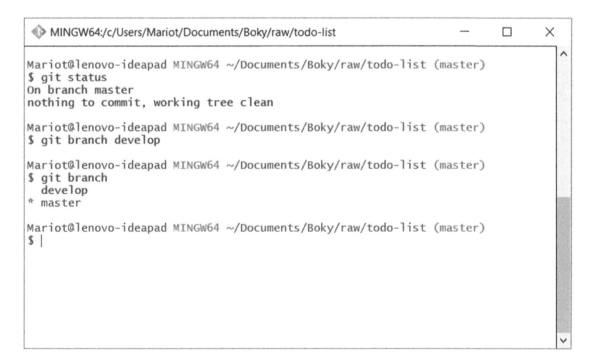

Figure 11-2. List of branches in our project

You will notice that we still are on the master branch because we haven't made anything other than creating a branch. Now let's switch to it.

You already know the command to switch between versions. Well, we will use the same command to navigate between branches. Simply use "git checkout" with the name of the branch as parameter.

```
$ git checkout <name>
```

So, if we want to switch to the develop branch, we will have to execute:

```
$ git checkout develop
```

Note   Like when we navigated between versions, you can't switch branches if you have uncommitted changed files. Commit before you move. Or use a technique called "stashing" that we will see in later chapters.

After checking out the new branch, you will get a confirmation message from Git and you can also check the result of git status to make sure. Figure 11-3 shows the result of those commands.

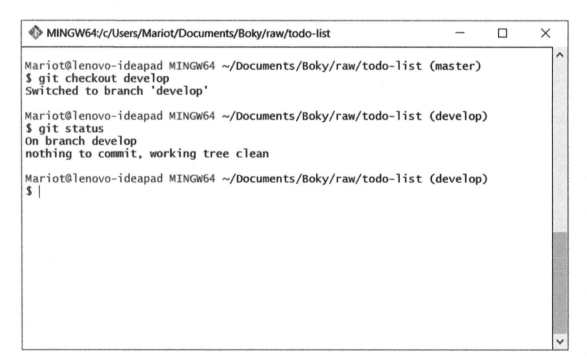

Figure 11-3. *Switching branches*

EXERCISE: CREATE A TESTING BRANCH

A simple exercise before we move out to the next battle. It's very straightforward as all the answers are in this section. The exercise is to create a branch named "testing" where we will test our project before merging all the commits to the master branch. You have to

- Go back to the master branch

- Create a new branch named "testing"

- Switch to the new branch

Tip   To immediately switch to a new branch after creating it, use the option "-b" with the git checkout command. For example, "git checkout -b testing" is the same as "git branch testing" and then "git checkout testing."

Deleting a branch

You had fun creating the testing branch? Good. It's time to delete it because we already have a testing branch: develop. That's where we will merge our patching branches and all the testing will be done there.

You can delete a pushed branch, meaning a branch that is present on the remote repository, by checking "delete branch after PR merged" when creating a Pull Request. This will delete the remote branch but your local branches will be unchanged. You will have to delete your local branches manually.

To delete a branch, simply use the same command as to create one but with the option "-d."

```
$ git branch -d <name>
```

So, to delete our testing branch, we will use

```
$ git branch -d testing
```

Just like a real tree branch, you don't cut the Git branch you are currently standing on. Check out another branch before deleting the branch; and for this reason, you can't have less than one branch in a project. If you try anyway, you will get an error like the one shown in Figure 11-4.

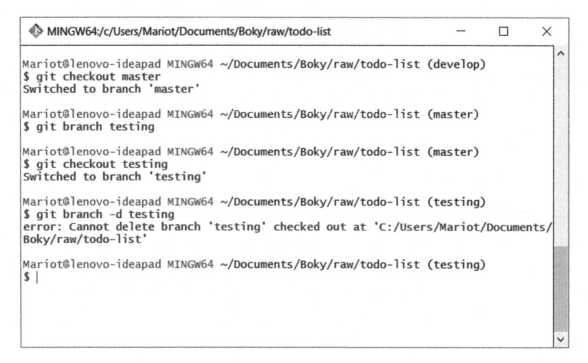

Figure 11-4. *Deleting current branch*

Thus, you have to check out the master or develop branch before deleting the testing branch. If you did it correctly, you should get a result like mine as shown in Figure 11-5.

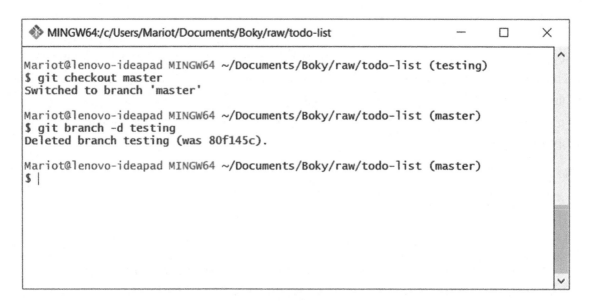

Figure 11-5. *Deleting of a branch (we hardly knew ye)*

Take note of the confirmation message, it gives you the SHA-1 name of the branch you just deleted. Since the branch we created and deleted contained no commits, it just referenced the last commit of the current branch. Let's check the history log to confirm this. Execute the git log command to get the list of the latest commits, just like in Figure 11-6.

Figure 11-6. *Commit name check*

You will see that the last commit name and the branch name is the same; this is because we haven't made any commit in our branch. You will also see on the history log where the branches are originating from. In this example, the develop branch originates from the 80f145c commit; it's the branch's parent.

Merging branches

We talked a lot about merging branches in this chapter but we haven't made a single merge. Let's change that.

Let's imagine that you want to improve the README file of the project by adding a few information. This task is already listed in our GitHub issues so no problem about that. The next step is to create a new branch from the development branch so we can merge them later. You have to create a new branch from the develop branch instead of the master because we won't touch the master branch until everything is properly tested. If everything is clear and clean, we will merge the development branch into the master branch.

It's clear then, let's create the new branch where we will work on. Let's name it "improve-readme-description." Don't forget to checkout out the develop branch before creating a new branch from it. We will thus have to execute

```
$ git checkout develop
$ git branch improve-readme-description
```

Now that the branch has been created, switch to it so we can begin to work. To switch to the new branch, just use the checkout command.

```
$ git checkout improve-readme-description
```

Perfect! Now we have a branch named "improve-readme-description" that originates from the develop branch. We like branches so much that we created a branch from a branch!

Now let's get to work. Open the README.md file and change its content to

```
# TODO list
A simple app to manage your daily tasks.
It uses HTML5 and CSS3.

## Features
* List of daily tasks
```

Now, stage the file and get ready to commit. I'll let you choose the commit message, but don't forget to put a reference to the issue you are trying to resolve! The next steps are thus

```
$ git add README.md
$ git commit
```

Nothing new here as every command is the same of any branch. The only slight change is that the branch name is different on the commit description. You can see it on my result shown in Figure 11-7.

Figure 11-7. *Committing on another branch*

After you made the commit, check the Git history to put all of we did in perspective. Execute the git log command to see our project history.

```
$ git log
```

Tip   Use the option "--oneline" when using git log to get a prettier result.

Your project history log should look like mine as shown in Figure 11-8 after you committed.

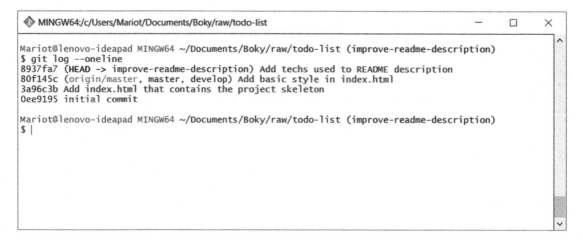

Figure 11-8. *History log after committing on a branch*

As you can see in the figure, HEAD now points to the last commit of our new branch; it means that every commit we will create will have that as a parent. You will also notice that the master and develop branch didn't change; that's because we only worked on our newly created branch.

Now that we are satisfied with our fix, let's merge the branch to the develop branch so we can test it. To merge our branch into develop, we first have to check it out. So, navigate there by using the git checkout command.

```
$ git checkout develop
```

Now let's try to merge the branch into the develop one. Merging just means reproducing all the commits on one branch on another. To do so, we will use the git merge command followed by the name of the branch be merged.

```
$ git merge <name>
```

Since we are looking to merge "improve-readme-description" into "develop," our command to execute on the develop branch is

```
$ git merge improve-readme-description
```

This command will recreate your commits from "improve-readme-description" into "develop." So, you will get a similar result as a commit confirmation. Check Figure 11-9 for an example.

```
MINGW64:/c/Users/Mariot/Documents/Boky/raw/todo-list                          —    □    ×

Mariot@lenovo-ideapad MINGW64 ~/Documents/Boky/raw/todo-list (improve-readme-description)
$ git checkout develop
Switched to branch 'develop'

Mariot@lenovo-ideapad MINGW64 ~/Documents/Boky/raw/todo-list (develop)
$ git merge improve-readme-description
Updating 80f145c..8937fa7
Fast-forward
 README.md | 4 ++--
 1 file changed, 2 insertions(+), 2 deletions(-)

Mariot@lenovo-ideapad MINGW64 ~/Documents/Boky/raw/todo-list (develop)
$ |
```

Figure 11-9. *Merge result*

Let's recheck the git log to have a clearer idea of what happened. You will get a similar result to mine after executing "git log --oneline" that is shown in Figure 11-10.

As you can see, HEAD now points to develop because it's the checked-out branch. You can also notice that develop and improve-readme-description now point to the same commit; that's because of the merge.

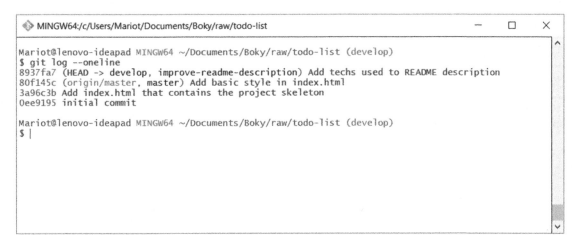

```
MINGW64:/c/Users/Mariot/Documents/Boky/raw/todo-list                          —    □    ×

Mariot@lenovo-ideapad MINGW64 ~/Documents/Boky/raw/todo-list (develop)
$ git log --oneline
8937fa7 (HEAD -> develop, improve-readme-description) Add techs used to README description
80f145c (origin/master, master) Add basic style in index.html
3a96c3b Add index.html that contains the project skeleton
0ee9195 initial commit

Mariot@lenovo-ideapad MINGW64 ~/Documents/Boky/raw/todo-list (develop)
$ |
```

Figure 11-10. *History log after merge*

Congratulations on your first merge! It won't be so easy next time (hint: merge conflicts, they appear when the same line of code has been modified in different commits)

Pushing a branch to remote

Branches are not only made for working locally, you can also publish them to the world by pushing them to the remote repository. For example, let's push our development branch to GitHub so everyone can see our progress.

The command to pushing a branch to remote is (you guessed it!) git push, just like what we learned in a previous chapter. The command is

```
$ git push <remote_name> <branch_name>
```

The remote name hasn't changed; it's still "origin." It's the branch name that is different this time. Instead of master, we are going to push the develop branch. So, the command will be

```
$ git push origin develop
```

Since you've already pushed to remote before, the result shown in Figure 11-11 is familiar to you.

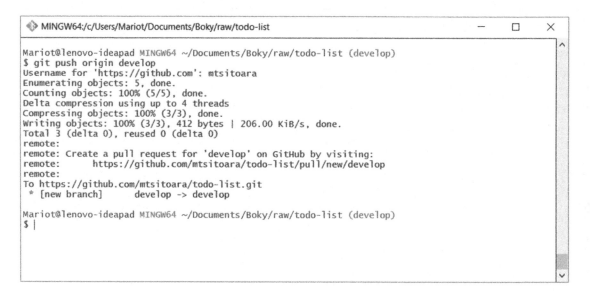

Figure 11-11. *Pushing to a remote branch*

As you can see, there is a little difference in the result: it gave us a link to create a pull request, that is, ask for permission to reproduce the commits on develop to master. Take note of the link because we are going to learn about Pull Requests in the next chapter. ☺

If you return to GitHub to check your project page, you will also have the call-to-action button about creating pull requests. Ignore them for now and instead navigate between your master branch and the develop one. You can check Figure 11-12 for an example of a project page after a new branch has been pushed.

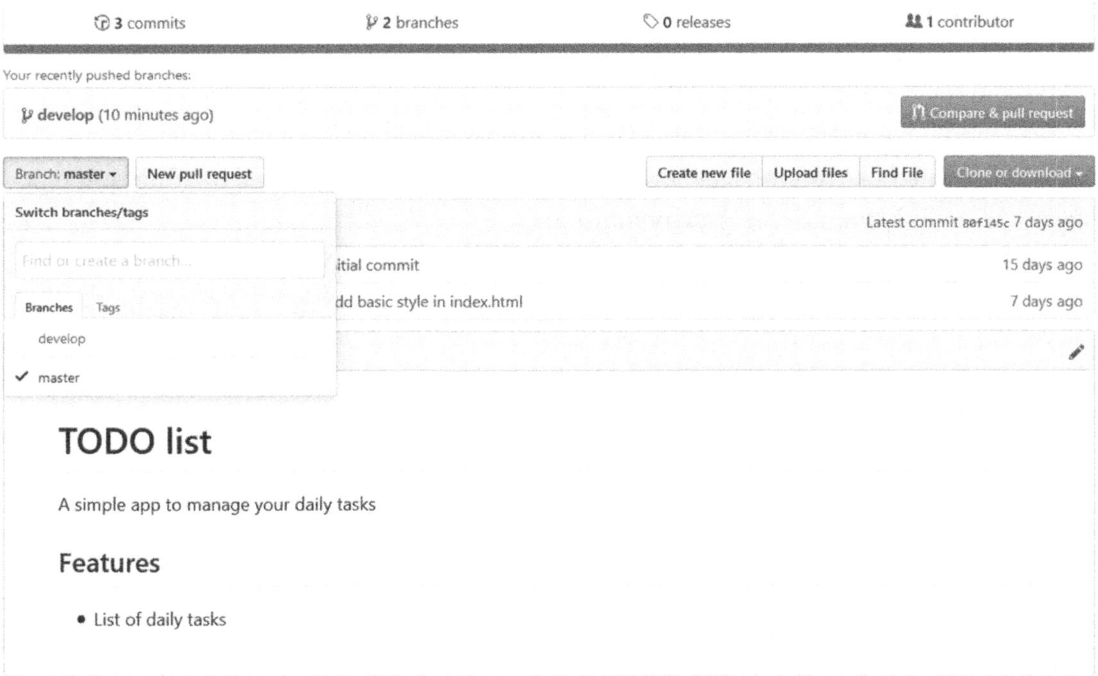

Figure 11-12. *Our new project page*

It is all about branches for now. You now know how to create, merge, and delete them. And most importantly, you have a basic knowledge of the GitHub workflow: create a branch, work on that branch, and create a pull request.

Now, you may ask yourself: "But didn't you promise us code reviews and pull requests? Did we even use the workflow?" You are absolutely right. We didn't use the workflow because we used the direct approach: directly messing with the branches. In a real-world project, you won't commit and push directly to the master or the development branch like we did earlier. Instead, you will use Pull Request to merge branches together. That way, your work can be reviewed by your coworkers before you can merge them to the development or master branch.

Summary

This chapter dealt with what makes Git a powerful tool for project management: branches. Branches are necessary in a fast-paced development as you will probably work on many issues at the same time. Keeping all those changes in the same place is a recipe for disaster. For example, you need to start in a clean environment to fix a bug or introduce a feature; trying to do both at the same time will seriously increase the risk of introducing more bugs.

The main takeaway of this chapter is the importance of using a workflow when developing with Git. And those workflows all use branches to separate the different types of work necessary for a clean issue resolution.

We've seen how to create, check out, and delete a branch. Now, let's learn more about Pull Requests and Code Review, so we can propose changes in our master branch!

## CHAPTER 12

Better Project Management: Pull Requests

In the last chapter, we learn about the typical GitHub workflow; the majority of companies use a variation of this workflow for their day-to-day work. We also learned a lot about branches and how to use them. But there is one thing we didn't get a chance to review: how to combine those two concepts. The answer is simple: Pull Requests and Code Reviews.

The previous chapter provided a lot of reasons why using a traditional approach to code management (everybody commits to the same branch) is a bad idea. But since we work alone in our current project, we don't see the inconveniences yet. But they are here, and they take a lot of time to resolve; so, trust me, it's better to follow the workflow.

This chapter will show you how to implement the workflow that was presented to us in the earlier chapter. We will use our newly created branches to introduce changes to older branches. We will also learn about code review and how to manage them.

Why use Pull Requests?

Many developers who don't follow a particular workflow say that it's a waste of time because it takes away precious development time. There is a truth in that statement because following the workflow means waiting for other people to review your code. But you have to keep in mind that you don't have to wait around doing nothing while waiting for a review, you can directly go on and solve another issue! That's why branches are so powerful in Version Control Systems; you can work on multiple issues at the same time. With the workflow, you can begin to work on an issue, ask for some ideas or directive from your peers, and then work on another issue when waiting for responses. After you receive the necessary feedbacks, you can continue to work on the first issue and repeat this

© Mariot Tsitoara 2020
M. Tsitoara, *Beginning Git and GitHub*, https://doi.org/10.1007/978-1-4842-5313-7_12

process until all the issues are resolved. Using the workflow will also let you begin working on an issue even if the information about what to do is not complete yet; you can work on an issue and stop for more info midway into it. And one last thing: having someone else reread your code is the best way to reduce bugs; the time you gain by not chasing bugs everywhere is greater than the time you gain by directly committing to master.

The GitHub workflow is also the preferred way of work of Open Source contributors. It would be very ugly if anyone could push commits directly to a branch without any review. Instead, each contributor has a working clone of the project and can propose changes that other contributors will review and discuss.

So, in conclusion, working using the GitHub workflow is the best way of working and using it will greatly reduce your bugs. And as we've seen in the last chapter, using branches is only the first step, so you have to use Pull Requests to complete the workflow. Let's learn more about them!

Overview on Pull Requests

Pull Requests, as useful as they are, are a fairly easy-to-understand concept. Submitting a Pull Request, or PR, is just asking for permission to apply all the commits in a branch to another branch. But we're moving too fast. Before learning about Pull Requests, we have to learn what a "pull" is.

Pull

In Git terminology, a pull is just the opposite of push (give yourself a high five if you guessed that!). Push takes your branch and copies all its commits to a remote branch and creates the branch if it doesn't exist on the server yet. Pull is just that, but backward: it looks at a remote branch and copies the commits on it to your local repository. It's just an exchange of commits: push if it's from local to remote and pull if it's from remote to local.

The syntax is very similar too:

```
$ git pull <remote_name> <branch_name>
```

So, for example, if you wanted to get the commits from the master branch on GitHub, you would have to execute the command while checking out the master branch:

```
$ git pull origin master
```

Make sure to always be on the branch corresponding on the one you are pulling before running any command. So, in this case, you have to check out master before running git pull. After executing the command, you will get a result like mine as shown in Figure 12-1.

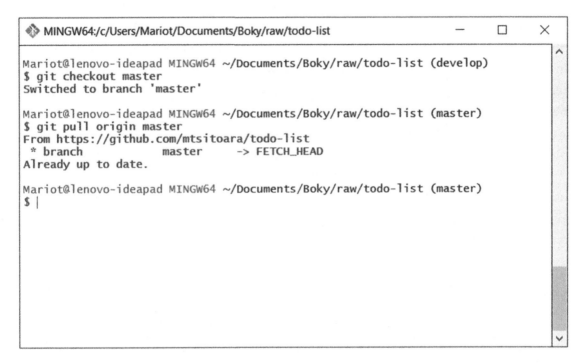

Figure 12-1. *Pulling master from origin*

Since you have the same commits on your local repository and on GitHub, nothing happened. But once you start working with other people, you will have to pull their branches on your local machine to review their changes or simply review the changes on GitHub.

It's basically it! Pulling is just copying commits from a remote branch to a local one. And don't worry, you will have more occasions to play with git pull soon.

What does a PR do

Now that we know more about pulling, we have a clearer idea of what a Pull Request is. A PR is just asking for permission to execute a pull action on a remote repository. But pulling a branch is not enough for the action to be complete: you also have to merge the branches together.

Remember when we merged a patch branch into the development branch? A PR is just asking for permission to do that. You can do everything you want with your local branches, but when you deal with upstream branches (branches in the remote repository), you have to use a little bit of civility and ask for permission first. This assures that every fix committed in the main branches is properly tested and reviewed.

So, to put it together, a Pull Request is a request you make to get GitHub to perform those actions: pull your patching branch and merge it with another branch. For example, in our project, we have currently three local branches (master, develop, and improve-readme-description) and two remote branches (master and develop). If we made any new commits to improve-readme-description and we wanted to merge it with develop, we would open a PR. After the PR is accepted, GitHub will perform the following actions: pull the improve-readme-description branch and then merge it with the develop branch.

You might ask yourself: "If the endgame of a Pull Request is to merge branch, why not call it Merge Request?" Well, many people (including other Git hosting services like GitLab) call it Merge Request. It means the same thing. In this book, we will use the two terms interchangeably.

Create a Pull Request

Let's get down to business! Creating a new PR is very easy; you just need two branches: one to work on and another to merge into. Let's do it!

First, let's create an issue to work on. So go to GitHub and create an issue called "Improve the app style." Yes, we've had a similar issue previously, but since we've already solved that issue, we are going to open a new one. It's not a good idea to recycle issues because it will make it harder to follow your progress.

After you've created the issue, it's time to go back to your Terminal because each PR begins with a branch. We are going to create a branch named "improve-app-style" from the latest development branch, which is develop. As we saw in the last chapter, the way to create a new branch from another is to check out the source branch and execute the branch creation command. So, we have to execute those commands one after another:

```
$ git checkout develop
$ git branch improve-app-style
$ git checkout improve-app-style
```

After executing those three commands, you will find yourself with the new branch checked out, just like in Figure 12-2.

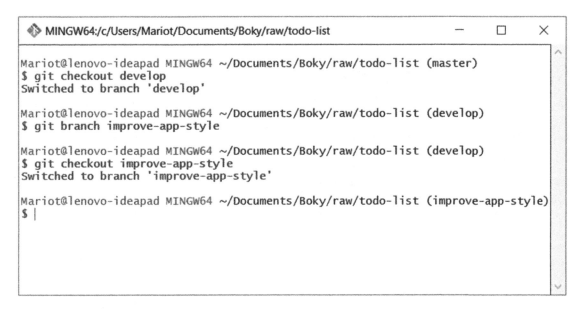

Figure 12-2. *Creation of a new branch*

Within our newly created branch, let's work on the issue. Open index.html and replace its contents to

```
<!doctype html>
<html>
    <head>
        <meta charset="utf-8">
        <title>TODO list</title>
        <style>
            h1 {
                text-align:center;
            }
            h3 {
                text-transform: uppercase;
            }
```

```
        ul {
            margin: 0;
            padding: 0;
        }
        ul li {
            cursor: pointer;
            position: relative;
            padding: 12px 8px 12px 40px;
            background: #eee;
            font-size: 18px;
            transition: 0.2s;
        }
        ul li:nth-child(odd) {
            background: #f9f9f9;
        }
        ul li:hover {
            background: #ddd;
        }
    </style>
</head>
<body>
    <h1>TODO list</h1>

    <h3>Todo</h3>
    <ul>
        <li>Buy a hat for the bat</li>
        <li>Clear the fogs for the frogs</li>
        <li>Bring a box to the fox</li>
    </ul>

    <h3>Done</h3>
    <ul>
        <li>Put the mittens on the kittens</li>
    </ul>
</body>
</html>
```

Then, stage the file and prepare to commit. Put something very simple as a commit message, no need to reference the issue; we'll do this later. As a commit message, you can simply put: "Add basic color changes on item rows." As usual, you will get a confirmation message as shown in Figure 12-3 after the commit.

Figure 12-3. *Commit confirmation*

Now it's time to push it to GitHub. As we've previously seen, we will have to use the git push command, followed by the remote name and the branch name. So the command will be

```
$ git push origin improve-app-style
```

After you've pushed your branch to GitHub, you will get another familiar confirmation message. You can check Figure 12-4 for an example of this.

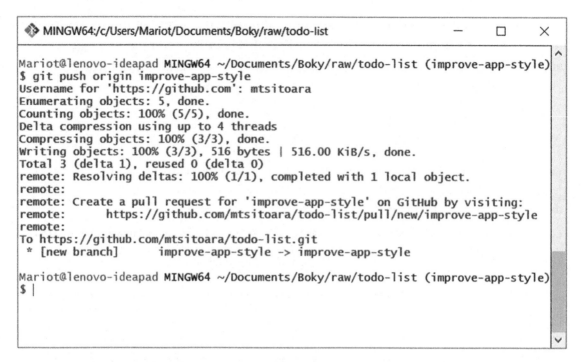

Figure 12-4. *Pushing the branch to GitHub*

As you can see on the confirmation message, Git directly shows you a link to follow so you can create a Pull Request. But let's create a PR with another way: directly on GitHub.

Go to your project page and look for something different in the presentation. After a recent push to a new branch, your project page should like the one shown in Figure 12-5.

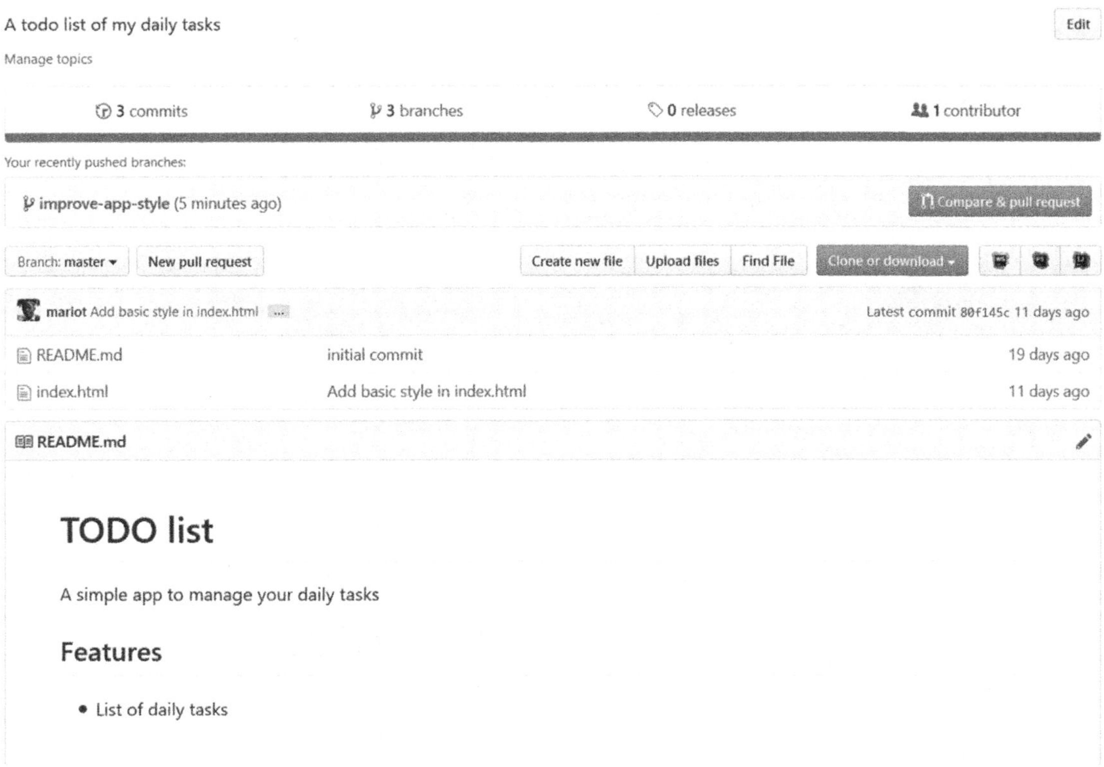

A todo list of my daily tasks   Edit

Manage topics

| ⓣ 3 commits | ⅄ 3 branches | ◇ 0 releases | ⩗ 1 contributor |

Your recently pushed branches:

⅄ **improve-app-style** (5 minutes ago)   🗂 Compare & pull request

| Branch: master ▾ | New pull request | Create new file   Upload files   Find File   Clone or download ▾   🗎 🗎 🗎

🐯 **mariot** Add basic style in index.html ⋯   Latest commit 80f145c 11 days ago

| 📄 README.md | initial commit | 19 days ago |
| 📄 index.html | Add basic style in index.html | 11 days ago |

📖 README.md   ✏

TODO list

A simple app to manage your daily tasks

Features

• List of daily tasks

***Figure 12-5.** Project page after a recent push*

As you can see, there is a new call to action on the page, right above the list of branches. It shows the name of the branch that you just created and a big button for creating a PR. Click the button to continue; you should get to the Pull Request creation form, just like in Figure 12-6.

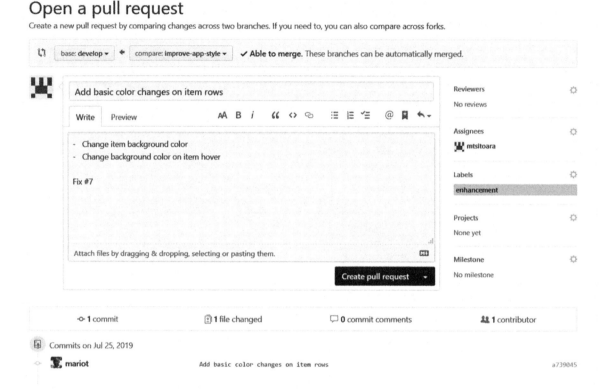

Figure 12-6. Pull request creation form

You can note that the PR creation form is very similar to the issue creation form. On the right, you can find the same information about assignees and labels; they work exactly the same. On the bottom of the page, you can see the commits to be applied by the Pull Request; and if you scroll down, you'll find the differences between the versions. Check Figure 12-7 for an example of this.

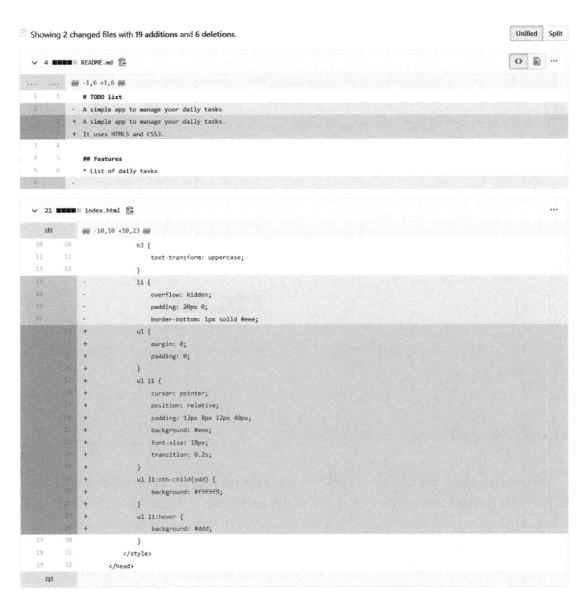

Figure 12-7. *Differences between versions*

But you might ask yourself why there are two commits to be applied. It's because of the target branch. If you examine Figure 12-6 closely, you'll find that the base branch for the PR is master. This is not what we want, as we are targeting the develop branch. Go ahead and change the base branch to develop. After you change it, the page will reload, and you'll get a different result, shown in Figure 12-8.

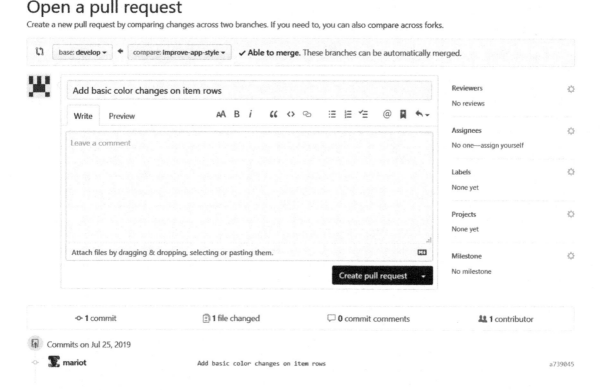

Figure 12-8.   *Pull Request on develop*

As you change it, notice that the PR name has also changed; that's because the PR name takes the last commit message as a default name. But you can change it if you want, especially if you have multiple commits in one PR. Remember one thing about PR name: it should be as clear and straight to the point as commit messages. Your PR name should respond to this question: "What will this PR do if I merge it?" So take a good care of your PR name and description so that the reviewers can know which problem you are trying to solve without reading your code.

You can expand your PR explanation on the description textbox, and don't hesitate to provide more information about the changes. You should put the keywords to closing issues there. Check Figure 12-9 for an example of this.

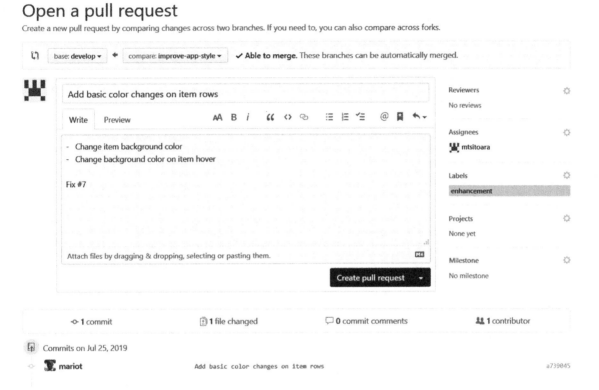

Figure 12-9. *A completed Pull Request*

Once you are ready, click "Create pull request" to get it done; you will arrive at a page similar to the one shown in Figure 12-10.

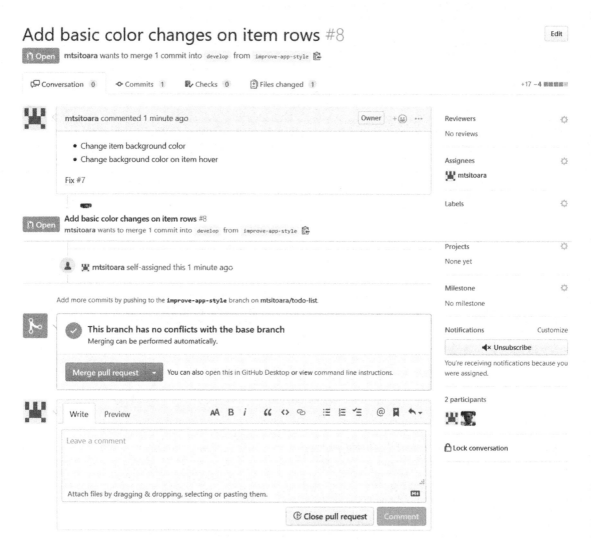

Figure 12-10.   *Your new Pull Request*

Again, this view is very similar to its Issues counterpart, even the PR number follow the Issues number. The only difference is the button to merge the pull request. If you click this button, the PR will be accepted, and the branches will be merged. But don't do that yet! Let's play around with our PR before merging it.

Now that our PR is submitted, it's time to review it! Put down your developer hat for a second and put on your tech lead hat, it's time to do a Code Review!

Code Reviews

Code Reviews are one of the best features of GitHub. Long gone where the days where you had to schedule a one-on-one meeting with your Tech Lead so they could check your code. No need to send each other long chains of emails (with a long list of annoyed people on the Cc list) for each change request in the code. Now, everything is done in GitHub. Let's see!

Give a Code Review

In Figure 12-9, you had a glimpse of the Code Review process. You saw all the changes done to the files compared to the current version but you couldn't interact with them yet. In this section, you will learn how to review your co-contributors' code.

You can see in Figure 12-10 that the PR page has many sections, just like the Issues page. You have to click "Files changed" to begin the Code Review. You will then arrive at a page similar to the one shown in Figure 12-11.

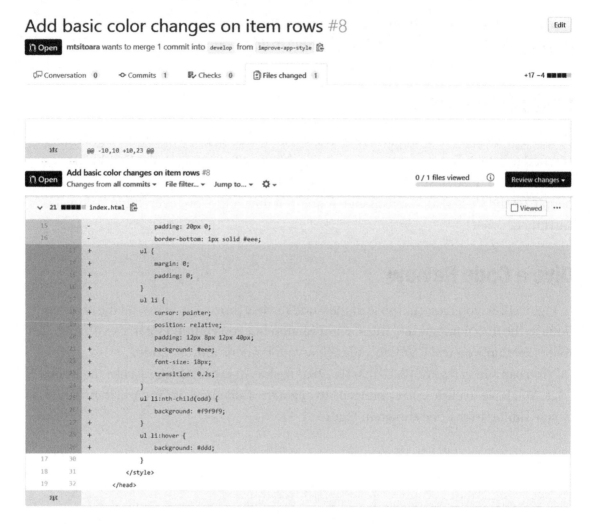

Figure 12-11. *The Code Review section*

This view should remind you of the git diff results, because it's essentially the same thing. It shows you the differences between the versions in detail, which means that you will see what has been added, removed, or replaced.

Leave a review comment

Now, let's pretend to review this code. During code reviews, you can comment on the whole changes or a specific piece of code. For example, let's put a comment on the "ul li" CSS definition on line 17. As you move around your cursor on the code review change, a little "plus" icon follows it. It means that you can comment there. Let's do that. Place your cursor on line 17, and when the "plus" icon shows, click it. It will open a small comment section like in Figure 12-12.

Figure 12-12. *A code review on a line*

As always, you can make all kinds of comments on this section with the help of Markdown syntax. For this example, we are going to put this comment: "Make the list items unselectable for a cleaner UX. Use `user-select: none`." You should check the preview before you leave the comment, just like in Figure 12-13.

Figure 12-13. *Comment preview*

If you are satisfied with your comment, click "Start a review" to go to the next step. The comment will show on the Review page, and there will also be a reply button on the comment, just like the result shown in Figure 12-14.

Figure 12-14. *The posted comment*

Using this button, the developer can discuss the comment with the reviewer before beginning to rework on the PR. You can make more comments if you want, because comments are essentially what constitute a Code Review. If you are satisfied, click the "Finish your review" button on the top of the page. You will again be greeted with a small section, just like the one shown in Figure 12-15.

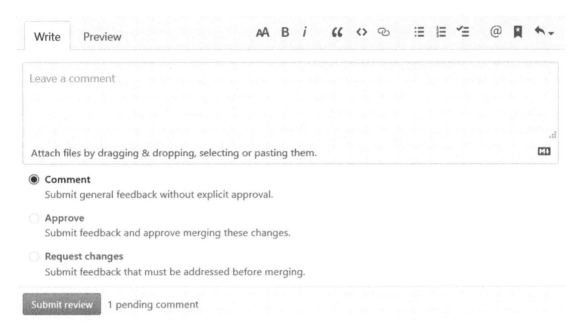

Figure 12-15. *Finishing the review*

Upon finishing the review, you will get three choices: Comment, Approve, or Request changes. Since it's our own Pull Request, we cannot approve or request change on it, so we'll just choose the default option, which is a general feedback on the changes. Let's put: "Don't forget to take account different browsers" as a comment and submit the review. You will once again go back to the PR details page as shown in Figure 12-16.

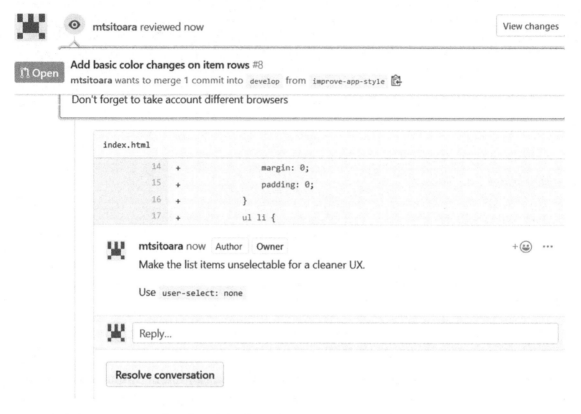

Figure 12-16. *Your completed Code Review*

The PR details page will show you the different comments left by the reviewer and also the general comments for the whole PR. Let's resolve these comments.

Update a Pull Request

The comment left by the reviewer suggested that we should change some code before our PR is accepted. So, let's do that! Let's update our PR by pushing new commits to the patching branch.

Note   The patching branch is also called topic branch, because each branch should have its own topic to resolve.

Open index.html once again and change its contents to this:

```
<!doctype html>
<html>
    <head>
        <meta charset="utf-8">
        <title>TODO list</title>
        <style>
            h1 {
                text-align:center;
            }
            h3 {
                text-transform: uppercase;
            }
            ul {
                margin: 0;
                padding: 0;
            }
            ul li {
                cursor: pointer;
                position: relative;
                padding: 12px 8px 12px 40px;
                background: #eee;
                font-size: 18px;
                transition: 0.2s;
                -webkit-user-select: none;
                -moz-user-select: none;
                -ms-user-select: none;
                user-select: none;
            }
            ul li:nth-child(odd) {
                background: #f9f9f9;
            }
            ul li:hover {
                background: #ddd;
            }
```

```
            </style>
        </head>
        <body>
            <h1>TODO list</h1>

            <h3>Todo</h3>
            <ul>
                <li>Buy a hat for the bat</li>
                <li>Clear the fogs for the frogs</li>
                <li>Bring a box to the fox</li>
            </ul>

            <h3>Done</h3>
            <ul>
                <li>Put the mittens on the kittens</li>
            </ul>
        </body>
</html>
```

Stage the file once again and commit the project with the message: "Make the list items unselectable." Then, push the branch to GitHub again. Check the previous section if you are lost in this exercise. Hint: git push origin improve-app-style.

After you pushed the branch, go back to the PR page again. You will notice a new comment on the details page. Check Figure 12-17 for an example of this.

Figure 12-17. *New changes detected by GitHub*

After each commit you push, GitHub will update the PR to reflect the changes applied to the branch; click "View changes" to review the new changes. You will once again arrive on the Code Review page but with a little twist: you will only notice the new changes, meaning the changes that you haven't seen yet. This makes it easier for the reviewer to follow the progression of the PR.

Since we don't have any additional comments, go ahead and click "Finish review" and then give a general comment. In a work environment, you won't review your own code so the Approve choice would be available. But since we're working alone, just give a general comment like "Good job!" since the developer worked really hard. The general comment will appear on the PR details page just like in Figure 12-18.

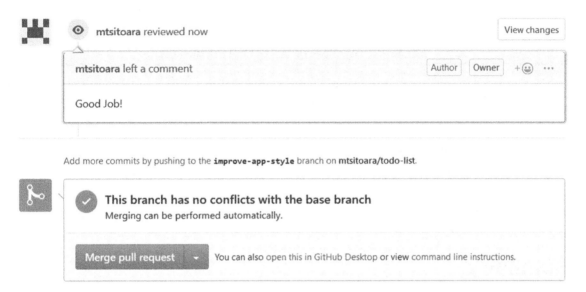

Figure 12-18. *A final comment has been made*

Now, we can safely merge our branch to the base branch because our code is properly reviewed. Click the big green button to accept and merge the PR. You will be asked for a confirmation before the branch is merged. After you confirm it, the branches will be merged and the PR closed. You can even delete the source branch if you want, just as Figure 12-19 shows.

Figure 12-19. *Pull Request accepted*

Whether or not you want to delete the branch is up to you. Sometimes, teams don't delete the branches until a tester has confirmed that all is well.

"But why isn't my issue automatically closed?" you ask. That's because the fix in the develop branch, which is not the default branch. Only fixes merged in the default branch (master) will close issues automatically. But since you are worried about that issue, let's do a little exercise before we go to the next chapter.

EXERCISE: MERGE DEVELOP INTO MASTER

Let's pretend a tester tested our new feature and said that it was okay to release. So, we have to merge develop into master. The exercise is

- Go back to the project page

- Open a PR to merge develop

- Accept the PR and merge

Summary

Congratulations on getting your first PRs accepted! (but it would be more impressive if you didn't accept them yourself). This chapter has been quite long, but you need to understand it completely to benefit from the awesome features of GitHub. For your next issues, open a PR instead of committing directly to master. And remember that in most professional settings, committing on master is not only discouraged but denied by default by GitHub. Each change must come from a Pull Request.

You should be comfortable using PR by now; if not, reread the first sections of this chapter. The one thing to remember is a pull request is just a fancy way of asking for permission to apply commits on a branch.

You may have some questions now: "What if somebody else pushed some changes in the base branch before I complete my PR?", "What if someone else modified the same file as me?", or "What if I'm tasked to resolve another issue while I'm working on a PR?" Those questions are very pertinent indeed; that's why we'll cover them in the next chapter. We will deal with Merge Conflicts and how to solve them. But before learning how to solve them, we will learn how to avoid them altogether! Let's go!

PART III

Teamwork with Git

CHAPTER 13

Conflicts

The last chapter introduced us to the wonderful world of Merge Requests. You should know what their use is and why it is a good idea to use them. Even if they are a fairly simple concept to grasp, they also come with some shortcomings that are hard to ignore.

You are mostly done with your journey; you've come a long way. But there are still things that you need to learn before continuing your path all by yourself. You need to learn what problems you're going to have along the way. We are going to talk about those problems in this chapter. First, we will re-review how branch merging works, and then we will present the problems you'll most likely run into in your career. Finally, we'll see the common solutions for those problems. Don't be afraid of Conflicts because they're easy to resolve; they're just annoying.

How a merge works

Let's rewind a little and go back to the basics: what does a merge do? A merge takes each commit in a branch and applies them on another. Simple, right? Well, a well-planned merge goes smoothly most of the time. But even if you plan every last detail, there is something you can't control: what other people do.

Don't forget that Git is a distributed Version Control System, meaning that every contributor has their own copy of the project and can do anything to their local repository. Everyone can change every file as there is no "file lock" like on some VCSs. This means that there are instances where multiple people have made changes to the same file. Bringing all those changes together necessitate a merge.

Before going to the next section, you have to remember one thing: only merge a branch when you are sure that the commits in that branch are final. Merging a branch that contains unfinished work defeats the purpose of branching—having a clear history. Opening a Pull Request even if you aren't planning to actually merge the branches is okay; but actually merging them uncompleted is not.

© Mariot Tsitoara 2020
M. Tsitoara, *Beginning Git and GitHub*, https://doi.org/10.1007/978-1-4842-5313-7_13

As we said earlier, a merge begins with a branch. Most of the time, it's a branch that you don't have on your local repository yet. So, you have to pull it from origin (the default name for a remote repository).

Pulling

Let's revise the pulling command the second time. Pulling means copying a remote branch to the local repository. For example, we have merged a branch into develop and master but have not done anything to our local branches. It means that we are "behind" in the history timeline as there are commits in the remote repository that we don't have.

In fact, the word "behind" is a little misnomer because, as we established, every repository is independent and there are no central repositories in Git. We chose to have a master remote repository because it makes it easier to work in teams. But, concretely, you can exchange commits as you like; the concept of being "behind" was invented just to make developers' lives easier.

Let's try to pull master into our local repository. Remember that you need to have finished the exercise from the last chapter (merging develop into master) before doing the next steps on this chapter. First, check out your local master branch and make sure it's clean.

```
$ git checkout master
$ git status
```

If you didn't do anything funny on your working directory, you should get the same result as shown in Figure 13-1: a clean directory.

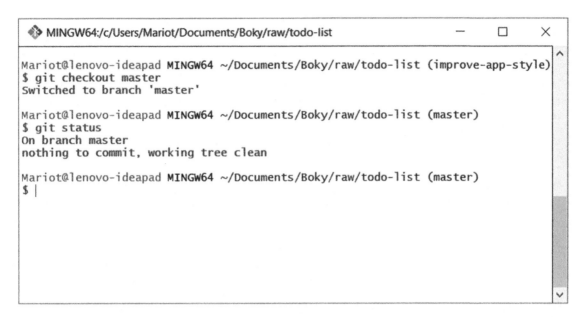

Figure 13-1. *A clean directory is needed before a pull*

Now, let's check the history log before we make any change.

```
$ git log --online
```

This will result in the output of the master branch history. It will not have the recent changes we made because those changes are only in the remote repository right now. The master history log should look like the one shown in Figure 13-2.

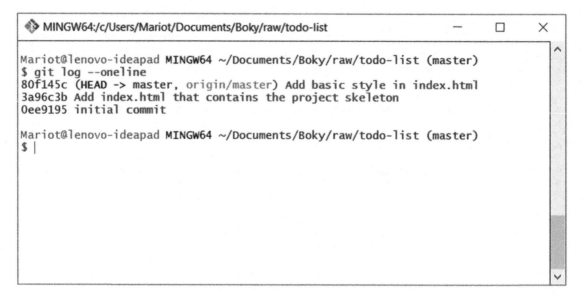

Figure 13-2. *The history log before the pull*

As you can see in Figure 13-2, the HEAD is pointed at the last commit of the branch right now (and most of the time, it will be that way). According to this result, our local master branch and the remote master branch are on the same level, meaning that they contain the same commits. We know that this isn't true because we've made changes on the remote master. Our local Git repository doesn't know that because we haven't fetched any commits from the server yet. Let's do that.

As we've seen last chapter, pull and push command work the same way: you just have to pass the remote repository name and remote branch name as parameters. So the command will be

```
$ git pull origin master
```

After executing this code on a clean working directory, you will get the result shown in Figure 13-3.

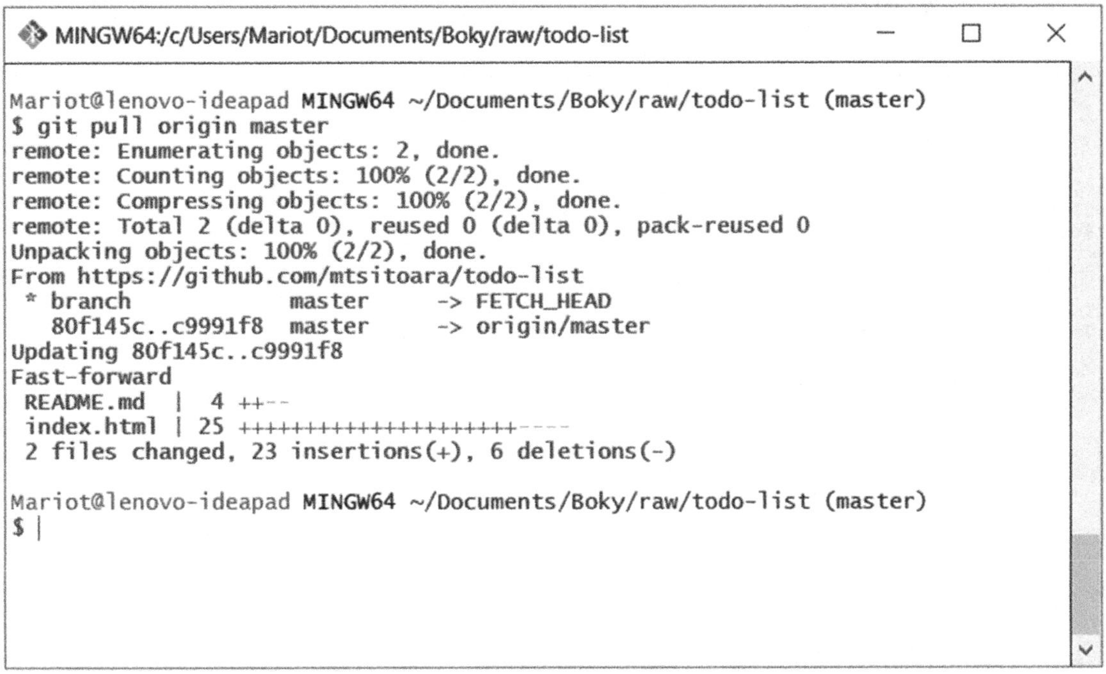

```
MINGW64:/c/Users/Mariot/Documents/Boky/raw/todo-list          —    □    ×

Mariot@lenovo-ideapad MINGW64 ~/Documents/Boky/raw/todo-list (master)
$ git pull origin master
remote: Enumerating objects: 2, done.
remote: Counting objects: 100% (2/2), done.
remote: Compressing objects: 100% (2/2), done.
remote: Total 2 (delta 0), reused 0 (delta 0), pack-reused 0
Unpacking objects: 100% (2/2), done.
From https://github.com/mtsitoara/todo-list
 * branch             master     -> FETCH_HEAD
   80f145c..c9991f8   master     -> origin/master
Updating 80f145c..c9991f8
Fast-forward
 README.md  |  4 ++--
 index.html | 25 +++++++++++++++++++++----
 2 files changed, 23 insertions(+), 6 deletions(-)

Mariot@lenovo-ideapad MINGW64 ~/Documents/Boky/raw/todo-list (master)
$ |
```

Figure 13-3. *Pulling master from origin*

Fast-forward merge

After you've pulled master from origin, you will get a summary of the operation. You will see the number of files changed and the type of merging that has been done. Here, the type is "fast-forward," and it's the easiest type of merge. Fast-forward means that the commits on the remote branch were on the same timeline as the local branch, so Git only had to move HEAD to the last commit of the origin branch. Remember when we talked about commits being linked to another by parent-child relationships? If Git sees a link between the commits on the first branch and the branch to be merged, a fast-forward merge is done, meaning that only a move of pointer is necessary, which makes Git very fast. You should always strive to use fast-forward as a method of merging as it's the easier and, most importantly, cleanest for the history log.

Talking about the history log, let's check it out to see the changes we've fetched from the server. Once again, use the "--oneline" option to get a prettier result.

```
$ git log --oneline
```

This will give you the result shown in Figure 13-4.

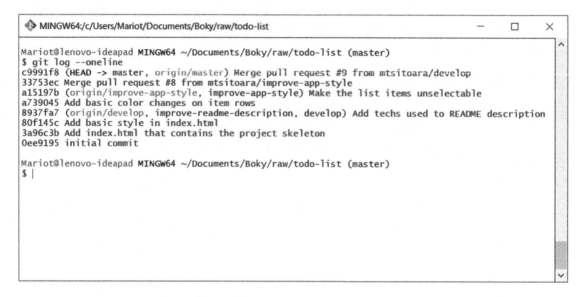

Figure 13-4. *History log after pulling from origin*

You got extra commits! Commits from the remote branch were merged into your local branch. Now, your local master branch points to the same commit as the origin branch.

Let's unpack all of this. First, let's talk about the branch colors. Green branches are your local branches, whereas red branches are remote. Remote also have two names as their names are combined with the remote repository name.

You can see that improve-readme-description, develop, and origin/develop are on the same level. We know this isn't correct because we changed develop from GitHub. Git won't know that changes were until you pull the develop branch from origin.

You will notice that there are commits you didn't make on this history, namely, "Merge pull request #8 from mtsitoara/improve-app-style" and "Merge pull request #9 from mtsitoara/develop." They are called merge commits and they are created by Git when you merge two or more commits. In our project, we merged improve-app-style into develop and then develop into master. Each of these merges produces a merge commit.

Just like normal commits, you can show more information about it by using the git show command. Let's show the first merge commit.

```
$ git show 33753ec
```

This will result in a familiar view for us: the commit intel view. You should get the same result as shown in Figure 13-5.

```
 MINGW64:/c/Users/Mariot/Documents/Boky/raw/todo-list

Mariot@lenovo-ideapad MINGW64 ~/Documents/Boky/raw/todo-list (master)
$ git show 33753ec
commit 33753ecaebae2ba1c3ffdc1e543d372385884c78
Merge: 8937fa7 a15197b
Author: mtsitoara <52602645+mtsitoara@users.noreply.github.com>
Date:   Fri Jul 26 01:25:47 2019 +0200

    Merge pull request #8 from mtsitoara/improve-app-style

    Add basic color changes on item rows
```

Figure 13-5. *The detailed view of a merge commit*

This view isn't particularly interesting because it only shows the commit parents and the user that did the merge. One thing to remember, though, is the committers and the merger can be different people. And you should put your keywords resolving issues in the merge commit message rather than the commit messages. Most of the time, a commit won't be enough to solve a problem; so, put those keywords into the pull request message so the issue is only closed when the branch has been merged.

The history log shown in Figure 13-4 is pretty, but it doesn't really show the concept of branches and merges. A graph would be more appropriate, and there's a parameter for that in the git log command. The parameter is "--graph" and you should use it with "--oneline" to get the best results.

```
$ git log --oneline --graph
```

This command will produce simple graphs like the one shown in Figure 13-6.

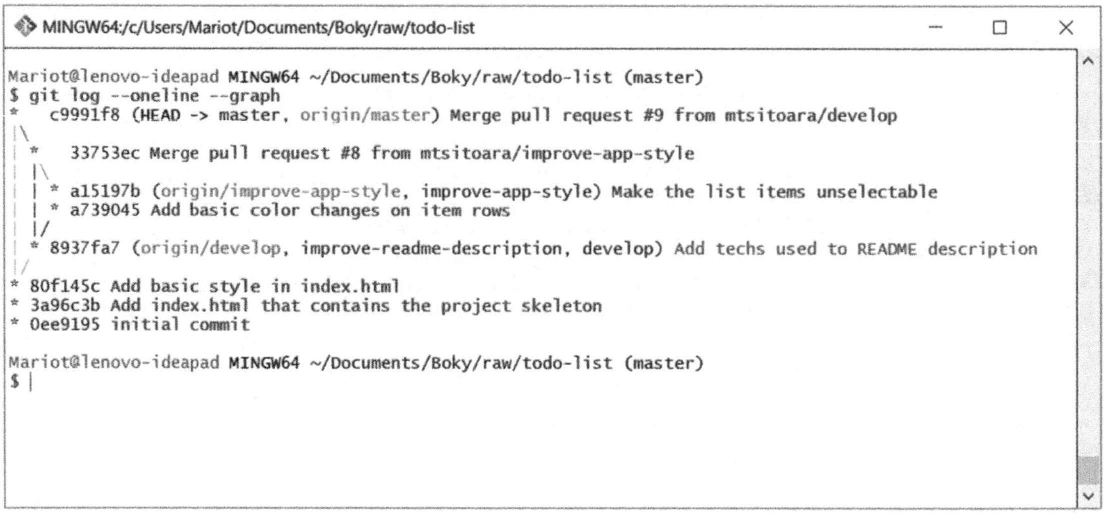

```
 MINGW64:/c/Users/Mariot/Documents/Boky/raw/todo-list                —    □    ×

Mariot@lenovo-ideapad MINGW64 ~/Documents/Boky/raw/todo-list (master)
$ git log --oneline --graph
*   c9991f8 (HEAD -> master, origin/master) Merge pull request #9 from mtsitoara/develop
|\
| *   33753ec Merge pull request #8 from mtsitoara/improve-app-style
| |\
| | * a15197b (origin/improve-app-style, improve-app-style) Make the list items unselectable
| | * a739045 Add basic color changes on item rows
| |/
| * 8937fa7 (origin/develop, improve-readme-description, develop) Add techs used to README description
|/
* 80f145c Add basic style in index.html
* 3a96c3b Add index.html that contains the project skeleton
* 0ee9195 initial commit

Mariot@lenovo-ideapad MINGW64 ~/Documents/Boky/raw/todo-list (master)
$ |
```

Figure 13-6. *The history graph of our project*

As you can see, the log graph provides a more detailed history of our project. Each asterisk represents a commit, as always. But there's a new type of element shown on this graph: branches. You can see that we diverged from the master branch and created the develop branch, which in turn diverged into the improve-app-style branch. We pushed two commits on that branch and then merged it back to develop. After that, we merged develop into master.

When you work on a project that uses a lot of branches and merge often (as you should), it is best to use the graph view as it's clearer than a traditional view. Also, the colors are pretty.

For a much cleaner history log, I suggest you delete the local improve-readme-description branch.

```
$ git branch -D improve-readme-description
```

Deleting an already merged branch presents little risk; but many developers don't do it often in case they need to rework on it later. Most of the time, this doesn't happen. A good rule of thumb is to only delete branches when you are sure that you won't need to check it out again to test something.

What we've done here is the simplest form of merging: a fast-forward. But remember that after you diverged from a branch (like we've done on master and develop), you are in a completely separate zone. You won't get any update from the other branches unless you ask for them. This also means that the other branches will evaluate independently from your branch. By the time you make a pull request on a branch, it may have changed already. For example, multiple contributors can make new branches from develop and work on their own issues. They won't be done at the same time so each PR will be accepted one after another. That's where the trouble begins: your target branch will change outside your influence while you work on your issue. The reality that you are working with may change by the time you are finished with your changes. Maybe multiple people changed the same files in their respective branches. This will happen a lot in your career, and many times, a PR won't go as well as ours did in this chapter. Those problems are called "conflicts," and resolving is essential to your Git journey. Let's do it!

Merge conflicts

The best way to understand merge conflicts is to create one. So, let's mess up our project! First, check out our local develop branch. Since we haven't touched this branch, it should still be clean right now.

```
$ git checkout develop
```

The first thing we are going to do is to check the history log.

```
$ git log --oneline --graph
```

You will get the same result as previously because we haven't pulled from origin yet. This result is shown in Figure 13-7.

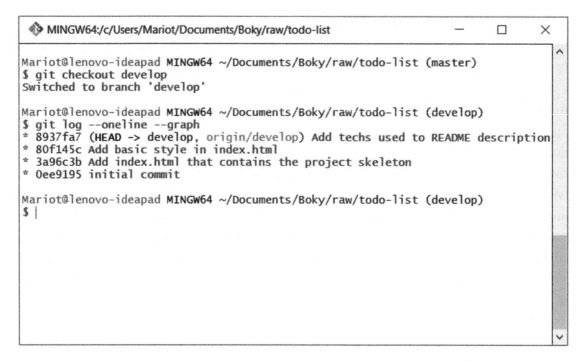

Figure 13-7.   *Develop history log before pull*

Nothing spectacular here, just a good old log without any problem. Since we deleted the improve-readme-description branch, there isn't any branch left in the develop history log.

The log says that develop and origin/develop is on the same state; but this isn't true because we changed it from GitHub. But instead of pulling from origin, we are going to make changes in our branch first, changes that will cause conflicts with the changes from origin.

Open index.html and replace its contents with the following code:

```
<!doctype html>
<html>
    <head>
        <meta charset="utf-8">
        <title>TODO list</title>
        <style>
            h1 {
                text-align: left;
            }
```

```
        h3 {
            text-transform: capitalize;
        }
        li {
            overflow: hidden;
            padding: 22px 0;
            border-bottom: 2px solid #eee;
        }
    </style>
</head>
<body>
    <h1>TODO list</h1>

    <h3>Todo</h3>
    <ul>
        <li>Buy a hat for the bat</li>
        <li>Clear the fogs for the frogs</li>
        <li>Bring a box to the fox</li>
    </ul>

    <h3>Done</h3>
    <ul>
        <li>Put the mittens on the kittens</li>
    </ul>
</body>
</html>
```

Run git diff to review your changes. We only made small changes so it shouldn't be a big deal, right?

```
$ git diff
```

The result is very familiar to us because we see it all the time on GitHub and on git show. Your result should be the same as mine as shown in Figure 13-8.

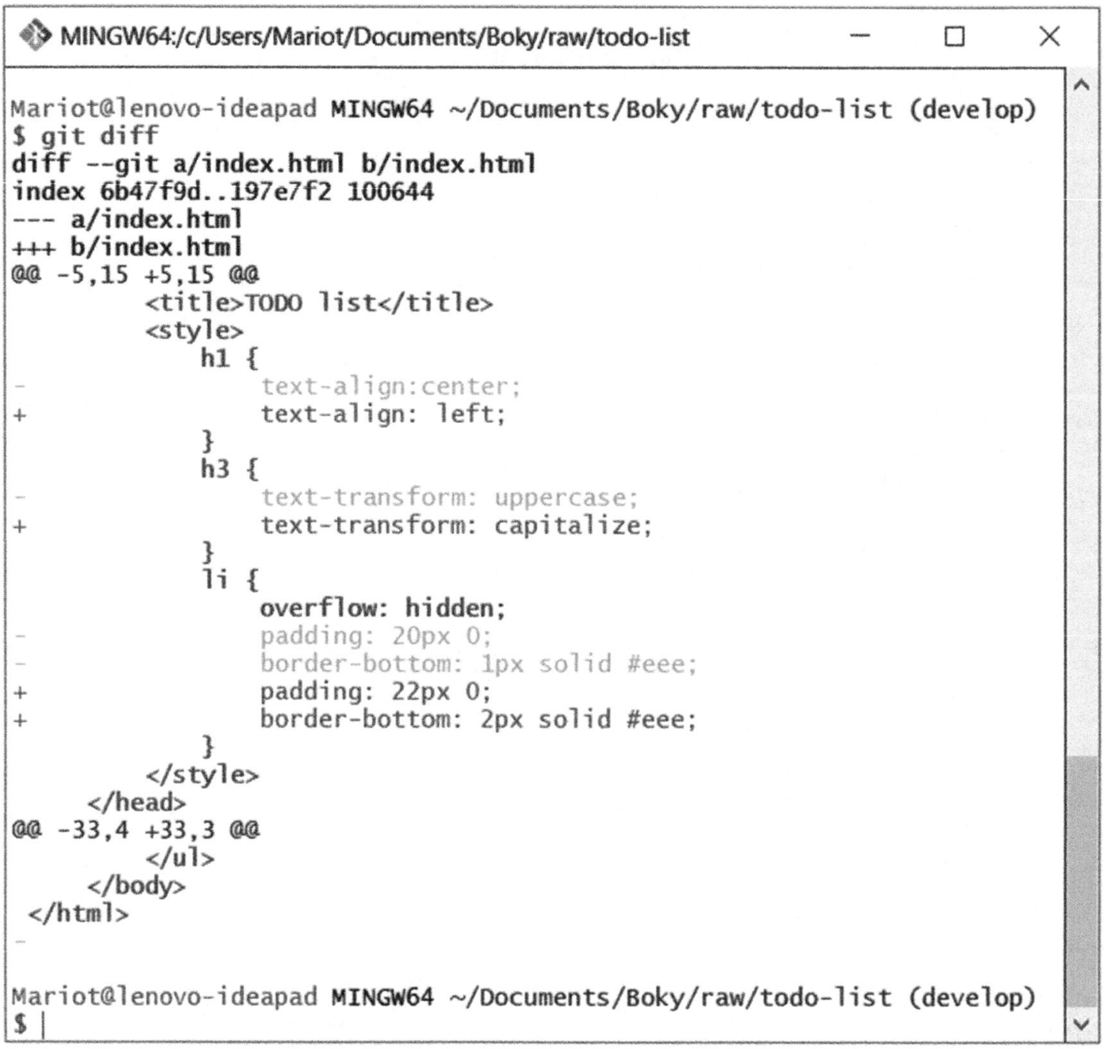

```
MINGW64:/c/Users/Mariot/Documents/Boky/raw/todo-list        —    □    ×

Mariot@lenovo-ideapad MINGW64 ~/Documents/Boky/raw/todo-list (develop)
$ git diff
diff --git a/index.html b/index.html
index 6b47f9d..197e7f2 100644
--- a/index.html
+++ b/index.html
@@ -5,15 +5,15 @@
        <title>TODO list</title>
        <style>
            h1 {
-                text-align:center;
+                text-align: left;
            }
            h3 {
-                text-transform: uppercase;
+                text-transform: capitalize;
            }
            li {
                overflow: hidden;
-                padding: 20px 0;
-                border-bottom: 1px solid #eee;
+                padding: 22px 0;
+                border-bottom: 2px solid #eee;
            }
        </style>
    </head>
@@ -33,4 +33,3 @@
        </ul>
    </body>
 </html>
-

Mariot@lenovo-ideapad MINGW64 ~/Documents/Boky/raw/todo-list (develop)
$ |
```

Figure 13-8. *Difference between develop and the working directory*

Nothing new here. Let's add the changed file to the staging area and then commit the current project.

```
$ git add index.html
```

Tip   Is opening your text editor for each commit tiresome? Well, you can skip it if you are on a hurry. To commit the project while skipping the commit message edition phase, you can pass the commit message as a parameter:

```
$ git commit -m "<commit_message>"
Don't forget the `-m`!
$ git commit -m "Change CSS to introduce conflicts"
```

Caution   Using the shorthand form of the git commit command can maybe save you a few seconds, but it makes it easier to make mistakes because you won't have the chance to review your changes before committing. I highly suggest only using it when you only have one changed file. Plus, you can't use it to write a multiline commit message.

This won't produce any result that we haven't seen before. As you can see in Figure 13-9, we get a standard result because there is no conflict yet.

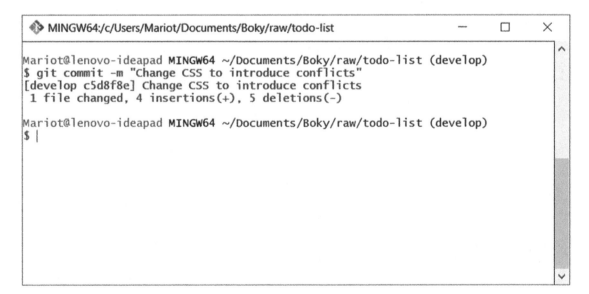

Figure 13-9. *The commit that will introduce conflicts*

To produce the conflict, we need to get the commits that we pushed on develop when we merged a branch into it.

Pulling commits from origin

We've already seen the pull command in action, but, in this scenario, we will get a little problem from it: we changed the same file across different commits. This will produce conflicts and we have to resolve those before you can complete the pull. Remember, pull just means to copy remote commits into your local repository.

Let's start by directly pulling develop from origin. Again, the command is very similar to the push command. You just need the remote repository and branch name.

```
$ git pull origin develop
```

The result we get is very different from everything we've seen earlier. Instead of a result of a completed action, we got a conflict and we are stuck between two states. You can check Figure 13-10 for an example of this.

Figure 13-10. *Merge conflict during the pull command*

Let's unpack this result one by one. First, we have the URL that is being used for the pull so, nothing spectacular here.

Next, we have the first action being performed by Git. That action is called "fetch," and its role is to copy the chosen branch from remote to the local repository. This branch is then stored into a temporary storage called FETCH_HEAD. Just like HEAD is a reference to the last commit we are working on, FETCH_HEAD references to the tip of the branch that we just fetched from origin.

The next action is a basic merge, just like we've seen before. We fetched the remote branch and it's time to merge it with the current branch. The action details the merge to be performed: the branches develop and origin/develop. It even specifies the commits that would be used. Your commit names will be different, but to verify the first commit, you just have to check the commit log:

```
$ git log --oneline
```

You will find the commit name on the second to the last commit as shown in Figure 13-11.

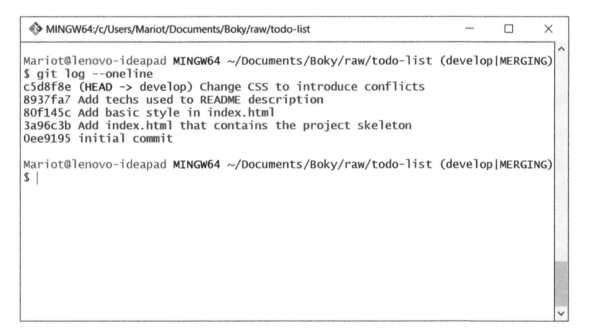

Figure 13-11. *The second to the last commit will be used for the merge*

Note that the merge will not use the last commit because it's the commit that we are working on, the one that introduced the changes.

Figure 13-10 also references another commit for the merge, and you can find that commit on origin/develop. Go to your project page on GitHub and select the develop branch to see the history log of the remote branch. You can also directly access it with your GitHub link like `https://github.com/mtsitoara/todo-list/commits/develop`, for example. You will get a view of the last commits just like in Figure 13-12.

mtsitoara / todo-list
Watch 0
Star 0
Fork 0
<> Code
Issues 3
Pull requests 0
Projects 0
Wiki
Security
Insights
Settings
Branch: develop
Commits on Jul 26, 2019
Merge pull request #8 from mtsitoara/improve-app-style
mtsitoara committed on 26 Jul
Verified
33753ec
Make the list items unselectable
mariot committed on 26 Jul
a15197b
Commits on Jul 25, 2019
Add basic color changes on item rows
mariot committed on 25 Jul
a739045

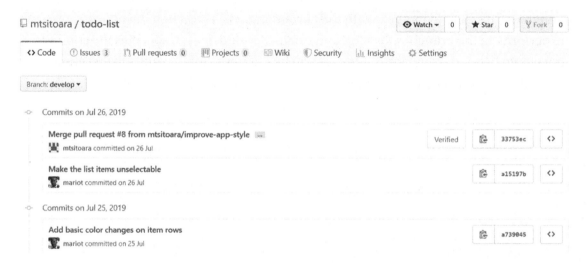

***Figure 13-12.** The commits on origin/develop*

As you can see, the second commit referenced in Figure 13-10 is the last commit of the remote branch, the one that has been created by our previous merge on GitHub. To get even more information, you can click it and get the details of the commit. Check Figure 13-13 for an example of this.

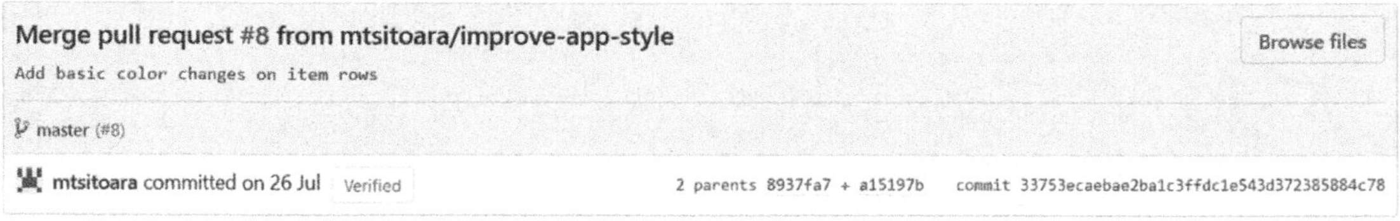

Merge pull request #8 from mtsitoara/improve-app-style
Add basic color changes on item rows
Browse files
master (#8)
mtsitoara committed on 26 Jul
Verified
2 parents 8937fa7 + a15197b
commit 33753ecaebae2ba1c3ffdc1e543d372385884c78

***Figure 13-13.** More info on the merge commit*

You can see in Figure 13-13 that this commit has two parents; that's because it's a commit created by the merge of two branches. You can also see that one of the parents is also referenced in Figure 13-10 because it was the last commit pushed before we merged the branches on GitHub.

Let's go back to Figure 13-10. In the next section of the result, Git tries to "auto merge" the branches, meaning that it tried to merge the branches automatically. This goes smoothly when different files or different parts of the files have been changed by the branches to merge. But since it found conflicts, the merge has failed. And it's up to us to resolve this.

Git tried to merge our local develop branch with FETCH_HEAD, but since both branches contain changes to the same parts of index.html, you have to decide which changes to keep. We'll see how to do that in the next section.

The last information that should be noted from Figure 13-10 is the state in which our local repository is. If you look at the left part of the console, you will find that the repository in the "develop|merging" state instead of the standard "develop" branch. This means that there are still unresolved conflicts in the project and the merge (and, by extension, the pull) is not done yet. You can check the status for more information about the current state of the repository.

```
$ git status
```

This will get you a new result that we haven't seen before, shown in Figure 13-14.

```
MINGW64:/c/Users/Mariot/Documents/Boky/raw/todo-list          —     □     ×

Mariot@lenovo-ideapad MINGW64 ~/Documents/Boky/raw/todo-list (develop|MERGING)
$ git status
On branch develop
You have unmerged paths.
  (fix conflicts and run "git commit")
  (use "git merge --abort" to abort the merge)

Unmerged paths:
  (use "git add <file>..." to mark resolution)

        both modified:      index.html

no changes added to commit (use "git add" and/or "git commit -a")

Mariot@lenovo-ideapad MINGW64 ~/Documents/Boky/raw/todo-list (develop|MERGING)
$ |
```

Figure 13-14. *Status of the merge*

This result is very easy to read and provides great advices for the next steps. First, it tells us the things we should do next: fix conflicts and commit the project. Then, it tells us the way to abort the current merge if we decide to chicken out of the conflict. In many occasions, this is a good idea as we can work on the local branch to resolve the conflicts that we know will arise. For example, we can abort this merge, revert the commit that introduced the conflicts, and then pull again. We will then have an automatic merge without any conflict. But that is too easy and reasonable for us, so, let's do this the hard way!

Next, we have a list of the files concerned by the merge. Here, only index.html is concerned and it has been modified in both branches. Let's open it to see the conflicts. You will see big changes in it as shown in Figure 13-15 and Figure 13-16.

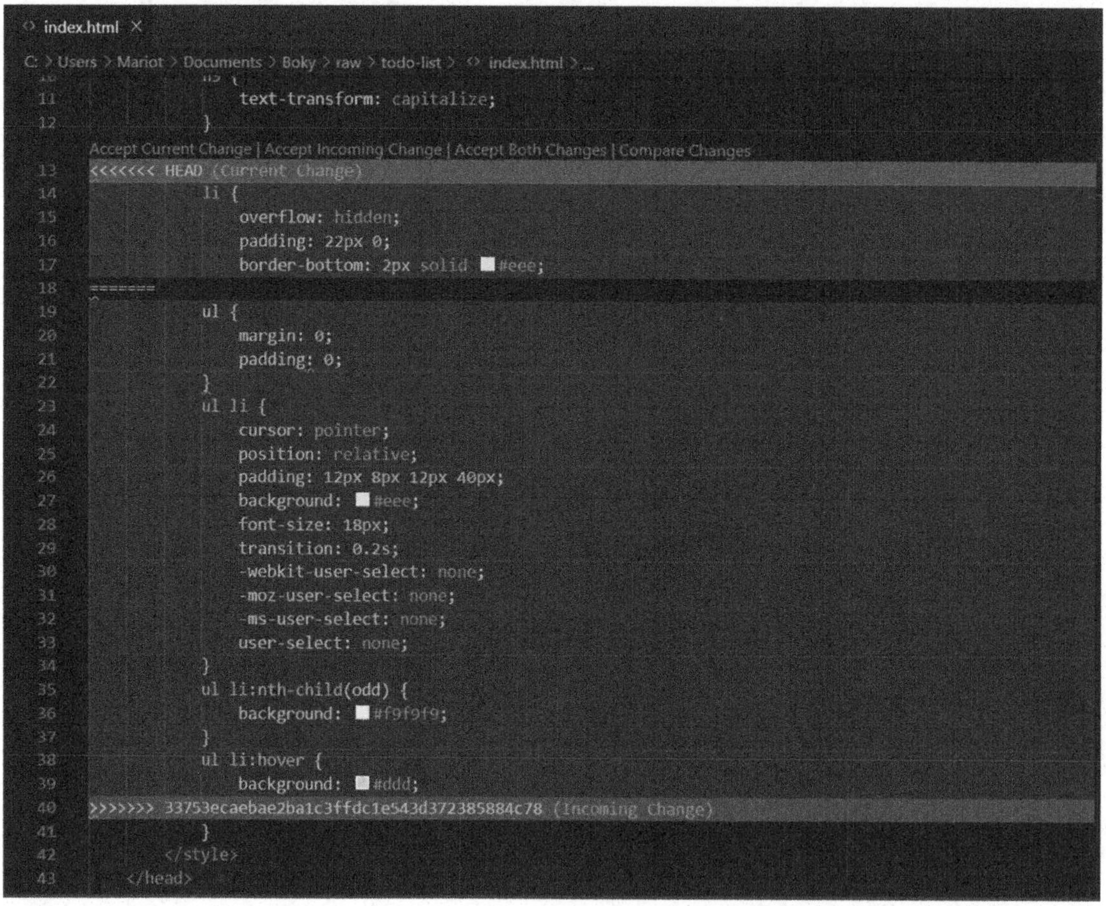

Figure 13-15. *index.html in Visual Studio Code*

```
 MINGW64:/c/Users/Mariot/Documents/Boky/raw/todo-list
<html>
    <head>
        <meta charset="utf-8">
        <title>TODO list</title>
        <style>
            h1 {
                text-align: left;
            }
            h3 {
                text-transform: capitalize;
            }
<<<<<< HEAD
            li {
                overflow: hidden;
                padding: 22px 0;
                border-bottom: 2px solid #eee;
=======
            ul {
                margin: 0;
                padding: 0;
            }
            ul li {
                cursor: pointer;
                position: relative;
                padding: 12px 8px 12px 40px;
                background: #eee;
                font-size: 18px;
                transition: 0.2s;
                -webkit-user-select: none;
                -moz-user-select: none;
                -ms-user-select: none;
                user-select: none;
            }
            ul li:nth-child(odd) {
                background: #f9f9f9;
            }
            ul li:hover {
                background: #ddd;
>>>>>>> 33753ecaebae2ba1c3ffdc1e543d372385884c78
            }
        </style>
    </head>
index.html [dos] (00:11 25/08/2019)
```

Figure 13-16. *index.html in Vim*

You will notice the three big lines dividing your code in the file. Those lines are always the same in every code conflict but different text editors might render them differently. For example, an IDE like Visual Studio Code will render the code with different colors and even add some button to interact with the code (shown in Figure 13-15). In contrast, a very simple text editor will show the lines as usual lines of code and might mess up with your color schemes. In Figure 13-16, I used Vim without any additional tools, so the rendering is a little bit bland; but many plugins can be used to fix this.

Resolving merge conflicts

Let's begin by explaining what those three lines mean. The "<<<<<<<" and the ">>>>>>>" lines delimit the region where there is a conflict. Keep in mind that a file can have multiple conflicting regions.

Those regions are separated by the "=======" line, which shows the code from the two branches. The first part is the code that you have on your current branch; the second part is the code on the branch that you are trying to merge.

So, we have two conflicting codes in our file. First is the code on develop, and second is the code on origin/develop. To resolve the merge conflict, we have to edit the file as to only have one changeset. It doesn't mean that you have to choose between the two changesets, it just means that there can be only one left at the end; you can merge them if need be.

In our case, it would be best to keep most of the second part because we've already vetted and accepted those changes. But there are also some things we can keep from the first part. So, the best course of action is to copy the code we need from the first part and copy it into the second part. The code will then become

```
<!doctype html>
<html>
    <head>
        <meta charset="utf-8">
        <title>TODO list</title>
        <style>
            h1 {
                text-align: left;
            }
```

```
        h3 {
            text-transform: capitalize;
        }
<<<<<<< HEAD
        li {
            overflow: hidden;
            padding: 22px 0;
            border-bottom: 2px solid #eee;
=======
        ul {
            margin: 0;
            padding: 0;
        }
        ul li {
            cursor: pointer;
            position: relative;
            padding: 12px 8px 12px 40px;
            background: #eee;
            font-size: 18px;
            transition: 0.2s;
            -webkit-user-select: none;
            -moz-user-select: none;
            -ms-user-select: none;
            user-select: none;
            overflow: hidden;
        }
        ul li:nth-child(odd) {
            background: #f9f9f9;
        }
        ul li:hover {
            background: #ddd;
>>>>>>> 33753ecaebae2ba1c3ffdc1e543d372385884c78
        }
    </style>
  </head>
```

```
    <body>
        <h1>TODO list</h1>

        <h3>Todo</h3>
        <ul>
            <li>Buy a hat for the bat</li>
            <li>Clear the fogs for the frogs</li>
            <li>Bring a box to the fox</li>
        </ul>

        <h3>Done</h3>
        <ul>
            <li>Put the mittens on the kittens</li>
        </ul>
    </body>
</html>
```

As you can see, we've only copied one line from the first part, because the second part was already almost completed. Now is the time to clean the file of the unnecessary part. First, we can remove the first part of the code conflict (between <<<<<<< and =======) because we don't need them anymore. Then we can just remove the remaining line (>>>>>>>) because it doesn't make sense to have it anymore. The file will then become

```
<!doctype html>
<html>
    <head>
        <meta charset="utf-8">
        <title>TODO list</title>
        <style>
            h1 {
                text-align: left;
            }
            h3 {
                text-transform: capitalize;
            }
            ul {
```

```
            margin: 0;
            padding: 0;
        }
        ul li {
            cursor: pointer;
            position: relative;
            padding: 12px 8px 12px 40px;
            background: #eee;
            font-size: 18px;
            transition: 0.2s;
            -webkit-user-select: none;
            -moz-user-select: none;
            -ms-user-select: none;
            user-select: none;
            overflow: hidden;
        }
        ul li:nth-child(odd) {
            background: #f9f9f9;
        }
        ul li:hover {
            background: #ddd;
        }
    </style>
</head>
<body>
    <h1>TODO list</h1>

    <h3>Todo</h3>
    <ul>
        <li>Buy a hat for the bat</li>
        <li>Clear the fogs for the frogs</li>
        <li>Bring a box to the fox</li>
    </ul>
```

```
        <h3>Done</h3>
        <ul>
            <li>Put the mittens on the kittens</li>
        </ul>
    </body>
</html>
```

The file is back to normal! With a merge of the conflicting codes and no more of those three big lines. Now, you can continue the merge process. If you forgot the next step, you could run git status again (or check Figure 13-14).

So, now that the file is ready, we have to stage it.

```
$ git add index.html
```

After that, you have to commit the project as usual.

```
$ git commit
```

You will be greeted by the familiar commit message view but with a little twist: the commit message will already be written. Check Figure 13-17 for an example of this.

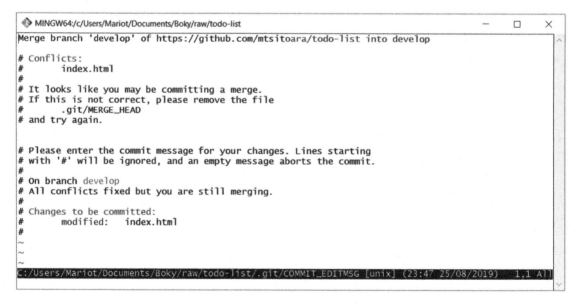

Figure 13-17. *The default commit message*

Of course, you can always modify the commit message, but I suggest leaving the default one unless you are following a personal or company guideline. You can save the commit message and move on.

If you look at the command result (shown in Figure 13-18), you will see that you are back on the develop branch and you are no longer in "merging" state.

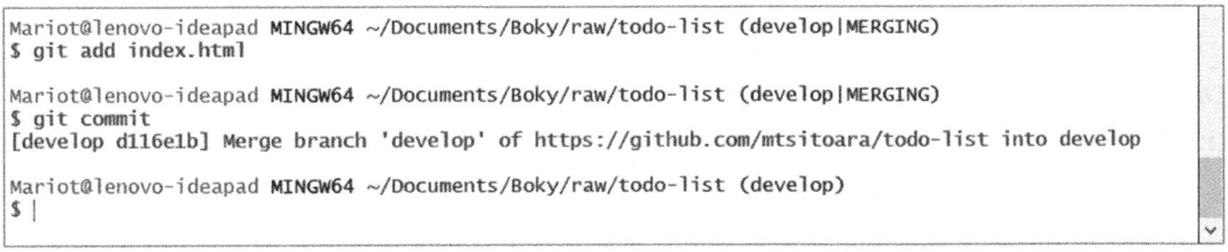

```
Mariot@lenovo-ideapad MINGW64 ~/Documents/Boky/raw/todo-list (develop|MERGING)
$ git add index.html

Mariot@lenovo-ideapad MINGW64 ~/Documents/Boky/raw/todo-list (develop|MERGING)
$ git commit
[develop d116e1b] Merge branch 'develop' of https://github.com/mtsitoara/todo-list into develop

Mariot@lenovo-ideapad MINGW64 ~/Documents/Boky/raw/todo-list (develop)
$ |
```

Figure 13-18. *Back to normal state*

You can also check if the merge has been completed by checking the history log. Make sure to add a graph option for a beautiful result.

```
$ git log --oneline --graph
```

This will produce the stunning visual shown in Figure 13-19.

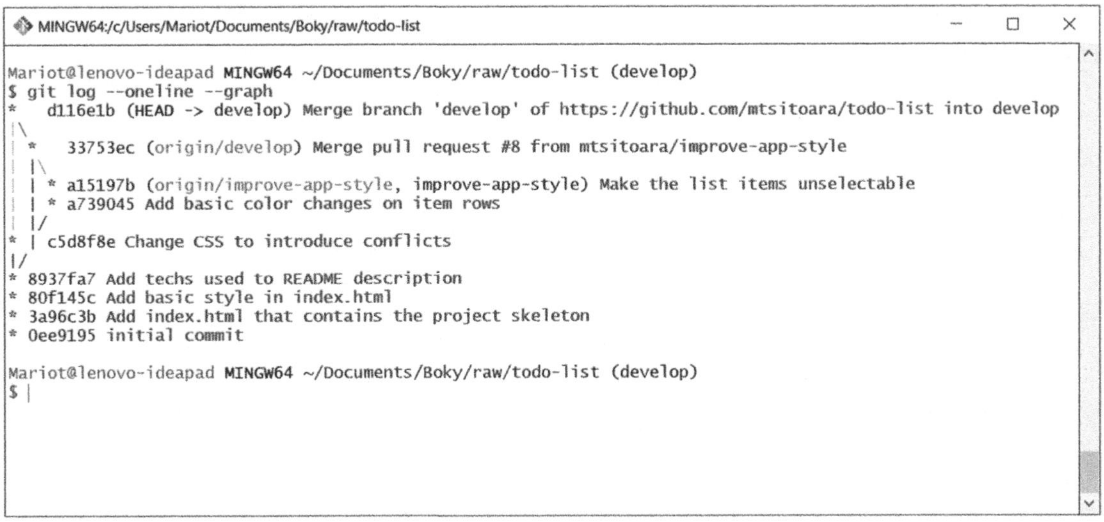

```
 MINGW64:/c/Users/Mariot/Documents/Boky/raw/todo-list                         —   □   ×

Mariot@lenovo-ideapad MINGW64 ~/Documents/Boky/raw/todo-list (develop)
$ git log --oneline --graph
*   d116e1b (HEAD -> develop) Merge branch 'develop' of https://github.com/mtsitoara/todo-list into develop
|\
| *   33753ec (origin/develop) Merge pull request #8 from mtsitoara/improve-app-style
| |\
| | * a15197b (origin/improve-app-style, improve-app-style) Make the list items unselectable
| | * a739045 Add basic color changes on item rows
| |/
* | c5d8f8e Change CSS to introduce conflicts
|/
* 8937fa7 Add techs used to README description
* 80f145c Add basic style in index.html
* 3a96c3b Add index.html that contains the project skeleton
* 0ee9195 initial commit

Mariot@lenovo-ideapad MINGW64 ~/Documents/Boky/raw/todo-list (develop)
$ |
```

Figure 13-19. *The recent history of our project*

You can see on that graph that when we merged the origin/develop branch, we imported all its history. So, it seems like we have a branch from a branch. In big Git projects, it happens all the time.

Summary

This is the biggest chapter of the book. Congratulations on getting there! We saw how to pull code from a remote server and how to solve conflicts when the same code region has been modified by two different branches.

The main takeaway concerning pulling is that it's actually two commands executed one after another:

- Fetching, which copies the remote branch into a temporary branch

- Merging, which merges the temporary branch into the current one

But merging sometimes throws conflicts when the two branches contain edits of the same code. To resolve those conflicts, you have to reopen the concerned file and decide which code to keep. Then, the rest is basic: staging and committing.

Merge conflicts are one of those things that are annoying but will sadly happen a lot in your career, so it's important to learn a lot about them. And since they are annoying, we are going to learn about how to reduce their appearances in the next chapter. Hang in there!

## CHAPTER 14

More About Conflicts

Last chapter was intense, wasn't it? We talked about what are merge conflicts and when would they happen. We also saw how to resolve them manually. Don't worry, this chapter will be much easier to digest. We are going to talk about how to get push your branch to remote after a merge conflict. Also, we are going to see some strategies to adopt to reduce the number of conflicts that might happen. Let's go!

Pushing after a conflict resolution

As we saw in the earlier chapters, pushing means copying our local commits to a remote branch. This means that every commit we have on local will be applied on the remote repository.

We saw in the last section that a pull action is just two actions executed one after the other: a fetch action that copies the remote branch into a temporary location and a merge action that merges the temporary branch to the local one. And since the pull and push actions are just the same but in different directions, it works the same way for pushing your local branch to origin.

So a push action is divided into two parts too: copy of your local branch to remote and the merge of the branches. The only difference between push and pull actions is just a matter of which actor performs the action: you or the server.

Under normal circumstances, the push goes smoothly as the merge is performed automatically using "fast-forward." Fast-forward is possible when the commits on your local branches can be linked directly with the commits present on the remote branch. For example, simply adding commits one after another on our master branch (like we've done until now) and then pushing them results in a fast-forward merge, no need to create a merge commit.

© Mariot Tsitoara 2020
M. Tsitoara, *Beginning Git and GitHub*, https://doi.org/10.1007/978-1-4842-5313-7_14

In our situation, this will happen as well as we only added new commits on our develop branch. And we won't have any problem unless we or someone else went in the past and changed history. Never attempt to do this.

That said, let's push our develop branch using the usual command.

```
$ git push origin develop
```

As expected, we will have the usual result shown in Figure 14-1.

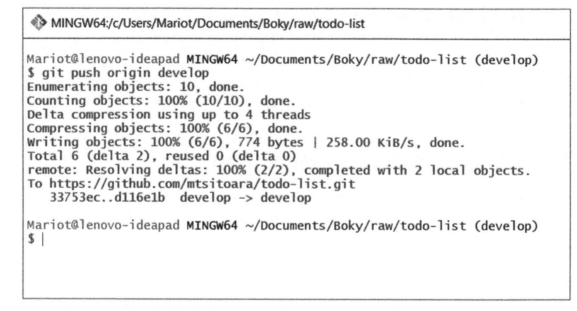

```
Mariot@lenovo-ideapad MINGW64 ~/Documents/Boky/raw/todo-list (develop)
$ git push origin develop
Enumerating objects: 10, done.
Counting objects: 100% (10/10), done.
Delta compression using up to 4 threads
Compressing objects: 100% (6/6), done.
Writing objects: 100% (6/6), 774 bytes | 258.00 KiB/s, done.
Total 6 (delta 2), reused 0 (delta 0)
remote: Resolving deltas: 100% (2/2), completed with 2 local objects.
To https://github.com/mtsitoara/todo-list.git
   33753ec..d116e1b  develop -> develop

Mariot@lenovo-ideapad MINGW64 ~/Documents/Boky/raw/todo-list (develop)
$ |
```

Figure 14-1. *Pushing our develop branch*

In conclusion, pushing a branch back to origin after pulling and merging the changes shouldn't result in an unexpected behavior. Unless someone changed history.

Review changes before merge

Before attempting any merge, the most important thing for you to do is to review all the changes that your branch will introduce. It's a crucial step that shouldn't be ignored because it will save your countless hours of battle against Git.

Check branch location

The first thing you need to make sure is your location. To merge two branches together, you must have the target branch checked out. For example, if you intend to merge develop into master, you would need to check the latter out first. So, the code would be (don't actually execute the second command now):

```
$ git checkout master
$ git merge develop
```

Review branch diff

Reviewing diff is not reserved for commits only! You can also use it to check differences between two branches, which is very handy in delicate situations like merging. The command is fairly simple:

```
$ git diff branch1..branch2
```

Note the two dots between the two branch names. This will show the differences between the two branches in a familiar diff view. Let's compare develop to master:

```
$ git diff master..develop
```

The result is very similar to our diff result when comparing commits. Check Figure 14-2 for such an example.

```
◆ MINGW64:/c/Users/Mariot/Documents/Boky/raw/todo-list                    —    □    ×

Mariot@lenovo-ideapad MINGW64 ~/Documents/Boky/raw/todo-list (master)
$ git diff master..develop
diff --git a/index.html b/index.html
index 2d27723..391ef94 100644
--- a/index.html
+++ b/index.html
@@ -5,10 +5,10 @@
         <title>TODO list</title>
         <style>
             h1 {
-                text-align:center;
+                text-align: left;
             }
             h3 {
-                text-transform: uppercase;
+                text-transform: capitalize;
             }
             ul {
                 margin: 0;
@@ -25,6 +25,7 @@
                 -moz-user-select: none;
                 -ms-user-select: none;
                 user-select: none;
+                overflow: hidden;
             }
             ul li:nth-child(odd) {
                 background: #f9f9f9;
@@ -50,4 +51,3 @@
         </ul>
     </body>
 </html>


Mariot@lenovo-ideapad MINGW64 ~/Documents/Boky/raw/todo-list (master)
$ |
```

Figure 14-2. *Differences between branches*

If you made a lot of changes and don't want to scroll too far, you can also view those changes on GitHub. Just push the branch and open a Pull Request!

Understand Merging

We've already seen many concepts about Git Merges, but let's review them to get a clearer view of this feature. As we saw earlier, merging is the act of combining two branches or, more correctly, pouring a branch into another.

Branches can be formed from any other branch, and when a branch has been created, it becomes independent from its parent. Changes done to either branch won't affect the other, until it's time to merge.

Let's imagine a situation where you create a child branch and made commits on that new branch. When the time to merge comes, several situations can arise.

If the parent branch didn't change (no commits were made) and you attempt to merge, a "fast-forward" merge will occur. A "fast-forward" merge is technically not a merge but just a reference change in Git. Remember that Git commits behave like chained lists, meaning that a commit contains a reference to the previous one. In fact, if the parent hasn't changed, Git just moves the reference to the parent forward (following the chained list), and the last commit in the child branch becomes the last commit of the parent branch. To put it simply, Git just appends the commits in the child branch to the parent branch. This is the easiest type of "merge" but also the most uncommon unless you work alone.

In contrast, if the parent branch has been changed (received commits), a fast-forward merge is not possible. What will occur is called a "true merge" or a "three-way merge." This is the type of merge that we've seen last chapter. This type of merge will create a new commit that has all the changes in the child branch and append that commit to the parent branch. This commit is called a "merge commit," and it has two parents: the parent and the child branches. If different commits from the parent and the child branches modified the same line of code, a conflict arises, and the developer must manually choose which changes to keep.

So, merges are just a fancy way to create commits containing all the changes in a child branch and appending it to the parent branch. It's very important to have a clear idea of it so we can reduce the frequency of merge conflicts.

Reducing conflicts

We saw last chapter that resolving conflicts can be painful and can also take a lot of time depending in their sizes. So, it will be beneficial to us to reduce their appearance to a minimum. We are going to see in this section the strategies to adopt to limit conflicts.

Having a good workflow

Most of the problems you will encounter in Git and GitHub can be avoided if you use a good workflow. We've already seen in the previous chapters the most common Git workflow but let's review it again.

The first thing to remember is don't commit directly to your main branches. To put it simply: every change you intend to introduce into your master or develop branches should be done by merging. And each merge must be introduced by a Pull Request. This way, you can receive feedback on your work as you work on it. It also gives testers a better way to track project changes. You should always use PRs to introduce changes in the main branches even if you work alone. This will provide a much clearer and cleaner history log of the project than simple commit messages.

Each Pull Request should have the resolution of an issue as a goal. Thus, a PR should do only one thing, be it a bugfix, a feature proposal, or documentation changes. Don't be tempted to fix several issues with a single PR. Do-it-all Pull Requests are the perfect recipes for merge conflicts.

One thing often overlooked by developers is line endings and file formatting. As we saw in Chapter 2, different OSs use different line endings. It is necessary for your team to discuss which ones to use for each project; most teams use Unix-style line endings so Windows users should configure their Git client accordingly. As for formatting, it is up to your team, but the only rule is that you must all use the same format for indentations and line returns.

Caution   Things might get heated when discussing tabs vs. spaces. Prepare your arguments in advance.

Aborting a merge

Many of your merge conflicts won't come from code clash; many will come from formatting and whitespace differences. For example, a trailing return space or the number of indentation spaces can introduce conflicts even though the code hasn't changed.

When confronted with these kinds of conflicts, the best move is just to abort the merge, roll back your formatting differences, and then try to merge again. As you saw earlier, the command to abort a merge is

```
$ git merge --abort
```

This won't destroy any of your commits, it will just cancel the merge and you'll stay at your current state.

Using a visual Git tool

When using a simple text editor, it might be difficult to resolve a conflict because most of the time, it messes up the code color scheme. A simple solution to that it is using specialized tools for Git. They can be IDE extensions or tools especially made for Git. Let's discover them in the next chapter!

Summary

This chapter was a simple reminder of what are merges and how are they used. We saw the various types of Git merge and the situations where they can appear. We also reviewed how a merge works and what is the goal: pour commits from a branch to another.

The main things to remember are the various ways to reduce merge conflicts. You may never get rid of them, but following those advices will keep their appearances to a minimum.

We've made a lot of progress in our Git journey, but we've done it using our plain and boring consoles. It's time to put more color in our Git projects so let's learn about Git GUIs!

## CHAPTER 15

Git GUI Tools

In the earlier chapters, we've seen a lot of the most important Git features and concepts. We've learned about commits, branches, pull requests, and merging. Using those concepts, you can already accomplish almost anything in Git. Only one small problem, though: we've only used the Terminal or Console window. In this chapter, you won't learn any new concept or feature; you will just learn how to apply what you already know with style ☺

First, we're going to investigate the default tools that come with Git, then learn more about IDEs that integrate Git, and lastly look at some specialized tools specially made for Git.

Default tools

If you've followed the installation steps from the Chapter 2, you already have those tools installed on your computer. If not, you can easily get them on our habitual software store. These default tools are shipped with Git to provide users very simple GUIs to browse their repositories and prepare their commits. They are available for almost any Operating Systems, so don't worry, they are available to you. They are presented in this book for historical reasons and because they come built-in into Git.

Committing: git-gui

The first tool we are going to see is called git-gui and it's a graphical committing interface for Git. You will use it to commit your project and review proposed changes. You can find more information about it on `https://git-scm.com/docs/git-gui`.

You can open it like you would open Git Bash: by the command line, context menu, or Start page. Choose whichever is the best option for you. On Windows and Debian-based OSs, you can open a Git GUI by navigating to the directory of the repository and right-clicking an empty space. Doing so will give you a result similar to Figure 15-1.

© Mariot Tsitoara 2020
M. Tsitoara, *Beginning Git and GitHub*, https://doi.org/10.1007/978-1-4842-5313-7_15

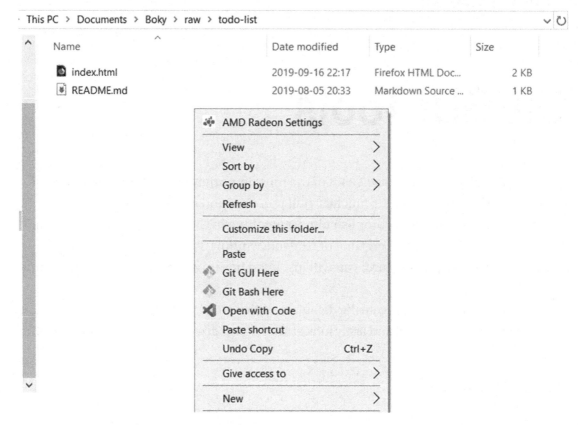

Figure 15-1. *Windows context menu*

As you can see, you can open Git GUI and Git Bash there. Go ahead and choose Git GUI. You will get a little program window that details your current working directory status. The window is presented in Figure 15-2.

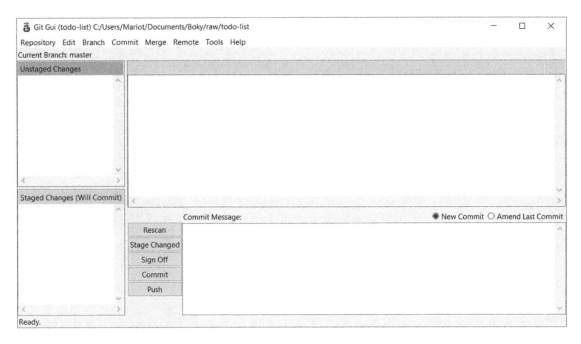

Figure 15-2. *Git GUI interface*

And if you don't want to use the context menu or can't, you can open it by opening a Terminal on the location of your Git repository and executing the following command:

```
$ git gui
```

The Git GUI interface is very lightweight and intuitive; and it's the same for each OS so everybody feels at home. It is divided in four parts:

- Top left is a list of edited files that have not been staged yet.

- Bottom left is a list of files that have been staged.

- Top right is a diff view.

- Bottom right is a commit message text area.

And since we haven't changed anything in our project, everything is empty. So, let's mess up our project with additional commits.

First, let's make sure that we are in master branch and then create a new branch from it. Go to the "branch" menu and select "checkout..."; it will open the selection window shown in Figure 15-3.

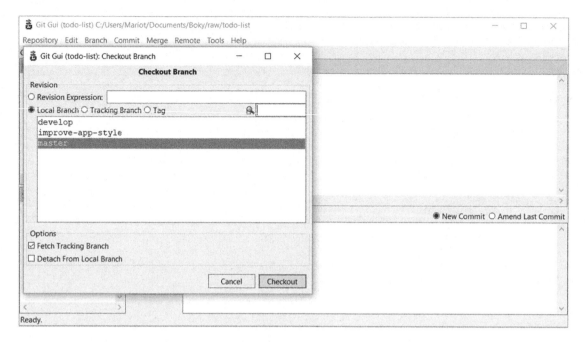

Figure 15-3. *Choosing a branch to check out*

You'll notice that when your cursor hovers above a branch, information about its last commit will appear. It will help you find the right branch, but shouldn't be necessary if you have good branch names. Check out master branch and then create a new one by selecting "create..." on the "branch" menu. You will get the branch creation window shown in Figure 15-4.

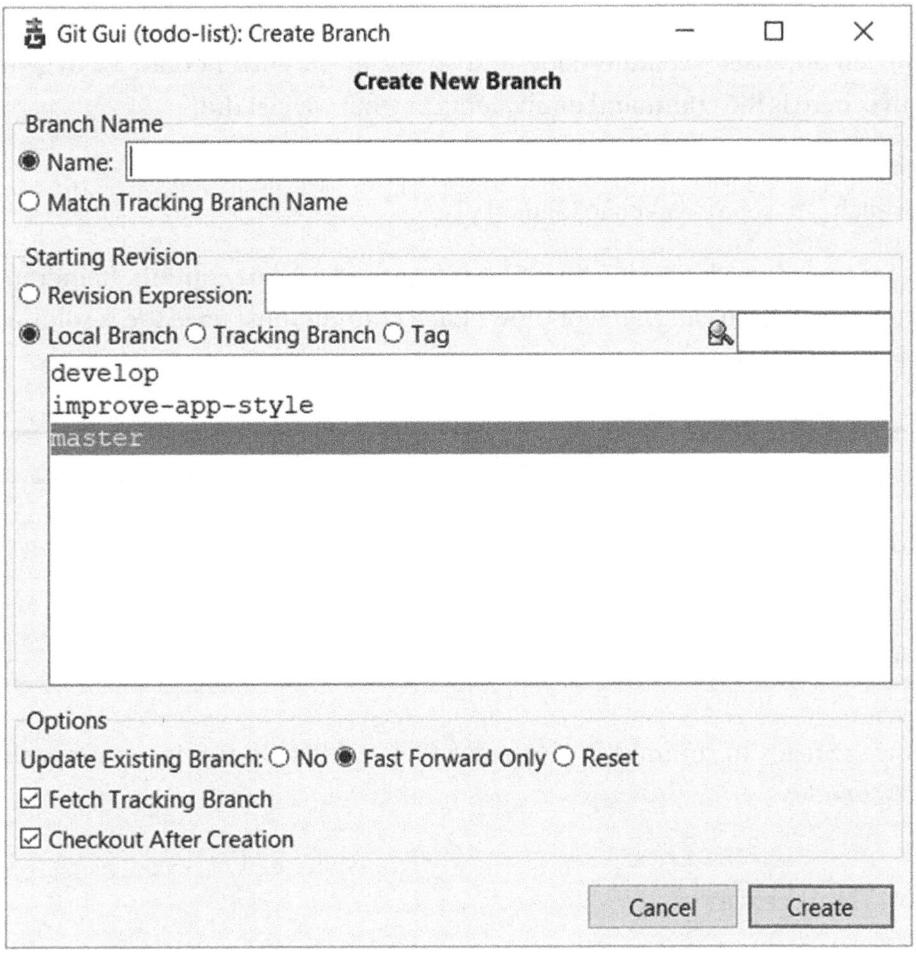

Figure 15-4. *Creating of a new branch*

The first input area is the most important: the name of your new branch. Name the branch "separate-code-and-styles."

The second input is a choice input where you have to select where you are going to create the branch from. In our situation, we are going to create a new branch from our local master branch; so choose "local branch" and select "master."

The third part are the options, which I recommend keeping the default options. With the default options, Git will fetch the latest commits on the remote (tracking) branch and then check out the new branch.

Now, you can click "Create" to see the result. You will see that the little message box on the top left now lists "separate-code-and-styles" as the current branch. To give you perspective, here is the command equivalents of what we just did:

```
$ git checkout master
$ git branch -b separate-code-and-styles
```

Now that we are in the correct branch, we can work on our commit. Remember our golden rule when discussing Git workflow? Each commit must have the resolution of an issue as goal. I'll let you create that issue.

EXERCISE: CREATE AN ISSUE

Go to GitHub issues.

Create an issue called "Separate code and styles."

Take note of the issue number.

Now we're ready to commit! Create a new file called "style.css" in your repository and paste in this code:

```
h1 {
    text-align:center;
}
h3 {
    text-transform: uppercase;
}
ul {
    margin: 0;
    padding: 0;
}
ul li {
    cursor: pointer;
    position: relative;
    padding: 12px 8px 12px 40px;
    background: #eee;
    font-size: 18px;
```

```
    transition: 0.2s;
    -webkit-user-select: none;
    -moz-user-select: none;
    -ms-user-select: none;
    user-select: none;
}
ul li:nth-child(odd) {
    background: #f9f9f9;
}
ul li:hover {
    background: #ddd;
}
```

Then, open "index.html" and change its content to

```
<!doctype html>
<html>
    <head>
        <meta charset="utf-8">
        <title>TODO list</title>
        <link rel="stylesheet" href="style.css" />
    </head>
    <body>
        <h1>TODO list</h1>

        <h3>Todo</h3>
        <ul>
            <li>Buy a hat for the bat</li>
            <li>Clear the fogs for the frogs</li>
            <li>Bring a box to the fox</li>
        </ul>

        <h3>Done</h3>
        <ul>
            <li>Put the mittens on the kittens</li>
        </ul>
    </body>
</html>
```

Save the two files and let's hop to Git GUI to see the result. You will see... nothing new! Because Git GUI isn't aware of our changes yet. Click "Rescan" near the commit message box to see the changes; you will get the result shown in Figure 15-5.

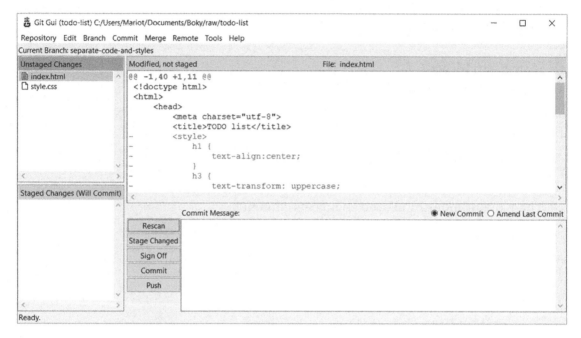

***Figure 15-5.** Changes shown in Git GUI*

Now we have our changes! You can see the list of modified files on the top left part of Git GUI, where the unstaged files are. You will notice that the files have different icons:

- An empty file icon for a new file (never been committed)

- A file icon for a modified file (has been part of a commit before)

- A "?" icon for a deleted file (has been part of a commit before)

Doesn't that view remind you of something? Well, it's the status view, of course! Clicking "Rescan" is the same as executing this command on the terminal:

```
$ git status
```

Here, we modified "index.html" and created "style.css." If you click the file names (not icons; don't click the icons yet), you will see the diff view change. Check Figure 15-6 for an example of the result that you would get after clicking style.css.

Figure 15-6. *Diff on the newly created style.css file*

It's certainly quicker than executing "git diff"! Also, it's easier on the eye if you have a lot of changed files. So clicking the file name is equivalent to executing these commands:

```
$ git diff index.html
$ git diff style.css
```

Now is then time to stage our files in preparation for the commit. Staging and unstaging a file is really easy: you just have to click its icon. Or you can also select the files you want to stage (by clicking their names) and choose "Stage to Commit" in the "commit" menu. Clicking the file icons is the same as executing these commands:

```
$ git add index.html style.css
$ git reset HEAD index.html
$ git reset HEAD style.css
```

See? Way quicker than typing commands!

We can finally commit our project! But first, make sure that all the files you created or modified are staged, meaning that they are on the bottom left section. Then, you can write your commit message on the bottom-right section of Git GUI, just like in Figure 15-7.

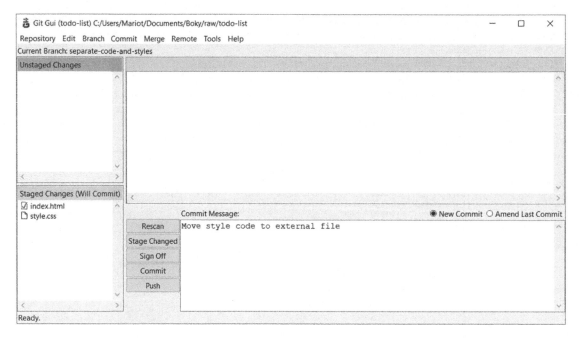

Figure 15-7. Writing of a commit message

Now with our files staged and our commit message written, we are ready to commit. Just click the "Commit" button near the commit message box. After you do so, Git GUI comes back to its normal, empty state. We've committed from the graphical tool!

Clicking the "Commit" button thus has the same result as this command:

```
$ git commit -m "Move style code to external file"
```

Since you are my best student (don't tell the others), I'll let you make another commit in our branch.

EXERCISE: MAKE ANOTHER COMMIT

Open README.md.

Add this line at the end of the file: "License: MIT."

Create a new file called LICENSE.

Copy the license text from `https://choosealicense.com/licenses/mit/` into the LICENSE file.

Stage both files.

Commit with the message "Add MIT license."

Oof! Now you have two commits on your new branch and it's time to push them to the remote repository. You have certainly guessed which button to click; it's "Push." Clicking it will give you the result in Figure 15-8.

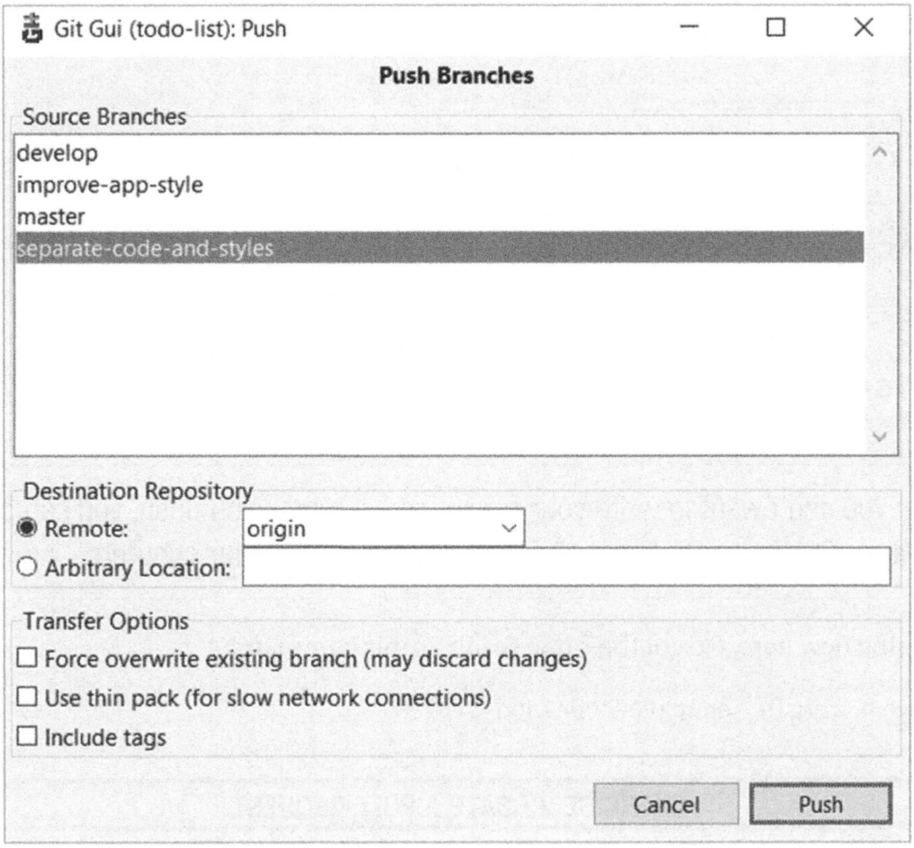

Figure 15-8. *Pushing a branch*

It's a straightforward interface; you just have to select the branch you want to push and the location where you want to push it.

The current branch is selected by default, so we don't have to change anything. The second section is the destination selection dropdown; and again, we don't have to change anything because we only have one remote repository. Ignore the options for now; we will see them in a later chapter.

Click push to push! If you are using an HTTPS authentication to connect with GitHub, you will be asked for your GitHub username and password and then get the result shown in Figure 15-9.

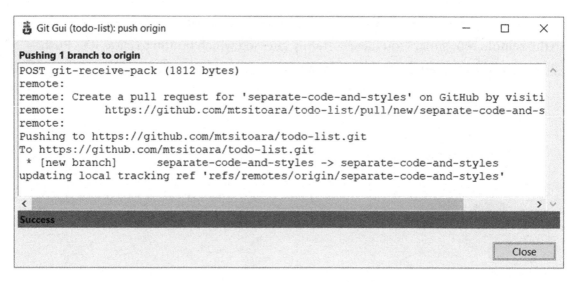

Figure 15-9. *Push result*

Tip   If you don't want to write your password each time you push, you can cache it or use an SSL authentication; all of this is explained in later chapters.

Nothing new here, we got the same result as this command:

```
$ git push origin separate-code-and-styles
```

EXERCISE: CREATE A PULL REQUEST

Follow the link you got after pushing.

Create a pull request with this description: "Fix #10" (replace the number with the issue number you created earlier).

Merge the PR.

Rejoice.

And that's how you commit with Git GUI! Simple, right? And very quick too. It's a great tool that can save you a lot of time when reviewing commits. Talking about commits, let's see the other default tool!

Browsing: gitk

In the previous section, we talked a lot about creating and pushing commits. Now, we are going to visualize those commits in their natural habitat: the repository. gitk is a simple tool to have a simple visual of your project history. You can think of it as an overpowered "git log" command. More documentation about gitk can be found on `https://git-scm.com/docs/gitk`.

Since you already have git-gui open, let's use it to open gitk. Simply choose "Visualize all branch history" from the "Repository" menu. Doing so will open gitk, and you will see the window shown in Figure 15-10.

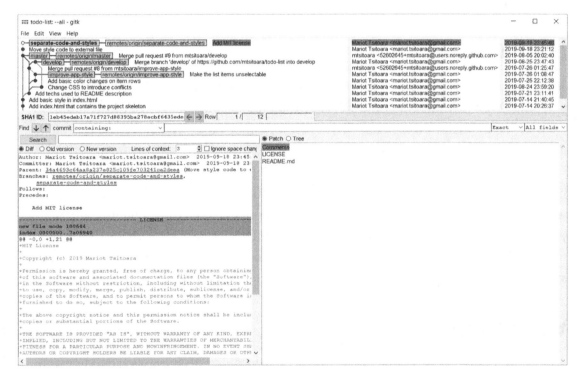

Figure 15-10. *gitk interface*

At the top of the window, you will find a list of all your project's commits, from all branches. It is presented in a nice graph view that you can reproduce on console with the command:

```
$ git log --oneline --graph
```

You can click the commits to get more information about them. Selecting a commit will update the views on the bottom of the window. The bottom left part is a diff view again, but with a twist: you can also choose to view the old or the new version of the files. The bottom right part is a list of all the files changed in the commit. You can click them to see the changes on the diff view. Clicking a commit is the equivalent of executing the following code:

```
$ git show <commit_name>
```

And that's it for gitk, the default browsing tool of Git! Since you can commit and browse with the default graphical tools now, it's time to present you to other tools.

IDE tools

As we saw in the previous section, committing with a graphical tool is very fast compared to typing in the console. But there still is a problem: you must leave your Integrated Development Environment to use them. Wouldn't it be nice if you could use the graphical tools directly from your editor?

It's possible with a lot of modern editors. I will present you to two popular IDEs that have Git integrated so you can use them for your future development. And if you don't want to use them or you are already in love with your current editor, chances are that your IDE also have integrated Git tools or plugins if it's modern enough. Each IDE has its own interface and user experience, so I won't go into detail in this section. I just want to show to what features are available.

Visual Studio Code

A very popular editor, Visual Studio Code, is a lightweight IDE supported by Microsoft; you can find it on https://code.visualstudio.com/. It's new so it has all the shiny new toys integrated in it; and Git is at the center of those. You can see the look and feel of VS Code in Figure 15-11.

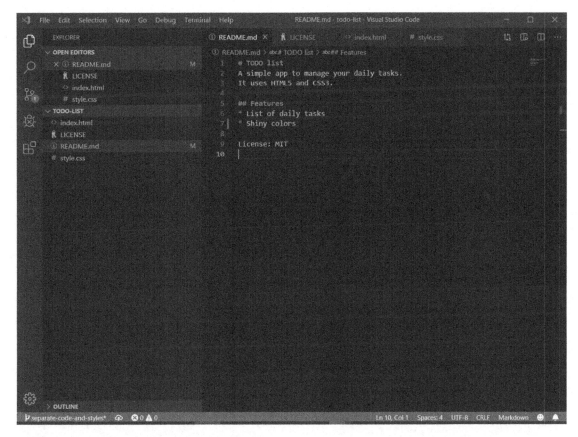

Figure 15-11. *Visual Studio Code*

It has the same interface as any other IDE but with a little bonus: you can see traces of Git here and there. First, if you change a tracked file (README.md here), the edited part is highlighted; no need to execute git diff anymore!

And at the bottom left of the window, you have the current branch name; if you click it, you can select the branch you want to navigate to or create a new branch. If you have unstaged files, there will be a little "∗" sign near your branch name and an "M" icon near the concerned file names. If you have staged push uncommitted files, you have a "+" sign.

Click the Source Control icon to access the Git Tab, shown in Figure 15-12.

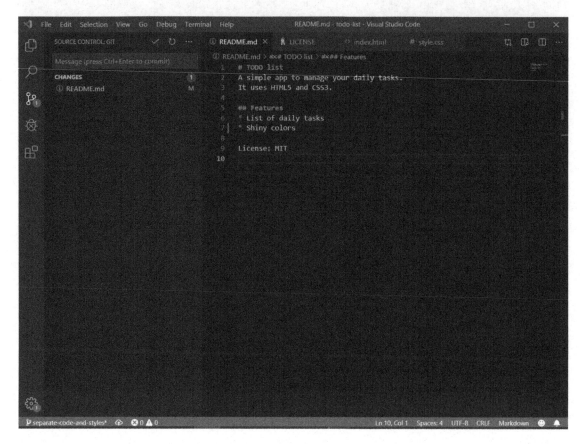

Figure 15-12. *Source Control view*

This view looks and works very much like git-gui, so I'll let you discover it yourself!

Atom

Atom is an IDE pushed by GitHub and it's also a very popular choice among developers. You can check it out on `https://atom.io/`. You can see its interface in Figure 15-13.

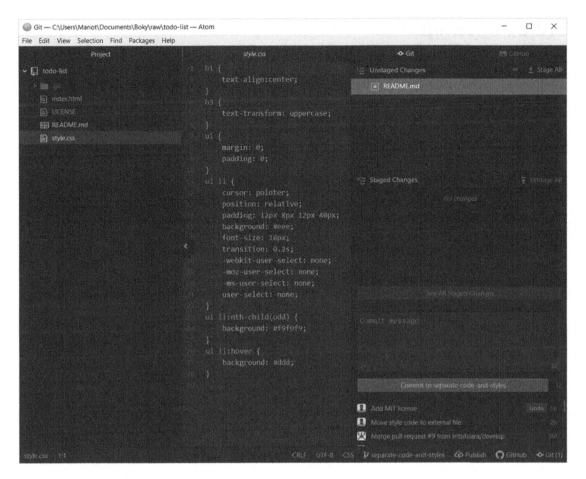

Figure 15-13. *Atom interface*

It has the same Git features as Visual Studio Code but with a little twist: you can link your GitHub account to it and create PR directly from the editor! Again, I'll let you discover.

Specialized tools

We saw the default Git tools and some IDEs that have Git integrated. Now, let's see some tools specially developed for Git.

GitHub Desktop

GitHub Desktop is the perfect tool for you if you like the default gitk and git-gui tools but hate their interface. Let's face it, the default tools are great, but their look feels odd in those modern times. GitHub Desktop (found on https://desktop.github.com/) has been created to replace those tools; it has all their features combined in one software. You can check Figure 15-14 for the interface of GitHub Desktop.

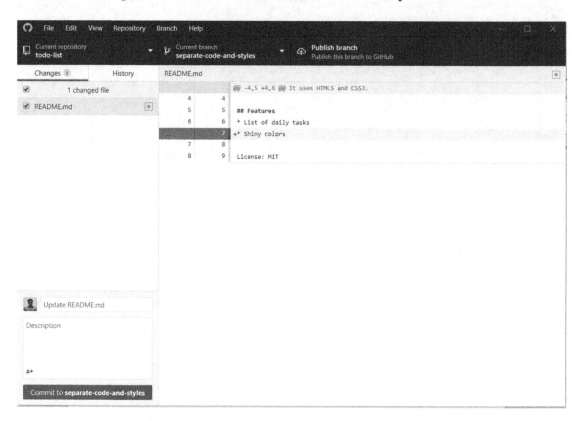

Figure 15-14. *GitHub Desktop*

GitKraken

GitKraken is a Git client created by Axolosoft that is becoming more and more popular. You can get it on its web site at www.gitkraken.com/. It's more advanced than all the other tools as its goal is the augmentation of developer productivity. It even has an integrated code editor! You can see its interface in Figure 15-15.

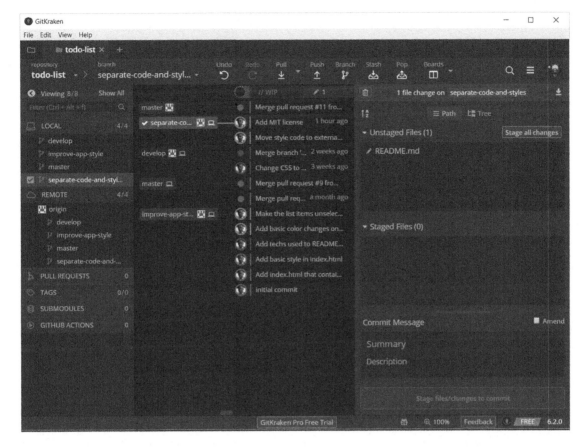

Figure 15-15. *GitKraken overview*

Again, the interface is the same as the others, but what distinguish GitKraken is its beauty: it's insanely gorgeous!

Summary

This chapter was fun, wasn't it? We learn a lot about how to use a graphical tool to make commits and browse them. We also discovered a ton of new tools that are available to us, be it integrated into an IDE or a specialized tool. And how can we forget about our good old default tool?!

You may ask yourself why not use the graphical tool from the very beginning? It's because using a tool without knowing the concepts behind them is counterproductive and a waste of time. Trust me, learning to use the Terminal was worth it! Talking about terminals, let's get back to it for some more advanced Git commands!

CHAPTER 16

Advanced Git

Last chapter, we learned how to do the basic Git features in a graphical context. Now, let's see some more Git commands that you won't be using as much as the others, but are powerful and necessary for a better productivity. Those are very easy-to-learn commands that will be useful to you if you ever made a mistake using Git.

We're going to see some common problems you will surely run into after a few times using Git. Then we'll see the easiest way to solve them. This is a pretty easy chapter but we're going to learn some powerful Git features.

Reverting

We've already seen how to revert a commit on the previous chapters. But most of time, all you want to do is reverting a single file to a previous state. This mostly happens when you've been coding for some time only to realize that your entire strategy was wrong. And instead of hitting Cmd-Z hundreds of time, it's better to revert the file.

You probably already know how to do this because Git tells you how to do it after you check git status. First, let's open README.md and then add some text in it.

```
# TODO list
A simple app to manage your daily tasks.
It uses HTML5 and CSS3.

## Features
* List of daily tasks
* Pretty colors

License: MIT
```

© Mariot Tsitoara 2020
M. Tsitoara, *Beginning Git and GitHub*, https://doi.org/10.1007/978-1-4842-5313-7_16

Now, let's see the status.

```
$ git status
```

As usual, you will see the status of your repository (shown in Figure 16-1).

```
MINGW64:/c/Users/Mariot/Documents/Boky/raw/todo-list          —    □    ×

Mariot@lenovo-ideapad MINGW64 ~/Documents/Boky/raw/todo-list (separate-code-and-styles)
$ git status
On branch separate-code-and-styles
Changes not staged for commit:
  (use "git add <file>..." to update what will be committed)
  (use "git checkout -- <file>..." to discard changes in working directory)

        modified:   README.md

no changes added to commit (use "git add" and/or "git commit -a")

Mariot@lenovo-ideapad MINGW64 ~/Documents/Boky/raw/todo-list (separate-code-and-styles)
$ |
```

Figure 16-1. *Git status after a changed file*

Nothing new here, but direct your attention to the directives shown above the modified file. As you can see, reverting a file to a previous state just means to check it out. The command is thus

```
$ git checkout -- <file>
```

This command will discard any change you've done to a particular file. Be careful when using it, as to not erase valuable code. It might be better to use the GUI so you can quickly get a detailed view of the current changes before discarding them. Let's try to discard our changes on README.md with the following command.

```
$ git checkout -- README.md
```

You won't get any response from this command, but if you check git status again, you will see that README.md is back to its previous state.

Stashing

Many times, you will want to navigate between branches but can't because your Working Directory is dirty. In this context, dirty means that you have uncommitted changed files, be they in modified or staged state. The only way to change branch is to first commit them. But most of the time, you won't be ready to commit yet because the issue at hand is not resolved yet.

One solution to this is to make a temporary commit, change branch, work on it, and then go back and amend the temporary commit. There are many problems attached to this method: first, your Working Directory will be clean when you commit, meaning that you won't know anymore which files were being changed. Second, it's a plain dirty and ugly method. That's not why the amend command was created.

The ideal solution is to use a technique called "stashing." Stashing means taking any modified tracked file in your Working Directory and put it away for later. That means that you will have a clean directory and can navigate around your repository, without having to commit your changes. Those changes are stored in a little database called "stash." You can think of the stash as a temporary repository for your unfinished commits. It's designed as a last-in first-out database, meaning that the last changes you stashed will be presented to you first. The best way to understand it is to try. So, let's change our README.md file again.

```
# TODO list
A simple app to manage your daily tasks.
It uses HTML5 and CSS3.

## Features
* List of daily tasks
* Pretty colors

License: MIT
```

If you check the status, you will see that README.md has been modified but is unstaged. You would get the same result as earlier (Figure 16-1).

Let's now suppose that while you work on this issue, an urgent one needs your attention. Obviously, you can't check the master branch now because your working directory is dirty and you can't revert your current changes because you haven't quite finished yet. The solution is to stash your current changes somewhere so you can have a clean directory to work with. To do this, you will have to use the stash command, which is very easy:

```
$ git stash push
```

Note   Just using the command "git stash" is the same as using "git stash push." It's recommended to use the full command because it's more intuitive and easier to understand.

This command will take your modified files, stage them, and create a temporary commit within the stash, leaving your working directory clean. Try it and you will get the same result as shown in Figure 16-2.

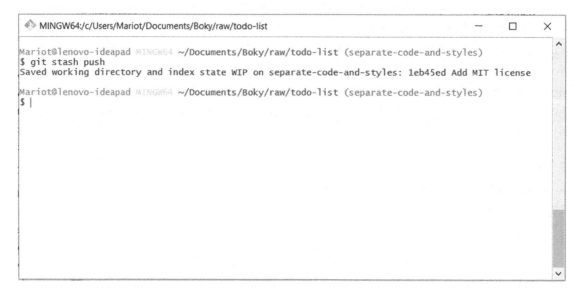

Figure 16-2. *Stashing current changes*

As you can see, your stashed changes were given a name and a description like a regular commit. It's normal because the stash is just a temporary repository that only has one branch. If you check the repository status, you will get a clean working directory as intended (shown in Figure 16-3); and you can finally navigate to other branches.

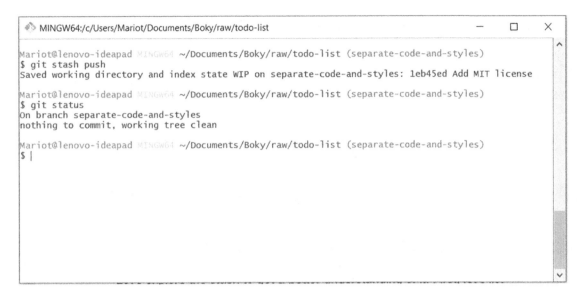

Figure 16-3. A stash push produces a clean working directory

Pushing changes into the stash can thus give you more freedom of movement without losing your current work. It's very useful in fast-paced development.

Caution   Even if this isn't a book about productivity, here is a little tip: if you find yourself jumping back and forth between issues, certainly your problem is your priorities, and resolving two issues at the same time will cost you precious time.

Since the stash is just a mini repository, you can thus execute most Git features on it, like checking the history log or getting a detailed view of the changes. Let's explore the stash to get a better understanding of it. First, let's show to history log by using the stash list command.

```
$ git stash list
```

This will get you a familiar, although a simplified, view of the history log, shown in Figure 16-4.

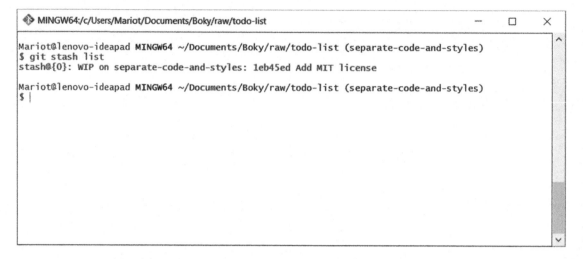

Figure 16-4. *List of stashed changes*

As we said earlier, this database works on last-in first-out, so if we made other changes to our working directory and stashed them, they will appear on top of our current stash.

You will notice in Figure 16-4 that each stash has a number. It's easier that way to interact with them, unlike commits where you must call them by their names. Let's see the detailed view of our stashed change by using the command stash show.

```
$ git stash show
```

This simple command will show you the files changed on the tip of the stash, meaning the last changes pushed unto it. Check Figure 16-5 for an example of this.

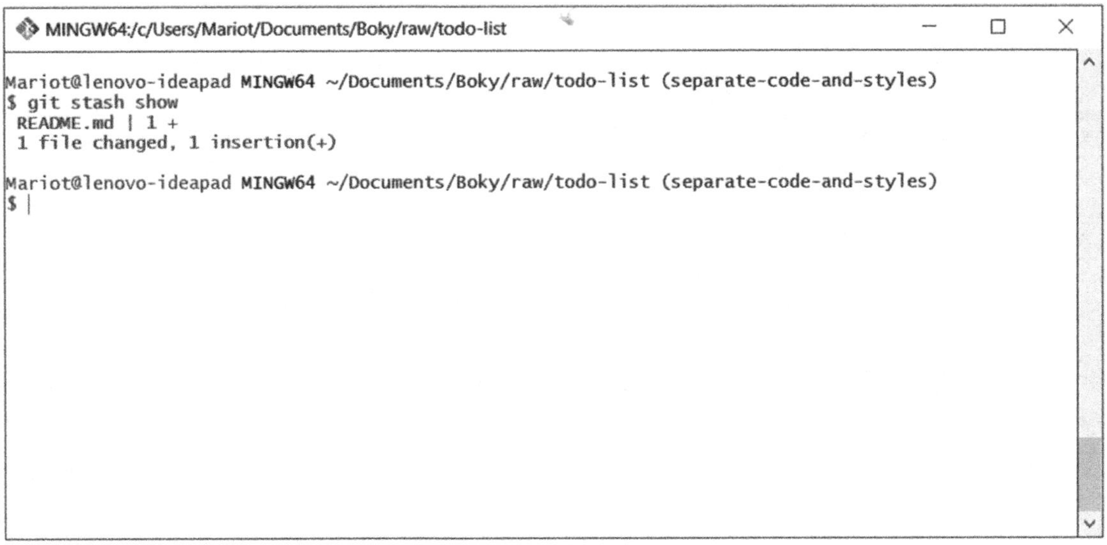

```
MINGW64:/c/Users/Mariot/Documents/Boky/raw/todo-list                          —    □    ×

Mariot@lenovo-ideapad MINGW64 ~/Documents/Boky/raw/todo-list (separate-code-and-styles)
$ git stash show
 README.md | 1 +
 1 file changed, 1 insertion(+)

Mariot@lenovo-ideapad MINGW64 ~/Documents/Boky/raw/todo-list (separate-code-and-styles)
$ |
```

Figure 16-5. *Detailed view of the tip of the stash*

The stash show command will just show you the description of the changes contained in the stash, but not much else. To see the changes, you must apply the stash. Applying the stash is very simple: just execute the following command.

```
$ git stash pop
```

This command will take the latest changes in the stash and apply it to the current branch. And as the name implies, popping the changes will take them out of the stash. So, if you only had one set of changes in your stash, it would be empty after you popped the tip. If you execute the previous command, the result you get will be the same as if you recreated the changes and then checked the status (shown in Figure 16-6).

```
MINGW64:/c/Users/Mariot/Documents/Boky/raw/todo-list                    —    □    ×

Mariot@lenovo-ideapad MINGW64 ~/Documents/Boky/raw/todo-list (separate-code-and-styles)
$ git stash show
 README.md | 1 +
 1 file changed, 1 insertion(+)

Mariot@lenovo-ideapad MINGW64 ~/Documents/Boky/raw/todo-list (separate-code-and-styles)
$ git stash pop
On branch separate-code-and-styles
Changes not staged for commit:
  (use "git add <file>..." to update what will be committed)
  (use "git checkout -- <file>..." to discard changes in working directory)

        modified:   README.md

no changes added to commit (use "git add" and/or "git commit -a")
Dropped refs/stash@{0} (8493c5ec10a605f41466fe4b535bb8289bd24f84)

Mariot@lenovo-ideapad MINGW64 ~/Documents/Boky/raw/todo-list (separate-code-and-styles)
$ |
```

Figure 16-6. *Popping the last set of changes*

We're then back at the beginning! But if we wished, we could have changed
branches, made commits, or pushed to origin without losing our precious changes.
Stashing is particularly useful when you want to set aside your current changes to do
some quick change elsewhere. As a rule of thumb, if you need to use more than one set
of changes stashed, you are doing something wrong with your workflow.

Resetting

I hope you won't use this feature often because it's very destructive! Sometimes, you
want to discard everything you've done and work on a clean plate, even if you've already
committed your project. To better understand it, let's create a commit and then discard it.

Make some modifications on README.md, stage it, and then commit the project, as
shown in Figure 16-7.

```
MINGW64:/c/Users/Mariot/Documents/Boky/raw/todo-list                        —    □    ×

Mariot@lenovo-ideapad MINGW64 ~/Documents/Boky/raw/todo-list (separate-code-and-styles)
$ git status
On branch separate-code-and-styles
Changes not staged for commit:
  (use "git add <file>..." to update what will be committed)
  (use "git checkout -- <file>..." to discard changes in working directory)

        modified:    README.md

no changes added to commit (use "git add" and/or "git commit -a")

Mariot@lenovo-ideapad MINGW64 ~/Documents/Boky/raw/todo-list (separate-code-and-styles)
$ git add README.md

Mariot@lenovo-ideapad MINGW64 ~/Documents/Boky/raw/todo-list (separate-code-and-styles)
$ git commit -m "Add a bad commit to project"
[separate-code-and-styles f719374] Add a bad commit to project
 1 file changed, 1 insertion(+)

Mariot@lenovo-ideapad MINGW64 ~/Documents/Boky/raw/todo-list (separate-code-and-styles)
$ |
```

Figure 16-7. *Add a bad commit to the project*

To put this into perspective, let's check the current history log after this commit by using the git log command.

```
$ git log --oneline
```

This command will show you the latest commits on this branch, just like in Figure 16-8.

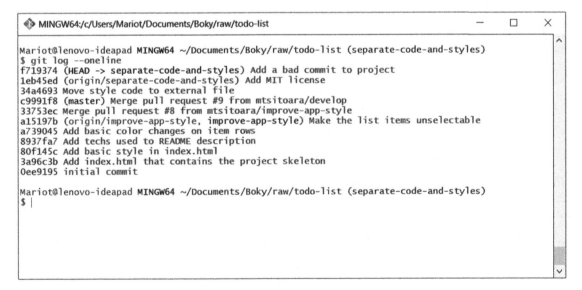

```
MINGW64:/c/Users/Mariot/Documents/Boky/raw/todo-list                        —    □    ×

Mariot@lenovo-ideapad MINGW64 ~/Documents/Boky/raw/todo-list (separate-code-and-styles)
$ git log --oneline
f719374 (HEAD -> separate-code-and-styles) Add a bad commit to project
1eb45ed (origin/separate-code-and-styles) Add MIT license
34a4693 Move style code to external file
c9991f8 (master) Merge pull request #9 from mtsitoara/develop
33753ec Merge pull request #8 from mtsitoara/improve-app-style
a15197b (origin/improve-app-style, improve-app-style) Make the list items unselectable
a739045 Add basic color changes on item rows
8937fa7 Add techs used to README description
80f145c Add basic style in index.html
3a96c3b Add index.html that contains the project skeleton
0ee9195 initial commit

Mariot@lenovo-ideapad MINGW64 ~/Documents/Boky/raw/todo-list (separate-code-and-styles)
$ |
```

Figure 16-8. *History log of the current branch*

As you can see, our latest commit sits on the top of our log. Notice that the HEAD reference is pointed to it; it means that our next commit (or branch) will have that commit as parent. You will notice also that the remote branch origin/separate-code-and-styles hasn't changed; that's because we haven't pushed our project yet.

But let's imagine that you are utterly dissatisfied with that last commit and want to do it over. Your only choice is then to reset the branch back to a previous state. To reset the project, we use the git reset command followed by the state of the project to reset to. You must use the option "--hard" to accomplish that, because it's a very dangerous command. For example, going back to the same state as the remote branch will require the following command:

```
$ git reset --hard origin/separate-code-and-styles
```

This command will erase EVERYTHING so the project can be brought back to a previous state. See in Figure 16-9 its result.

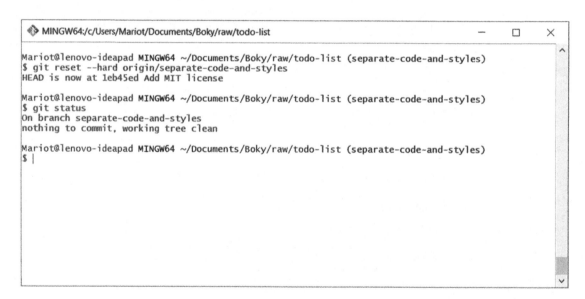

Figure 16-9. Status of the project after a reset

Your commits made after the target state, your current changes, and staged files will all be deleted as the "--hard" option overwrites everything on its path. It's the most dangerous command in Git and you should think hard before using it.

Resetting should only be done in the last resort. Prefer reverting the commit if possible or just straight-up continue to work on a new branch. When used carelessly, reset can destroy your data.

Summary

This chapter dealt with some advanced concepts of Git that will be useful to you when confronted to certain situations. You will need to use reset to revert a file back to a previous state without much effort; and of course, you can revert those changes using the GUI too. Stashing will be very useful too in case you need of a quick change of context. And finally, the hard reset is an all-powerful feature that is very destructive; don't unless you have no other choice.

This concludes our lesson about advance Git commands. Let's return to GitHub now, to discover some more features that can help us with our project management.

PART IV

Additional Resources

## CHAPTER 17

More with GitHub

We've seen almost every Git feature that you will use daily in the previous chapters. Now, let's turn our eyes to GitHub, which only served as a code hosting site until now. But we've already established that GitHub is so much more than that. You can use it to host documentation for your project and host software releases. You will also mainly use it as project management tool and a way to connect to your collaborators. Let's learn about those features.

Wikis

Your project can be the best in its category, but you would get nowhere if other people don't know how to use it or how it works. That's why documentations are important, especially in software development. GitHub provides a nice way to document your project: wikis.

GitHub wikis work mainly the same way as the world's most popular wiki: Wikipedia. Its goal is to provide in-depth information about your project: what does it do, how does it work, how can someone contribute...

Let's create a wiki page for our project so we can better understand it. Just go to your project main page and click "wiki"; you will arrive at the page shown in Figure 17-1.

© Mariot Tsitoara 2020
M. Tsitoara, *Beginning Git and GitHub*, https://doi.org/10.1007/978-1-4842-5313-7_17

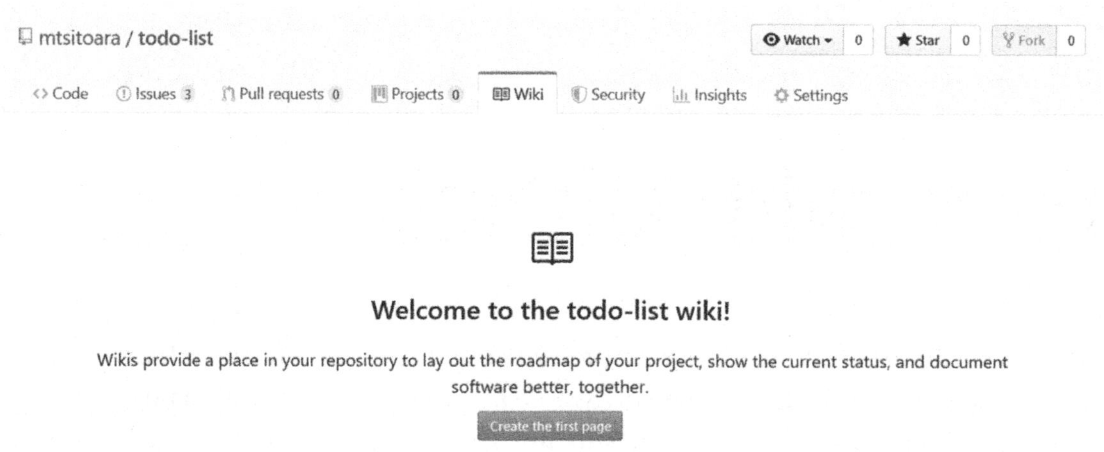

Welcome to the todo-list wiki!

Wikis provide a place in your repository to lay out the roadmap of your project, show the current status, and document software better, together.

Create the first page

Figure 17-1. *Wiki homepage*

You'll see a big call-to-action button on the wiki homepage, so click it to create your first wiki page. You'll arrive at the page creation page, shown in Figure 17-2.

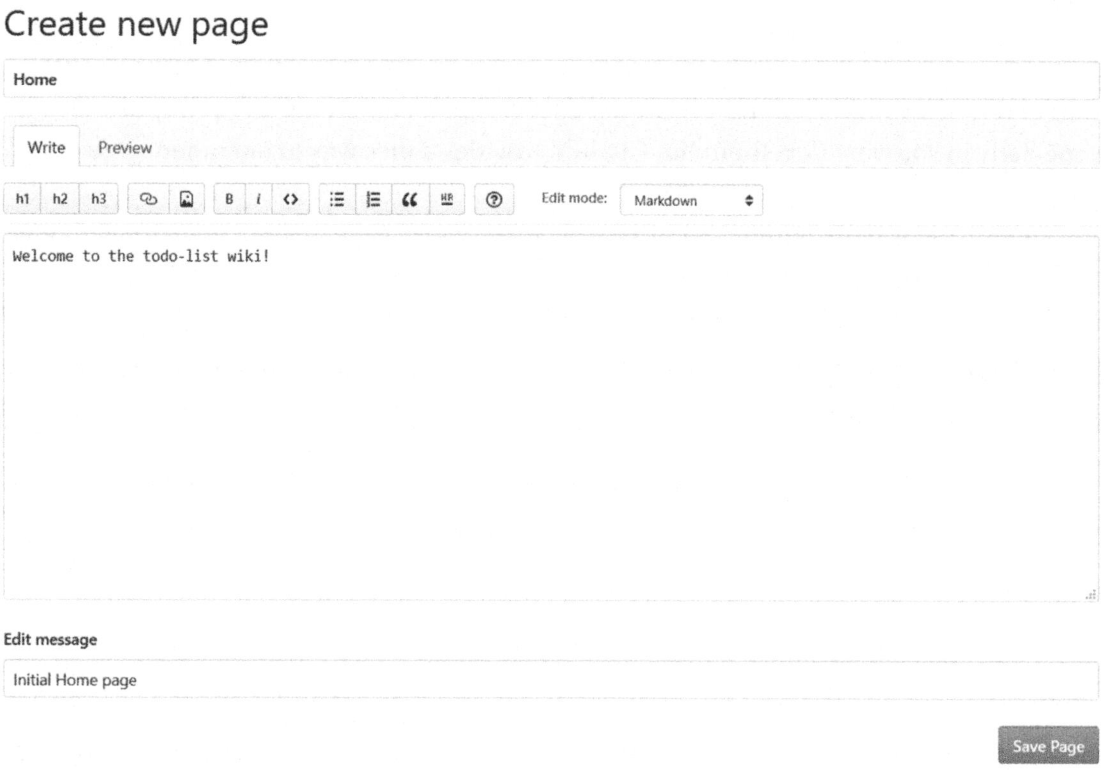

Create new page

Home

Write   Preview

h1 h2 h3   B i <> ≔ ≔ " ᴴᴿ ⑦   Edit mode: Markdown ⬍

```
Welcome to the todo-list wiki!
```

Edit message

Initial Home page

Save Page

Figure 17-2. *Creation of a page*

As you can see, it's a very simple view that is divided in three sections: the title, the content, and the edit message. Think of the title as a web page title, so it must adhere to the same standards: it must be clear and inviting. The content should be written in Markdown, just like README.md. You can choose to write the wikis in other formats, but Markdown is the recommended choice because so many editors already use it and it's so much easier to read. The edit message is just like commit messages, a simple description of your proposed changes.

Change the content in your wiki; here is an example:

```
# What is this

This is a simple app to track your daily goals

# Why another TODO app

Because that is never enough TODO apps in the world

# How does it work

Open `index.html` and update the goals as you wish

# How can I contribute to the project

You can contribute by forking the project and proposing Pull Requests.
Check [Issues](https://github.com/mtsitoara/issues) to see the current
areas that need help
```

Save the changes, and you will be redirected to the wiki homepage, shown in Figure 17-3.

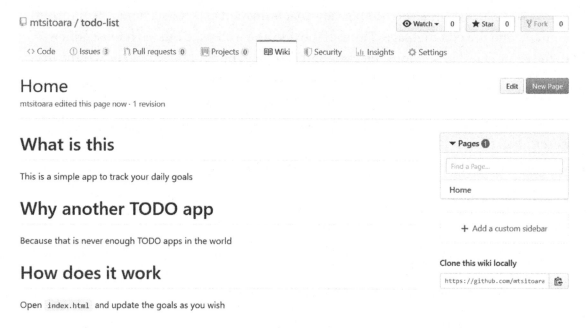

Figure 17-3. *Wiki homepage showing the newly created wiki*

As you can see, the wiki you just created is automatically visible on your project page, and each page you create will appear on the sidebar on the right.

You can make as many wiki pages as you like, but make sure they are comprehensible and useful; don't forget to add images and relevant links!

GitHub Pages

Put simply, GitHub Pages is a web site hosted for you on GitHub. You can use it to showcase a project, host your portfolio, or just use it as an online version of your resumé.

A GitHub Page can be for your personal account (portfolio and resumé) or for your projects (showcase). If you decide to use it for your account, you will only get to create a Page; but if it's for your projects showcase, you can create a Page for any of them. You can check https://pages.github.com/ for a better explanation of this.

Let's assume you want to create a Page to showcase you todo-list project. First, you need to head back to your project page and click "Settings"; you will access the page shown in Figure 17-4.

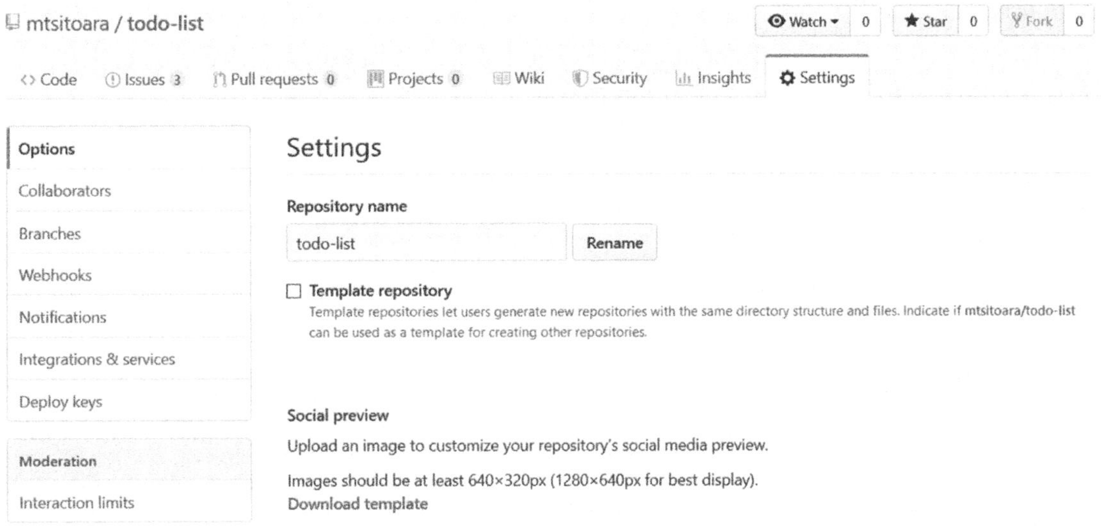

Figure 17-4. *Settings page*

Scroll down to the Pages settings, shown in Figure 17-5.

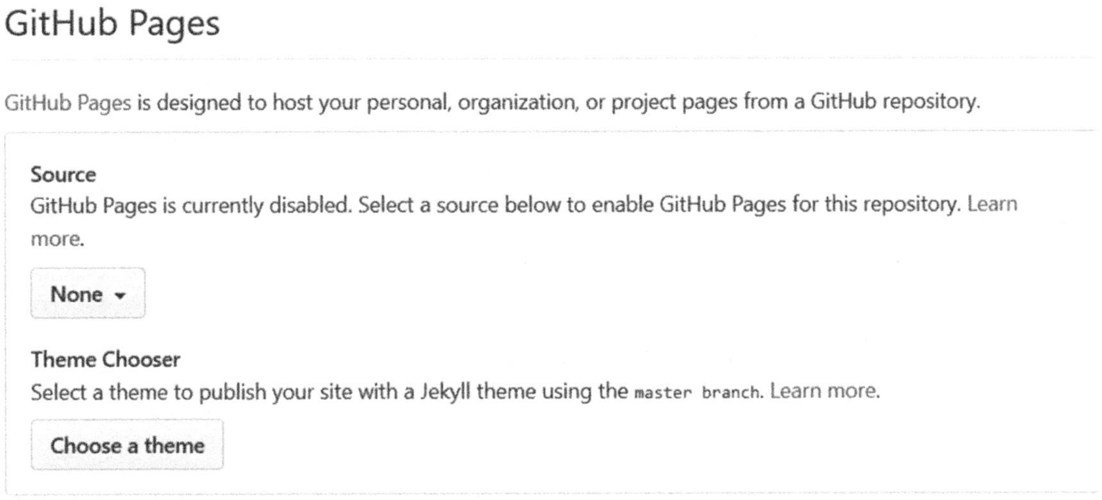

GitHub Pages

GitHub Pages is designed to host your personal, organization, or project pages from a GitHub repository.

Source
GitHub Pages is currently disabled. Select a source below to enable GitHub Pages for this repository. Learn more.

None ▾

Theme Chooser
Select a theme to publish your site with a Jekyll theme using the `master` branch. Learn more.

Choose a theme

Figure 17-5. *GitHub Pages settings*

The first option is a dropdown list containing the location of your Page source. You must host your page on the master branch, but you have two locations for the source files. One is directly on master; the other is on master under a directory called "docs." I recommend the second option as it's clearer to any visitor. We must then create that directory first.

Using GitHub or Git tools, create a file called index.html under a directory called docs. In the file, just write some basic HTML:

```
<!doctype html>
<html>
    <head>
        <meta charset="utf-8">
        <title>Docs</title>
    </head>
    <body>
        <h1>Docs</h1>
        <p>Example of documentation</p>
    </body>
</html>
```

This will be your documentation. Your master branch must thus look like mine as shown in Figure 17-6.

Figure 17-6. *Docs folder and index.html*

We can then go back to the settings page and select the source of the documentation. Select the docs folder as source, and the page will reload and show you a link like in Figure 17-7.

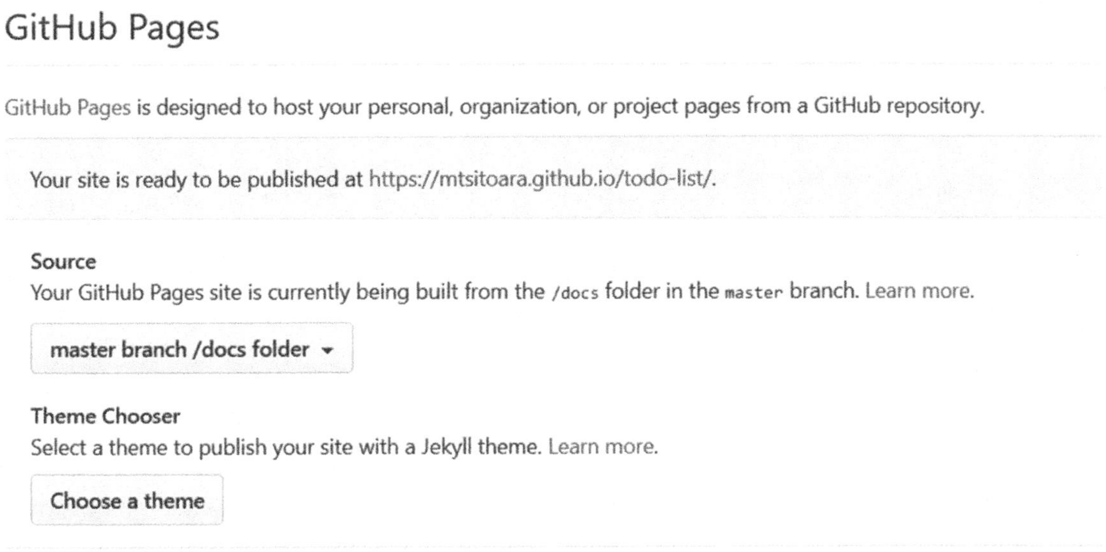

GitHub Pages

GitHub Pages is designed to host your personal, organization, or project pages from a GitHub repository.

Your site is ready to be published at https://mtsitoara.github.io/todo-list/.

Source
Your GitHub Pages site is currently being built from the /docs folder in the master branch. Learn more.

master branch /docs folder ▾

Theme Chooser
Select a theme to publish your site with a Jekyll theme. Learn more.

Choose a theme

Figure 17-7. *Page published*

If you follow the link shown to you, you will get a glorious view of your GitHub project page! The possibilities are then limitless as you can design your Page like any other static web site page! If you want better style, check `https://jekyllrb.com/`; it can help you generate GitHub Pages in no time!

Tip   Since your project is a static HTML page, you can point to it as the location of your Page; and you would get a real-time version of it!

Releases

Your project won't stay in development indefinitely; it must be released sooner or later. And what better platform to release your app than GitHub? It's very easy.

Go back to your project page again and click "Releases"; you will see the main page shown in Figure 17-8.

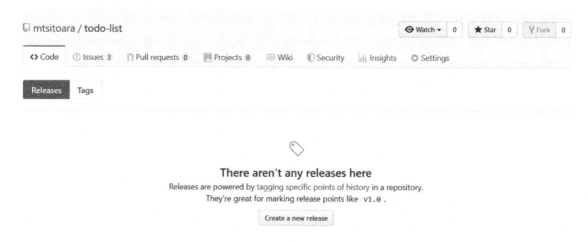

Figure 17-8.   Releases page

Let's create our very first release! Click the call-to-action button, and you will get the release creation view, shown in Figure 17-9.

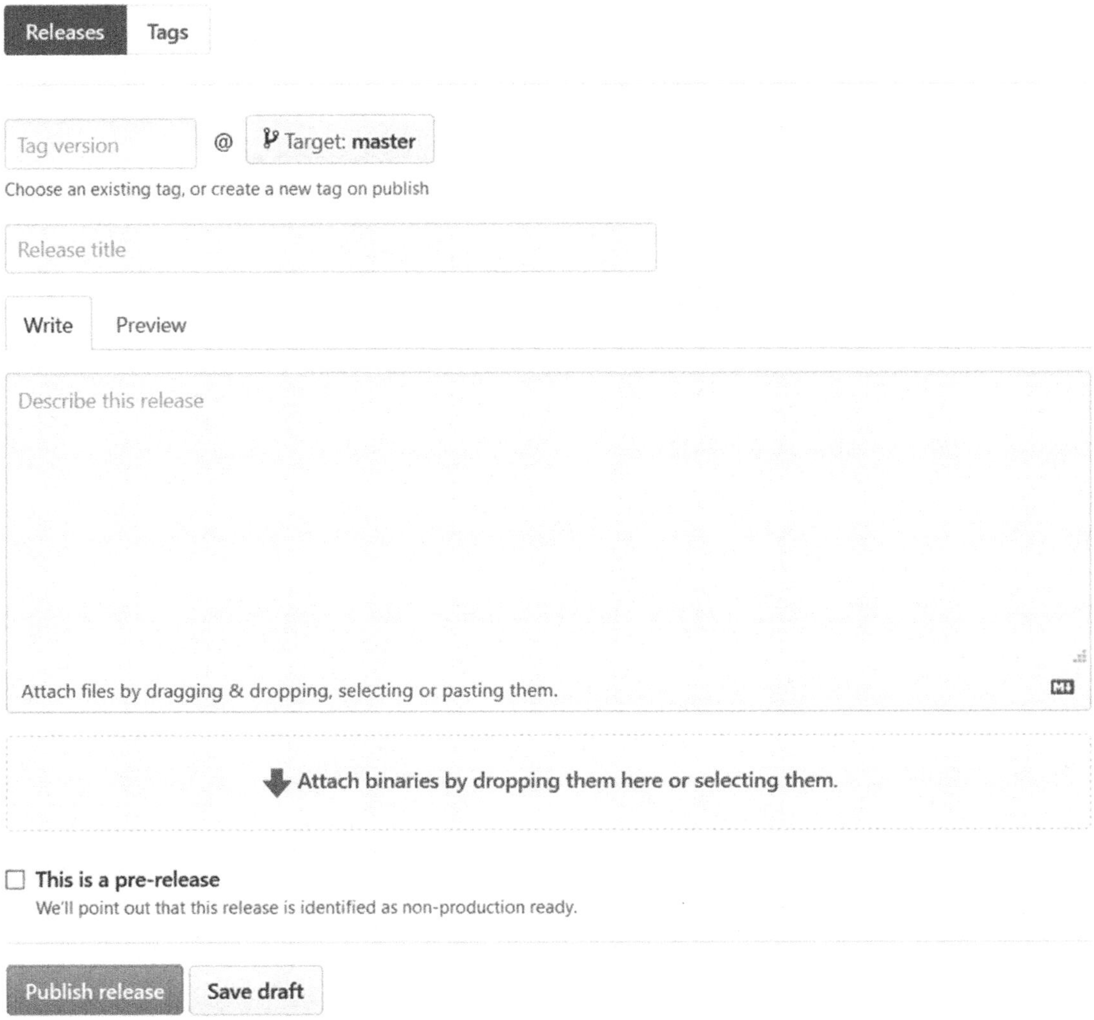

| Releases | Tags |

Tag version @ ⑂ Target: **master**

Choose an existing tag, or create a new tag on publish

Release title

| Write | Preview |

Describe this release

Attach files by dragging & dropping, selecting or pasting them.

⬇ Attach binaries by dropping them here or selecting them.

☐ **This is a pre-release**
We'll point out that this release is identified as non-production ready.

Publish release **Save draft**

Figure 17-9. *Release creation form*

It's a very easy form to fill as the sections are straightforward and clear. The main thing to do is to upload the release binaries by dropping them on the preceding form. Since our app is in HTML, let's attach compressed versions of our master branch. For installable apps, it will be a binary to be executed; for us, it will be zip and 7z files. Don't forget to change the target of the release if you need to. The default option is the master branch but you can point to another branch or a specific commit! The form will then be the same as the one shown in Figure 17-10.

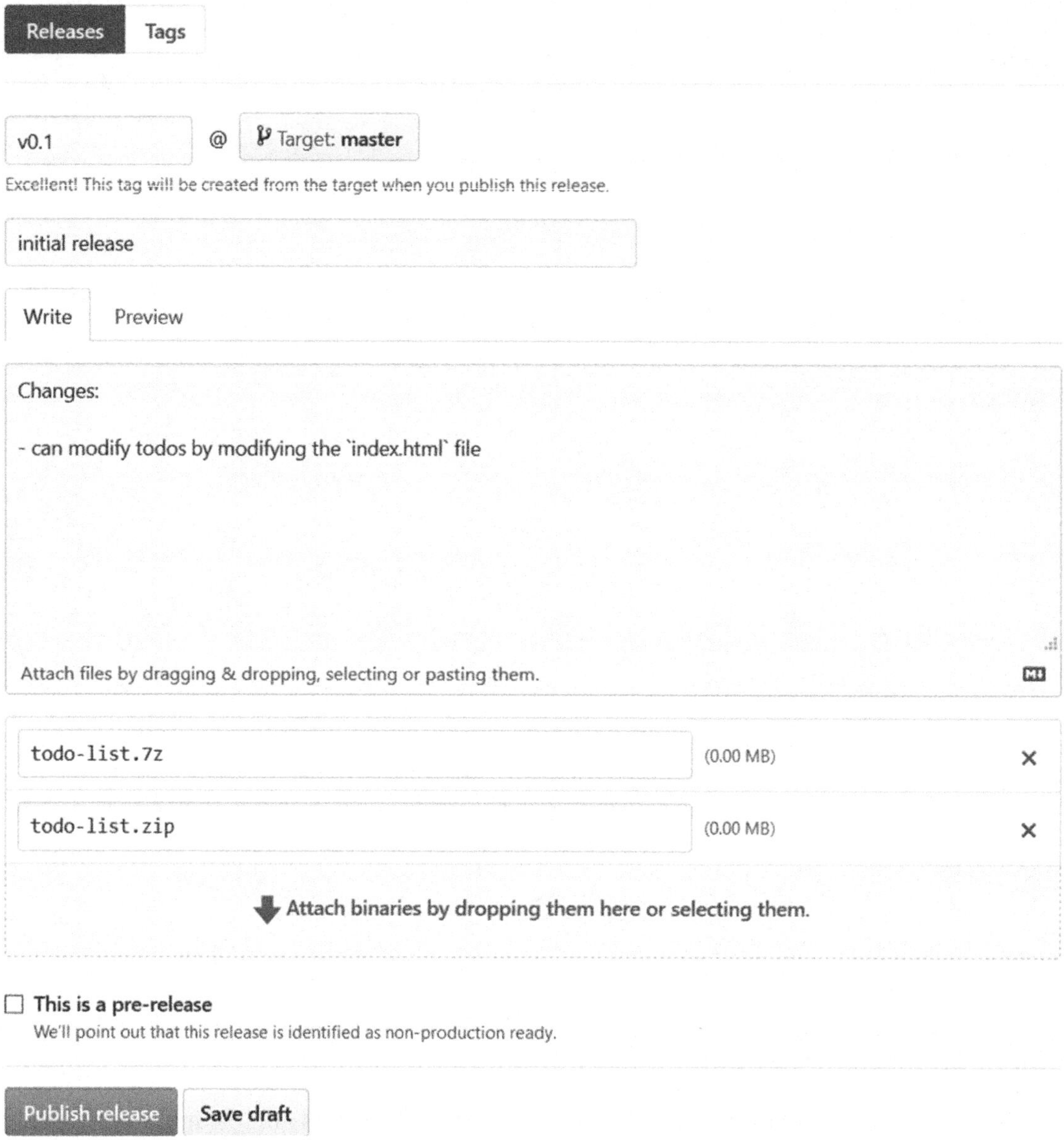

| Releases | Tags |

v0.1   @   ⴽ Target: **master**

Excellent! This tag will be created from the target when you publish this release.

initial release

| Write | Preview |

Changes:

- can modify todos by modifying the `index.html` file

Attach files by dragging & dropping, selecting or pasting them.

| todo-list.7z | (0.00 MB) | ✕ |
| todo-list.zip | (0.00 MB) | ✕ |

⬇ Attach binaries by dropping them here or selecting them.

☐ **This is a pre-release**
We'll point out that this release is identified as non-production ready.

Publish release   **Save draft**

Figure 17-10. *Filled release form with binaries*

Click publish to see the result. You will be redirected back to the Releases list and will see your new release there! Check Figure 17-11 for an example.

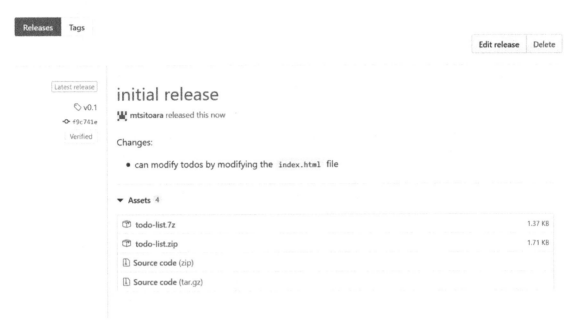

Figure 17-11. *List of all the releases*

As you can see, GitHub automatically bundles the source code with your release too! Be careful when creating a release; be sure to properly test and retest everything!

Project Boards

Project Boards are a very useful feature of GitHub because it provides a way to track and organize your project. For example, you can create cards for any new idea you have, so you can discuss them with your team later. But the main use of Project Boards is to track the advancement of your project. It goes beyond Issues, because Issues only describe a feature or a bug to be worked on; but Project Board can show you if someone is working on it or it's only a plan to be executed.

The best way to understand Project Boards is to directly experiment with them. So go back to your project page and select "Projects." You will get the empty project shown in Figure 17-12.

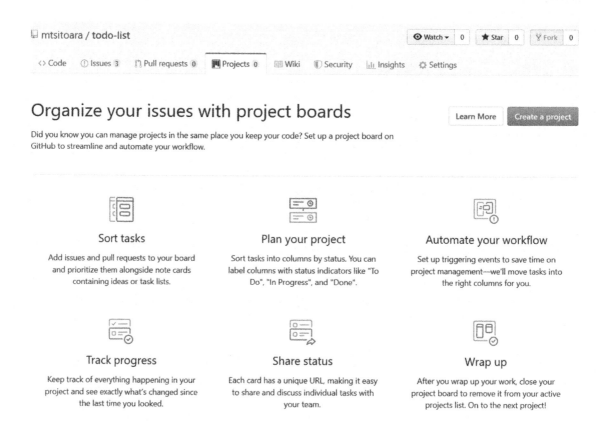

Figure 17-12. Projects main page

The project main page is still empty as we haven't created any project. It also shows you different situations where you would want to use Project Boards. Click "Create a project" to continue; you will get the view shown in Figure 17-13.

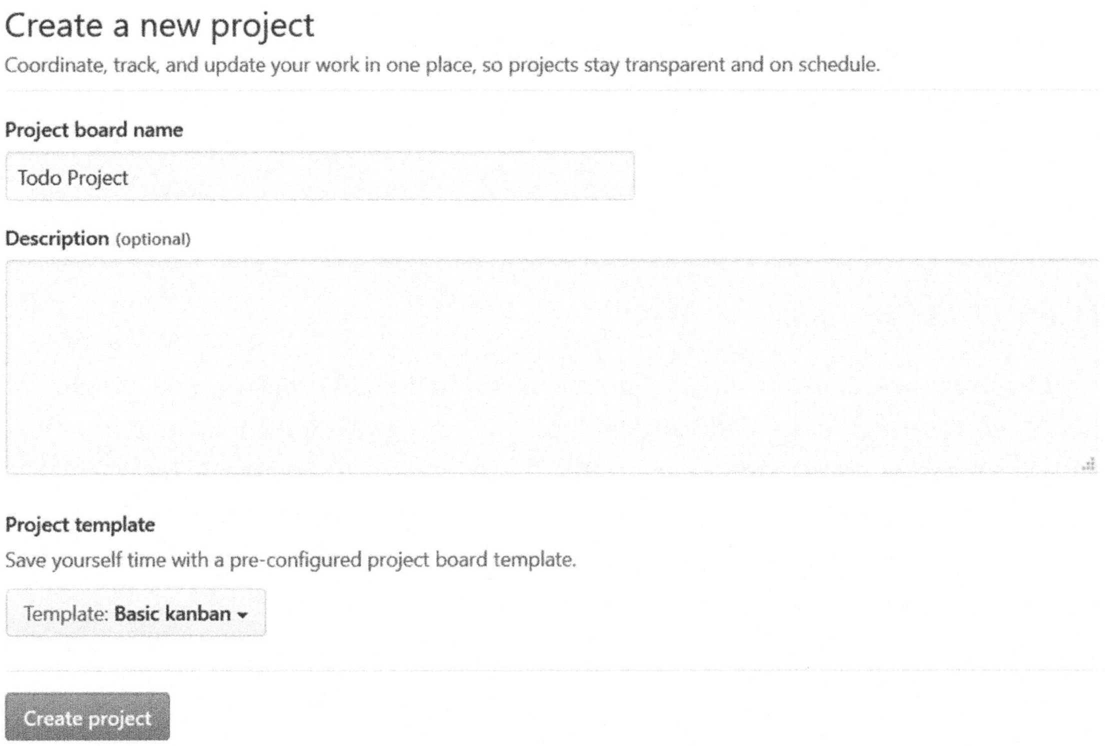

Create a new project

Coordinate, track, and update your work in one place, so projects stay transparent and on schedule.

Project board name

Todo Project

Description (optional)

Project template

Save yourself time with a pre-configured project board template.

Template: **Basic kanban** ▾

Create project

Figure 17-13. *Creation of a project*

Again, it's a very simple form. But direct your attention to the template: it's quite important. As a beginner, you should use the Basic Kanban template as it's a prefilled one. You can choose to create the boards yourself, but for now, let's stick to basics. Create the project, and you will see the semi-empty board shown in Figure 17-14.

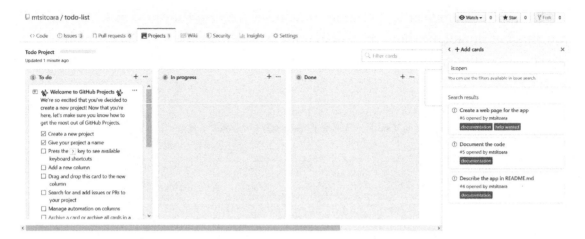

Figure 17-14. *New project created*

As you can see, there are three Boards created: "To do," "In progress," and "Done." Just like our app! At the right side of the screen, you can see a list of our open issues. Drag and drop those issues to their respective Boards. In the "To do" Board, you have a little example of what you can do with your Boards; it's not only for Issues but also for Pull Requests or simple notes. After you placed your Issues in the desired Boards, you will get a result like Figure 17-15.

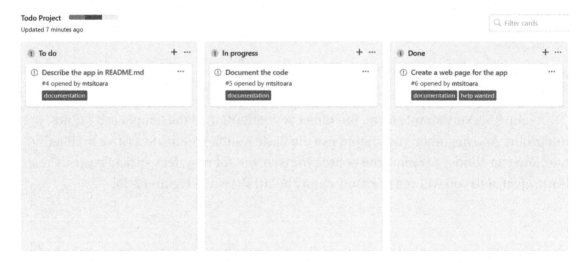

Figure 17-15. *Our first Project Boards*

A little bonus: as you move the Issues around the Board, the colored bar near the project name will change. It's a good way to track your progress!

But Project Boards are more than a project progress tracker! You can create Project Boards for many situations: release tracking, meeting notes, developer idea notes, user feedbacks... You can find in Figure 17-16 the Project Board for this book that you can also find on `https://github.com/mariot/boky/projects/1`.

Figure 17-16. *Current Project Board of this book*

I advise you to use Project Boards for your future projects because having a clear view of your progress is a sure way to success. If you are feeling dauntless, you can also check the Automated Kanban that automatically moves the cards for you! For example, every new Issue will be filled under "To Do," and every closed Issue will be moved to "Done."

Summary

This chapter took us away from Git for a little moment and we focused on GitHub. We've seen that GitHub is more than a store for your code, but a complete tool to manage and release your project. After this chapter, you should be able to dress a mini web site and have a little documentation of it. You should also have a first release of your app.

The most important feature shown earlier is the Project Boards. Use them to have a clear view of what you've done and where are you going. They seem simple but they are very useful in project management.

You've now mastered the basics of Git and GitHub. But there are still roadblocks in your path: you are still unsure of what awaits you in a real-world environment. In the next chapter, we will explore the problems you will surely face when working with others and how to resolve them. Stay tuned!

## CHAPTER 18

Common Git Problems

We've come a long way since our first Git command! We've learned a lot about basic and advanced Git features and when to use them. But since we are only humans, we're going to face a lot of problems during our Git journey. Most of these problems are the result of inadvertences, so just being aware of their existence is a big step forward toward avoiding them. But if you still run into them, here are the best solutions!

Repository

The repository is the backbone of your Git experience; everything begins and ends there. It's very difficult to mess it up, but in the slight chance something bad happens, here are some tips.

Starting over

This is the most radical "solution" in the chapter, and I hope you won't ever use it. This solution is basically a way to delete everything and start over! This should only be an option when you have a remote repository and you want to delete your local one for some reason. Reasons to do this include

- Change of work computers

- Unreadable sectors in hard drive

- Unrecoverable errors in ".git" directory

To start over, you just need to clone the remote repository with the git clone command:

```
$ git clone <repository_location>
```

© Mariot Tsitoara 2020
M. Tsitoara, *Beginning Git and GitHub*, https://doi.org/10.1007/978-1-4842-5313-7_18

The repository location is the HTTPS or SSH link to your remote repository; you can find it on your GitHub project page.

Cloning has the same effect as initializing a repository but with a big bonus: all history and commits will also be copied on your new local repository. And you won't need to precise the origin link anymore.

Change origin

Under normal circumstances, you would want to keep the remote repository's URL the same throughout your development. But there are certain circumstances where it's necessary to change it:

- Switching between HTTPS and SSH links

- Transfer of the repository to another host

- Addition of dedicated repository for release or testing

First, let's get some more information about our current remotes. To do so, use the git remote command with the "-v" option.

```
$ git remote -v
```

This will give you a list of your current remotes, as shown in Figure 18-1.

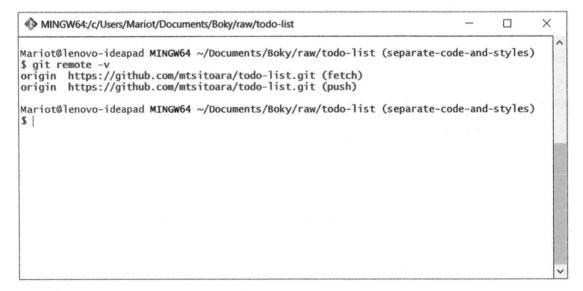

Figure 18-1. *List of current remotes*

Here, we only have one remote "origin" that points to a GitHub HTTPS link. To modify this link, you will need to use the set-url subcommand:

```
$ git remote set-url <remote_name> <remote_url>
```

For example, if I wanted to switch to SSH instead of HTTPS for my GitHub access, I would execute

```
$ git remote set-url origin git@github.com:mtsitoara/todo-list.git
```

Doing this will allow me to push and pull to-and-from GitHub without providing my username and password. The authentication will be done by two sets of keys: a private key that I keep on my local computer and a public key that I must upload to GitHub. If you are interested in using SSH for your authentication, please head over to GitHub help for more information depending on your Operating System (`https://help.github.com/en/articles/which-remote-url-should-i-use`). If you decide to keep using HTTPS but what to cache for password so you don't have to type it all the time, you can use a credential helper. Again, there is more information about this on GitHub help, depending on your Operating System (`https://help.github.com/en/articles/caching-your-github-password-in-git`).

Caution   If you change your remote name, don't forget to use the new name for every push and pull action.

Working Directory

You will spend most for your time on the Working Directory, and here again, there's not a lot of thing you can break.

Git diff is empty

This comes up a lot but it's not dangerous. Sometimes, you made a lot of changes and want to check the changes. But when you run git diff, the result is empty. Don't panic! Git diff only shows modified files, so if your file is staged, you won't see it there. To see changes done to staged files, you must run:

```
$ git diff --staged
```

> **Tip**   Using a GUI tool would help you greatly when reviewing changes.

Undo changes to a file

This will come up a lot when you'll use Git. Sometimes, you just want to revert a file back to its previous state without having to check out an entire commit and then copy-paste the code. We've already seen the command earlier:

```
$ git checkout <commit_name> -- <file_name>
```

This command will check out the file as it was on the commit and, thus, will change your Working Directory. Careful not to lose any uncommitted changes!

Commits

Most problems will arise when you'll try to commit your current project. But don't worry, there is always a simple solution for these kinds of problems. The most important thing to consider is: are the commands you are using destructive? Commands like reset or check out change your Working Directory, so please make sure that you know what you are doing before executing them.

Error in commit

This is a basic error in Git. After you commit your hard work, you'll sometimes notice that a little grammatical error found its way into your commit message or that you forgot to stage a file. The solution to these problems is to amend the commit, meaning that you will cancel the immediate commit and make a new one. The command is simple:

```
$ git commit --amend
```

The commit name will change because you are basically changing its content. That's why you should not amend a commit that you've already pushed to a remote branch, especially if somebody else works on that branch. This is rewriting history and you should never do it.

That said, if you've pushed your commit and are alone on the branch, you can amend a commit and try to push it again. But since the commit name changed, Git won't allow you to change history without a fight. You will have to erase all the history on the remote branch and replace it with yours, meaning that you will overwrite everything on the remote branch. That's why you should never amend a commit if you aren't alone on a branch. To push a branch with amended commits, you have the force it.

```
$ git push <remote_name> <branch_name> -f
```

The "-f" option forces Git to overwrite everything on the remote branch and replace it with your current branch history.

Caution   Rewriting history on a branch where somebody else is working is just plain rude and selfish. Don't do it.

Amending commits should only be used when you want to modify the commit message or add/remove a file. Don't amend a commit to change code.

Undo commits

If you committed on a branch but then realized it's the wrong one, you can undo it, but only when you haven't pushed to a remote branch.

The command is simple but dangerous: it's the reset command. But contrary to the "hard" reset where everything is cleared, a "soft" reset is necessary to undo the commit but keep the changes.

```
$ git reset HEAD~ --soft
```

The commit will then disappear, leaving you with some option to stash the changes and apply them to another branch.

Again, this is rewriting history and should not be used if you've already pushed to a remote branch.

Branches

You will need to work with branches a lot to have an optimized workflow. When working on a new feature or bugfix, your first instinct should be the creation of a branch. But the more you are getting comfortable with branches, the more you are likely to forget a little detail that can lead to problems. Here are the most common problems that you will encounter with Git.

Detached HEAD

HEAD is a reference to the current checked-out commit, meaning the parent commit of any future commit you will create. Usually, HEAD points to the last commit of the current branch; and all future branches and commits will have it as parent.

When you check out branches, the HEAD will go back and forth between the last commits of the branches. But when you check out a specific commit, you enter a state called "detached HEAD" which means that you are in a state where nothing you will create will be attached to anything. It's useless then to try to commit during that state as any change will be lost.

Git will tell you when you are in that state (like in Figure 18-2) so you won't ever be in that state unknowingly.

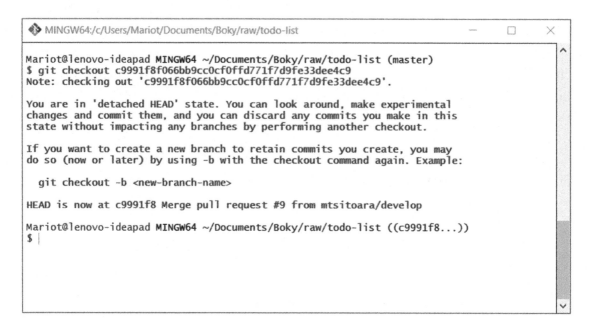

Figure 18-2. Checking out a commit

Checking out a commit is thus only needed to test something on your software. You can, however, create a branch from that specific commit if you want to keep the commits you intend to make. The command is the same as creating a branch from another branch:

```
$ git checkout -b <branch_name>
```

Worked on wrong branch

This happens a lot. The situation is usually like this: you receive a task and you are so eager to complete it that you begin to code immediately. You are already an hour into the task when you notice that you were working the master branch all along! Don't worry, it's very simple to resolve this.

If you modified some files on the wrong branch, you can directly create a new branch (and check it out) to take the current changes there. It's the same command again:

```
$ git checkout -b <branch_name>
```

This will create a new branch with your current changes and check it out. You can then stage your modified files and commit the project.

However, this won't work if you've already pushed the branch to a remote repository; history is history, don't change it. The only way to fix that is to revert the commit you push and live with that shame all your life.

Catch up with parent branch

When you create a branch from another (usually master), their histories are not linked anymore, so what happens in a branch doesn't have any incidence on the other. This means that while you are working on your branch, other people can commit on the base branch; and those commits won't be available to your branch.

If you are still working your branch but are interested in having those new commits on the base branch, you must first have a clean plate, meaning that you must commit your project (or stash your current changes).

You then have to check out the parent branch, pull the new commits, and then go back to your branch.

```
$ git checkout master
$ git pull origin master
$ git checkout <branch_name>
```

Safely on your local branch, you can then catch up to the parent branch. The concept is simple: Git will take out your current commits and create new branch from the tip of the parent branch; your commits will then be applied on your new branch. It would be like you create a branch from the latest commit of the master branch. The command is called rebase.

```
$ git rebase master
```

The commits on master might introduce conflicts in your branch, so be prepared to get your hands dirty. The resolving of those merge conflicts is the same as what we've seen previously: open each conflicted file and choose which code you want to keep; then you can stage them and commit.

You can find an example of rebase conflict in Figure 18-3, on which commits on master and test_branch both modified README.md.

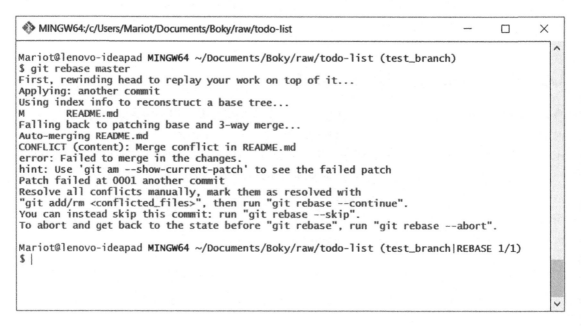

Figure 18-3. *Merge conflict during rebase*

As you can see, it's almost exactly like any merge conflict; and the resolution is the same:

```
$ git add <conflicted_files>
$ git rebase --continue
```

Here also, if you are not feeling brave enough for conflicts, you can abort the rebase and go back to the initial state.

```
$ git rebase --abort
```

If you work on a branch for a long time, it's a good idea to rebase from time to time, so you aren't left too far behind the parent branch. Of course, you can face merge conflicts, but those are more and more likely to appear the bigger your changes are. And if you delay rebases for a fear of conflicts, you will only set yourself up for failures because those conflicts will appear again when you'll attempt to merge the branches anyway. It's better to deal with small conflicts with a rebase from time to time than have to merge a lot of conflicted files at the same time on merge.

Branches have diverged

This will happen to you if you are using a bad Git workflow. As we said earlier, you should work on your own branch to resolve an issue, because multiple people committing on the same branch is the perfect recipe for disaster.

We say that two branches are diverged when you can't push to your remote branch anymore due to a history change. This happens when you committed on your local branch, but other people have pushed their commits on the remote branch before you. Come the time to push, Git won't let you because the last commit of the remote branch isn't part of your local history. You will get an error like the one shown in Figure 18-4.

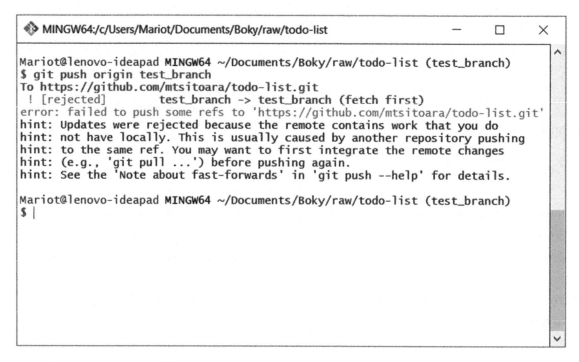

Figure 18-4. *Rejected changes*

Here is the most sensible solution: pull the commits for the remote branch and merge your changes. You will then have their changes on your history (after resolving the eventual merge conflicts) and can push afterward.

```
$ git pull origin <branch_name>
$ git push origin <branch_name>
```

This will give you an ugly history log, but at least all commits are saved. An example of this is shown in Figure 18-5.

```
MINGW64:/c/Users/Mariot/Documents/Boky/raw/todo-list            —    □    ×

Mariot@lenovo-ideapad MINGW64 ~/Documents/Boky/raw/todo-list (test_branch)
$ git pull origin test_branch
From https://github.com/mtsitoara/todo-list
 * branch             test_branch -> FETCH_HEAD
Auto-merging README.md
CONFLICT (content): Merge conflict in README.md
Automatic merge failed; fix conflicts and then commit the result.

Mariot@lenovo-ideapad MINGW64 ~/Documents/Boky/raw/todo-list (test_branch|MERGIN
G)
$ vim README.md

Mariot@lenovo-ideapad MINGW64 ~/Documents/Boky/raw/todo-list (test_branch|MERGIN
G)
$ git add README.md

Mariot@lenovo-ideapad MINGW64 ~/Documents/Boky/raw/todo-list (test_branch|MERGIN
G)
$ git merge --continue
[test_branch 6ea4096] Merge branch 'test_branch' of https://github.com/mtsitoara
/todo-list into test_branch

Mariot@lenovo-ideapad MINGW64 ~/Documents/Boky/raw/todo-list (test_branch)
$ |
```

Figure 18-5. *Merge local and remote branch*

The other solution is more brutal: overwrite everything on the remote branch and replace its history by yours. To do so, you must push using the "force" option.

```
$ git push origin <branch_name> -f
```

This results in lost commits and fistfight; don't ever do this.

Again, this shouldn't happen if you use a good Git and GitHub workflow.

Summary

This chapter is there to point you to the right solution when faced with common Git problems. Surely, you'll discover new, harder problems but it's a good way to start. The main thing to remember is always to check where you are before doing anything, especially committing.

But these problems shouldn't appear at all if you use the common Git and GitHub workflow. So, let's rediscover that in the next chapter. We've already talked about this in the earlier chapters, but it's time to review it after you've seen all the most used Git and GitHub features.

## CHAPTER 19

Git and GitHub Workflow

We've learned a whole lot in the last chapters, especially on the technical aspects of Git. You now know how to properly version your project and how to deal with eventual problems. We also looked a lot into the basics of project management with GitHub.

Now is the time to put all of this into perspective and prepare the perfect game plan for your project. In this chapter, you will be presented with a carefully crafted workflow that you should follow for a successful project. You can think of it as a "best practices" section or an "how-to" guide.

How to use this workflow

The workflow presented in this chapter was designed for both beginners and experienced users. It is also used a lot of time in Open Source projects so many developers use it already. Keep in mind that this workflow is not set in stone, and it can be tweaked to suit your demands, within reasons.

My suggestion is to follow the workflow religiously when you are still a beginner, so that you can get how it all works and what are the rituals to go through. When you are feeling a little bit experienced, you can modify the workflow a little bit if that make you more efficient; but never forfeit security for time. Bypassing some rituals might gain you some time, but if it leads to more bugs and merge conflicts, it would be counterproductive. After you've used Git and GitHub for a few years, you will become a Master of It and can create your own workflow, provided that what you will bring will make your team more efficient.

GitHub workflow

The most basic error you can commit when working with GitHub is to only think of it as a code hosting service, that is, using it just for sharing code between your collaborators or just to release your product to users. GitHub is such a powerful tool that it would be a colossal waste to not use it at its full potential.

© Mariot Tsitoara 2020
M. Tsitoara, *Beginning Git and GitHub*, https://doi.org/10.1007/978-1-4842-5313-7_19

Think of GitHub as your main project management tool. Every action you intend to make in your project should be tracked within GitHub, so you can go back and understand the history. You can't just go ahead and make some changes without properly documenting why you are making those changes. Here are then the golden rules of GitHub.

Every project starts with a project

When you are starting a new project, you should create a GitHub project just after creating the repository. You need to do this as soon as possible because using Project Boards is the best way to track your evolution. You should at least have one Kanban board to track the "to do" of your project. And you can use other boards to track user feedback or to dress a list of your random ideas. The main takeaway is to always keep what pass through your mind in writing, as you will most likely forget most of it.

Every action starts with an Issue

Issues are a good way to make note of what needs to be done on your project. When you notice a bug in your program, your first instinct shouldn't be to open your IDE to fix it but to create an Issue tracking it. The same thing goes with a feature idea, even if you're not sure if you will work on it in the future. Create an Issue to document your intent and you can close it after if you decide not to implement it.

This ritual implies that everything you do on your local Git should have the resolving of an Issue as goal. So, when you are working on something on your IDE, you should always ask yourself: "What Issue does this resolve?" If the answer is "none," you should create an Issue for it, no matter how small the task is.

No direct push to master

This is the main ritual that is very hard to follow but makes life so much easier for everybody involved in a project. The idea is simple: nobody should directly push commits to the master branch. The only way to introduce changes to master is by merging other branches into it.

The direct implication of this is that every change you create should be contained on its own branch before it can be merged into master. So, any new feature or bugfix should start in a branch and then merged into master when ready. "Ready" means properly reviewed and tested.

Any merge into master needs a PR

Since we can't directly push into master, the only choice is to merge branches into it. But you shouldn't blindly merge any branch branches into master either. You must create Pull Requests to propose the changes. That way, another team member can investigate your code to verify if all is well.

You should put references to Issue numbers that the PR resolves in the PR description, so the Issues are automatically closed when the PR is accepted.

Use the wiki to document your code

This might seem like a drag but it's the best way to document your code. The README file isn't enough (or adapted) for a full code documentation, so the wiki is needed. It may seem like a huge task, but the best way is to write the documentation at the same time as the code. So, you only need to write small changes from time to time. If you wait for a long time to decide to write documentation, you will be overwhelmed, and you will likely forget crucial information.

Git workflow

Let's now talk about Git. By now, you surely know all the most used features of Git; but using them at the right moment is the best way to avoid errors (and conflicts).

Always know where you are

This is very basic and, thus, very easy to forget. You should always know which branch you are on before making any change or executing any command. If you are using a modern IDE, your current branch should appear at the bottom of your screen. If not, nothing beats the old reliable git status!

Pull remote changes before any action

Pull the remote master branch before you create a branch from it. This will permit you to stay up to date with your coworkers and you will avoid most merge conflicts.

And when you are working on your local branch, you should also rebase from time to time as to receive the latest updates and thus reduce the number of merge conflicts in the future. As a bonus, your git log graph will be way prettier. ☺

Take care of your commit message

Please refer to Chapter 5 on commits to review how to write a good commit message. Don't underestimate this process because it will be the backbone of your history log. Writing a bad commit message might save you a few minutes at first, but come the time of a bugfix (it will come, trust me), you will waste countless hours searching for a commit that introduced bugs.

Don't rewrite history

Just don't. This is one of the worst things you can do when using Git within a team. If you change a commit and force push it to a remote branch, everything done to that branch will be overwritten by your changes. That means that if somebody else worked on that branch, they would have to discard everything that they've done and reset their local branch. If you really have to do it, be sure that you are the only one working on that branch.

Summary

Such a short chapter! But it's the best way to have a successful project. The main thing to remember is that GitHub is so much more than a code hosting service. You should use it to properly track your project evolution and to track any idea you or your clients might have. By following this workflow, you set yourself for success as you will avoid most problems with Git and GitHub.

You now have all the tools to succeed with Git and GitHub! All now depends on your imagination and courage. Use those tools properly and you will pilot your project into the best paths. Good luck!

Index

A

Atom, 234, 235

B

Branches, 142
  bugfix, 274
  commit, 145
  creation, 146–147
  deletion, 149–151
  diverged, 277, 279
  force option, 279
  HEAD, 146, 274, 275
  logic, 144
  parent branch, 146
    merge conflict, 277
    pull commits, 276
    rebase command, 276
  pull requests, 145
  push, remote, 156, 157
  switching, 147, 148
  wrong branch, 275

C, D, E

Code review, 173, 174
  comment
    finishing the
      review, 177
    PR details page, 177, 178

285

© Mariot Tsitoara 2020
M. Tsitoara, *Beginning Git and GitHub*, https://doi.org/10.1007/978-1-4842-5313-7

Made in United States
Orlando, FL
31 May 2022

18342313R00174